A LONG WAY
FROM
BROOKLYN

An Italian-American
Journey

John Tursi
Thelma Palmer

Some names and places have been changed to protect the innocent.

Published by Cave Art Press, Anacortes, WA 98221
An imprint of Douglass, Hemingway & Co., LLC
CaveArtPress.com

ISBN-13: 9781934199206

Editor and book designer: Arlene Cook
Manuscript readers: Réanne Hemingway-Douglass, Lisa Wright, Kathleen Kaska
All interior photographs courtesy of John Tursi
Cover photograph of Deception Pass by Arlene Cook
Maps by Ken Morrison

CONTENTS

LIST OF PHOTOGRAPHS

LIST OF MAPS

John Tursi and Thelma Palmer, 2010

INTRODUCTION

This book was originally published in 1989 by John Tursi and his friend and collaborator Thelma Palmer under the title *Long Journey to the Rose Garden*. Thelma, a retired English teacher, and John, a former Shell Corporation engineer, had long been friends, and as Thelma explains in her 1989 Preface (which follows this Introduction), she had heard some of his stories since she was a girl and knew they were "the stuff that books are made of." The pair worked together for three years: John related anecdotes from his hardscrabble childhood in Brooklyn, his two years as a CCC worker during the Great Depression, and his experiences in World War II; Thelma worked them into a cogent autobiographical narrative.

Though *Long Journey* was published privately, it sold reasonable well in Tursi and Palmer's home town of Anacortes, Washington, where John and his wife Doris were well known members of the community. After Don and I moved to Anacortes in 2000, we came across the book on the shelves of Watermark Book Company, our local bookstore. Upon reading it, we both felt strongly that it deserved a wider readership. The idea stayed with us, and after we started up our small publishing imprint, Cave Art Press, in 2013, we approached John and Thelma about re-issuing their book. Both were elderly by then—John was in his late nineties and living in a retirement home—but they agreed jointly to sell us the rights. John was very much looking forward to the publication of this new edition but, sadly, he did not quite live to see it, as he died on April 8, 2016, as the book was in the final stages of production.

Thelma's approach as co-author was to keep the text true to John's voice and vernacular. "It is his story, and I have written it almost exactly as he told it to me," she wrote in the original Preface. We at Cave Art Press have made a number of editorial changes, primarily in the interests of readability, but the stories themselves remain entirely John's. We have expanded the post-war content, but this too comes directly from John, from interviews Don and I conducted with him in 2010.

We also felt that the book needed a different title better suited to its contents. The original title, *Long Journey to the Rose Garden*, was explained almost as an afterthought in the 1989 edition: only on the very last page of the book was any mention made of John and Doris's volunteer efforts in their retirement years, and of the invitation that came their way in 1985 to attend a White House ceremony honoring outstanding senior volunteers. John was proud that his efforts were recognized in this way, particularly given his unpromising beginnings, and the prejudice he endured during and after the War as an Italian-American. He attended the Rose Garden ceremony shortly before he and Thelma began working on their book, and he undoubtedly saw the occasion, at that time, as the crowning achievement of everything in his life that had preceded it.

That morning in the Rose Garden in 1985 still represents a great moment in John Tursi's life—but he and Doris had a lot more living to do, as new causes arose that demanded their attention as volunteers and philanthropists. I have always felt, in any case, that John's story is about so much more than the specific achievements that led to the Rose Garden invitation. The book's new title, *A Long Way from Brooklyn*, is intended to reflect this. Above all, we hope readers enjoy this new edition of one remarkable man's life story.

Réanne Hemingway-Douglass
Don Douglass
Publishers, Cave Art Press
Anacortes, Washington, April 2016

PREFACE

When John Tursi first asked me to write his story, I thought it would be more work than I wished to do—even though over the many years of our friendship I had heard some of his adventures and knew they were the stuff that books are made of. One evening at a dinner party, I overheard him telling how his hunting rifles had been confiscated by the Anacortes Police Department the day after Pearl Harbor merely because he was of Italian parentage.

I was horrified at such blatant discrimination, and somewhere in the recesses of my mind, a distant memory began to come awake. A couple of days later, I remembered! I must have been about twelve years old when my mother took me into town to Doris Tursi's Kulshan Beauty Shop for my first hair appointment. I was sitting all wired up under the electric machine having my curls heated to permanence when the phone rang. As Doris hung up, I heard her say to an employee, "That was my husband. He just bought a hunting rifle." I was intrigued that I had incidentally heard about one of the rifles involved in the wartime infamy, and that made me begin paying more attention to John's stories.

When John related the story of his mother's death, I was deeply touched by the suffering of the children and shocked by the insensitivity of the mortician. I knew, then, I would write John's story for him, and though the two years I thought it would take to complete the book stretched into three, I have not been sorry.

Along the way, I learned many fascinating details of life In Brooklyn in the twenties: how children were purged on Saturday night; how pasta was shaped into "little ears" and "seashells"; how leeches were used; how to catch a sparrow; and how water-pipe joints were soldered in the tenements. I discovered John and I share memories of Fidalgo and Whidbey Islands that go back long before we knew one another, and re-living these memories together has been a delightful journey into the past. I also learned more than I ever suspected about the myriad services that John and Doris Tursi perform quietly for our community.

Most important of all, I learned much about the resilience of the human heart and how goodness can grow out of inauspicious beginnings. I re-learned what my Scandinavian parents taught me, that hard work and determination do pay off, and it is still possible to pull yourself up by the bootstraps in America.

Thelma Palmer
Guemes Island, Washington
August, 1989

DEDICATION

This book is affectionately dedicated to Doris Tursi and Darrell Palmer.

JT and TP, 1989

And to the memory of John Tursi, July 24, 1917 – April 8, 2016.

PART I

NEW YORK

1922-1934

Lower New York State, Including Suffern

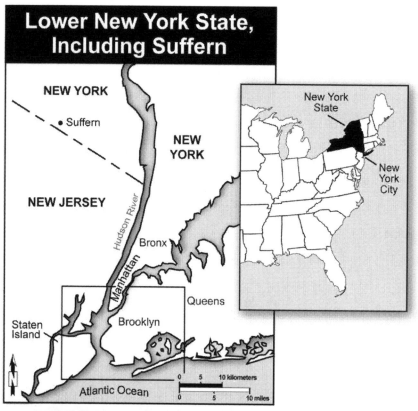

New York City / Brooklyn

Chapter 1

TWENTY-SEVEN FLOWER CARS

"*E mia casa!*" My first clear memory is of my mother shouting at my oldest brother, Tony. It was her house, Mama was saying, and she did not want to share it with just anybody. In particular, she did not wish to play hostess to a mysterious stranger, whom Tony had just informed her would be staying with us for a while.

Mama's words flew over my head. I was sitting on the linoleum floor pulling on my first lace-up shoes, eagerly anticipating our neighbor Tommy Chevi's funeral procession. Mama had told me Tommy would be buried that day, and I had wakened early, as excited as if I were going to Father Appo's to eat Eucharist-wafer leftovers and stack pennies. Tommy had been well-liked by everyone on our block, and his funeral was going to be outstanding. First would come the brass band in their black short-billed caps and high-collared jackets; then the casket in a horse-drawn hearse; next the mourners on foot; and, finally, the open touring cars filled with sprays and wreaths. The number of "flower-cars" always indicated how high up the social or criminal ladder the dead person had climbed. Tommy was sure to have plenty.

On this morning of the funeral, Papa had already left to harness his horse, Jim, and peddle ice down toward Borough Park. My six-year-old sister, Angelina, and my eight-year-old brother, Mike, were off to school. I was four, too young for school, and I thought just Mama and I were at home in our upstairs cold-water flat.

Then Tony came into the kitchen. I didn't pay much attention to him, because we had seen little of him since his return from the war in Europe, four years earlier. He was just a scowling shadowy figure who slipped in and out of the apartment. On most occasions, he completely ignored Angelina, Mike and me—the three youngest children, who had been born in America. Our older brothers, Antonio, Pasquali and Graziano, had been born in Italy and Tony, as the eldest, had replaced Papa as boss of the family, because, unlike Papa, he could speak English and was better able to cope with life in Brooklyn.

3

My view from the kitchen floor was of Tony and Mama's black shoes, the bottom of her long black skirt and of his black trousers. What they were saying and doing existed somewhere above my head in another world—until I caught sight of a revolver in Tony's hand.

I scrambled to my feet and clung to Mama's mourning skirt, which she always wore in honor of a miscarried baby.

Mama ignored me. "I tell you, your friend cannot stay here," she insisted to Tony in Italian.

"Shut up!" he snarled back.

"You will end up in jail, or you will be killed, Antonio." Mama was breathing hard by now. I had the feeling that if Tony weren't careful, she might take the stove poker to him.

Tony aimed his gun under the sink and twirled the barrel, checking to see that all chambers were loaded.

Mama attempted to finalize the matter: "The man must go, and that's that."

"Shut up!" Tony commanded again, and because he truly was the boss, Mama said no more.

Tony slipped the gun into his hip pocket and issued Mama his orders. "He'll stay here in my room until I tell you it is time for him to leave. You will take him three meals a day. No one will see him or speak to him." He finished by slamming a few bills and a handful of change onto the blue-checked oilcloth of the kitchen table. "Here is the money for the first week's food."

Tony then went back to the unseen visitor in his room, banging the door shut behind him.

Mama, defeated and mad, grabbed me by the shoulders and admonished me not to follow in my brother's footsteps. I took little notice of this advice. When she moved away to the sink, I slipped a penny off the table into my pocket and flew down the stairs to join the Niccoli boys, Francesco and Tommaso. They were waiting for me because we had agreed the day before to watch Tommy Chevi's funeral together and count the flower cars.

Tommy Chevi had returned to Brooklyn after World War I and moved in with his parents, a good Italian family across from us on 65th Street. He had served in the Navy and, like most immigrant kids who had no trade, he was attracted to the dangerous life and big money of gangsters. One of them, Frankie Yale, lived three blocks away and his gang was currently battling a rival Chicago gang that wanted to control the booze racket in New York as well as Chicago. Yale needed a bodyguard, so he hired Tommy as both bodyguard and chauffeur. Everyone in our neighborhood thought Tommy had been lucky. Yale was a thug, but he was a thug with a heart. Sometimes in the bitter cold of a New York winter, he would have a load of coal dumped on the corner of sixty-fifth and thirteenth for anyone who needed it. People swarmed around the pile with coal scuttles, burlap sacks and buckets, and the coal quickly disappeared. One time, when Frankie's gang thought they were hijacking a load of silk, the loot turned out to be a truckload of snow sleds. These, too, ended up on the corner so that every boy in the neighborhood was able to help himself.

Shortly after beginning his new job, Tommy drove up to the tenement where Yale lived with his wife and children. Frankie's wife saw Tommy on the street below and called out to him from her second-story window, inviting him to join them for dinner. As Tommy got out of Yale's Hupmobile sedan, another car sped by and riddled him with bullets that were probably intended for the Kingpin himself.

The day of the funeral was a fine one. The sun shone down between the tenement buildings, leavening the sense of solemnity in the air. The vestibule of Tommy's apartment house had been filled with wreaths and bouquets sent by family members and friends. From our stoop across the street we three boys especially admired the black funerary draping around the entry and the bright flower spray on the door.

"I saw them put that stuff up yesterday," Francesco bragged in Italian. As with my own family, most of the kids in our neighborhood knew very little English, so we mostly spoke Italian.

"I saw it, too," Tommaso chimed in, exhibiting his superior knowledge. "It was the undertaker who did it."

"Well, I saw Frankie Yale go up to Chevi's last night," Francesco said, continuing the game of one-upmanship. "He's the biggest gangster in the world."

But it was I, four-year-old Giovanni Torccio, who had the best news of all. "You know what I got?" I said loftily, "I got a penny!" Pulling the coin out of my pocket, I told them I would buy a treat for the three of us.

"Let's buy nigger babies. I like them best," Francesco said on the way to the candy store.

"*E mio soldo!*" I said. It was my penny, and I would buy with it what I wanted. We agreed that I would do the talking as we pulled our usual number on old man Moskowitz, the Italian-Jewish man who owned the store.

Once inside, we eagerly surveyed the possibilities: Indian nuts, corn candy, Tootsie rolls, two kinds of licorice whips, jelly beans, chocolate kisses, cinnamon-flavored sugar-coated peanuts, and chocolate-covered goobers.

"How much is this, *Signoro?*" I asked drawing the old man's attention to a tray of nigger babies on the bottom shelf in the corner. He told me, and then I pointed to the dark brown, naturally sweet bean-pods laid out on the counter tray.

"Could I buy three of these with my penny, *Signoro?* Then we could all have some." I pleaded with my eyes as well as my words, and as I continued to divert the storekeeper's attention, *mio compagni* stuffed their pockets with anything they could lay their hands on. In the end, I bought according to volume, as usual, getting roasted peas that *Signoro* Moskovitz measured from a small wooden cup into my hands.

We three boys then staked out our seats on the curb across from the Chevi apartment and shared the peas and pilfered sweets as we waited for the funeral to begin.

Mourners were gathering across the street, and six Navy men in full-dress uniform went into the apartment. A few minutes later they emerged with the flag-draped casket and slid it into the hearse that had just arrived.

"It's the 'dead-wagon'," Tommaso said, lapsing from Italian into Brooklyn-accented English.

"It ain't a 'dead-wagon.' It's a hoise," Francesco replied, in equally Brooklyn-esque tones.

This vehicle in which Tommy Chevi was to take his last ride was truly a fine one: glass windows and doors draped with black curtains trimmed in white tassels; a black shiny frame; and on the very top a "catlick" cross. The driver sat up front in charge of the great black horse, whose harness was decorated with ivory rings and brass knobs. Even the horse's hooves were ready for the occasion, having been blackened and painted with used motor oil.

The hired band arrived en masse and took their position in front of the hearse. When the first notes of the dirge sounded, we kids knew the long-awaited moment had come. We stood at attention and made the sign of the cross.

"*Nome di Padre, Figlio, e Spirito Santo. Amen,*" we said in unison as the procession began.

Off went the band and hearse up 65th Street and around the corner, circling the block before heading down toward Saint Rosalie's Church. We had positioned ourselves so everything would pass by us twice. Behind the hearse came the immediate family and closest friends, weeping and moaning, lurching and staggering under the weight of their grief. The more composed mourners supported the distraught as best they could. Neighbors and passers-by stood on the sidewalk, doffed their hats and silently crossed themselves if they were Catholic.

Then the "flower-cars" got underway and our excitement escalated. In the front seat beside each driver were the sprays and wreaths. The very largest floral pieces were arranged carefully in the back against the folded top of each car. The fragrant and colorful onslaught was the closest thing to a flower garden that we had ever seen.

"Look at those carnations," I said. All flowers were carnations to us.

"Here they come," shouted Tommaso.

"There's number one," shouted Francesco. He was the only one of us who could count, so the burden of responsibility was upon him. In case he lost track, I slipped a pea into my shirt pocket as each car passed. When the last car had passed, the band was already around the block and turning back up 65th Street. Francesco had counted twenty-seven flower cars, and the peas in my pocket matched his total. Twenty-seven flower-cars! That was the most we had ever heard of!

When I got home, Mama saw a couple of peas in my pocket and somehow got it out of me that I had stolen a penny. She gave me a good whipping and warned me that I would grow up to be just like Tony if I continued to take things without asking.

That night before we ate supper, Mama sent Angelina to Tony's room with a plate of food for our unseen guest. Angelina knocked on the door and a hand reached out and took the food.

At the table I told of the procession and the twenty-seven cars. Papa drank from the wine flask and passed it around to us kids. Mama frowned a lot—an expression I was to see on her face quite often during the month that the stranger remained hidden in Tony's room.

One morning I realized that no one had taken a breakfast plate to our unwanted guest, and I overheard Mama asking Tony who the man was and where he had gone.

"Shut up and don't ask questions," Tony growled, letting us all know that it was none of our business. The guest to whom we could not speak had slipped away in the night as mysteriously as he had come on the day of Tommy's funeral.

Chapter 2

ICEMAN'S ASSISTANT

Weekends were special. Every Saturday morning I would go with Papa on his ice route. We didn't have a clock, so we never knew the exact time, but Papa seemed to waken automatically in the mornings. We always left very early, without having breakfast. I was hungry, but I didn't think much about it because Papa usually ate only one meal a day.

I enjoyed going with Papa. He never showed any of us younger children much tenderness, but he never beat us either because Mama would not let him. She personally administered all of our beatings, and they were regular and no-nonsense.

Papa was a short man—about five-foot-six—and thin and wiry. He seldom smiled, perhaps because life in America had not turned out to be as rosy as he had expected. Life in Italy had been difficult, but Papa had lived among friends in the quiet of the countryside, amid the fragrance of the basil fields. Here in Brooklyn, he worked as hard as in the old country, but in a teeming, noisy city full of strange new ways. Adding to his difficulties, Papa did not speak English and was competing with thousands of other immigrants who had learned at least some of the language. No wonder his face was lined and his hair prematurely gray.

His most memorable features were his eyes—one was gray and the other was blue. This difference in color made him appear somewhat uncertain or vague, as though he saw the world in one way through the blue eye, and another through the gray. Otherwise, Papa looked like the rest of the immigrant ice peddlers. They all wore baggy black pants that ended two or three inches above the tops of their heavy shoes, and they draped hooded burlap capes over their shoulders. Made from feed sacks, the capes helped anchor the ice and gave a little protection against the cold.

On our way to the stable, I followed closely behind Papa, imitating the way he walked. His toes pointed out almost ninety degrees from his heels. I forced myself to stretch my own toes in the same way. I did this at a time when my bones were forming and still find myself walking more like a duck than a human.

Although we had gone without breakfast, Papa was careful to feed Jim, the horse, generously. Jim was a good-natured animal, and as Papa curried and harnessed him, I would dart back and forth underneath his belly, testing my courage and developing my agility.

Papa wore only his burlap sack for protection, but Jim had a black rubberized raincoat for rainy days and a handsome fringed net for hot days when the flies were bad. During the snows of winter, Jim had other special equipment—leather covers that fit over the tops of his hooves and held three delicate but strong chains across the underside of his feet so he would not slip.

After helping Papa load the wagon with blocks of ice, I would sit proudly beside him on the high seat. Most of his customers were in the Borough Park District, which was just three blocks away in distance, but miles away in wealth. These people lived in two-story row-houses and could afford to spend fifteen or twenty cents a day just for ice.

All morning, Papa cut the heavy blocks of ice into smaller pieces. He held these with tongs against the burlap on his shoulder as he carried them up the steps of the houses. Disappearing inside, he deposited his load into ice boxes and collected the pennies that supported our family.

When noontime came, we stopped to feed Jim, but there was no lunch for us. Instead, Papa lit up his short piece of Italian cigar, and I refreshed myself with bits of shaved ice.

At the end of the day, we went by Peter Bollo's feed store to pick up the hay and oats that Jim needed for the coming week. I was always fascinated by the old Jewish couple who lived in a small room just inside the door of the feed store. Their living quarters, partitioned off from the rest of the cavernous building, contained a two burner gas stove, a table with two chairs, and a cot on which only one of them could possibly have slept. They earned their living by mending burlap sacks for a penny apiece. The man wore a traditional black yarmulka and the woman her black shawl as they worked swiftly, reweaving the old sacks that had been torn or chewed by rats.

On one particular Saturday Papa stayed longer than usual talking with Mr. Bollo, whose soldier son had been killed while fighting in France. The grief-stricken Mr. Bollo was still waiting four years later for the body to be shipped home to him. To Papa, he said, "My Leonardo should be home any day now. The government said they would send him home to me soon."

Papa put a comforting hand on his shoulder. "I hear there is a boat in the harbor today. Surely your Leonardo is on it."

After this exchange, Papa bought a live rooster at the chicken market on our way home and presented it to Mama. From long experience, she knew exactly what to do with it. She deftly folded the bird's neck back over her index finger and cut the jugular vein open with a sharp knife. Then she held the chicken over a skillet and drained the blood to make a special Saturday night treat. Seasoned with a little salt, the blood was heated slowly until it clotted into a cake, which Mama divided among us. After not eating all day, we kids were starving, and the small squares of fried blood tasted wonderful.

We stood around watching Mama as she continued preparations for Sunday dinner. After the chicken had been plucked and the insides removed, she took out the intestines, split them with scissors, washed them, and cut them into small pieces. These were added to the liver, gizzard and heart and made into broth. The chicken feet were boiled and scaled, the head was plucked and cleaned and these, too, were added to the pot.

The next morning, Papa took Mike and Angie to Saint Rosalie's Church, where he earned a little money cleaning up after mass. I stayed back with Mama as she continued to prepare for our weekly feast. She rolled pasta dough into long pale ropes, cut them into half-inch pieces, and drew her fingertip deftly through the dough, which then appeared to fashion itself almost magically into *orecchiotelli* (little ears) or *scamaruchelle* (seashells). Mama worked quickly and silently, because life was serious with no time for idle talk or play with children.

By the time Papa, Mike and Angie arrived back from church, delicious smells filled our flat. The strongest of these came from a simmering sauce that Mama had made on an earlier day from *conserva di pomidoro* (tomato puree). This had been cooked, strained, and reduced into a thick paste. Mama preserved it in jars with leaves of basil and olive oil on top. Now, some of it simmered away slowly with onion, garlic and other herbs, tempting us almost beyond our ability to endure until dinner time.

Then it was time for me to go to the corner saloon and call Tony to dinner. I was happy to do this, not only because it meant we would eat soon, but because Tony would always tell the bartender to give me something to drink. Gimpy, the bar tender, had been wounded in the war

11

and he usually gave me a glass of water with a few drops of anisette in it. But I would not enter the bar until my presence had been acknowledged.

"The kid's here," Gimpy called to Tony as he saw me hanging around the door.

"Give him the usual." Tony's order was my invitation to go in.

While Gimpy prepared my drink, my eyes adjusted to the darkness of the saloon. I saw a group of men seated around a table playing cards. Each player had either a gun or a knife beside his cash pile, and everyone was serious. There was no joking around. Two of the men, Irish and Slug, sat across from each other. They were good friends who were constantly seen together around the neighborhood.

In spite of Prohibition, the men were drinking openly. Gambling was illegal also, but they were deeply involved in their cards and oblivious the fact that the door was open.

"Mama wants you to come home and eat," I said to Tony

"Okay, kid. I'll be right there."

I drank my anisette water and went home. When Tony arrived, everyone but Mama sat down to dinner. An Italian housewife always fed her husband first, her kids next, and herself last. Papa started dinner by taking a drink of homemade "Dago red" from a flask before passing it on to us kids. We were all expected to take at least one drink, so our blood would be strong and we would sleep well. The cherry-wood flask looked like a small barrel with a vent hole and a spout, and it took some practice to be able to drink from it. You had to plug the hole with your finger as you lifted the flask above your head, then unplug it at the right time so the wine would stream out of the spout into your open mouth. Papa was very good at this and held the flask up high so the wine trickled directly down into his swallowing gullet.

As the wine circulated, Mama served the soup. Papa was first and he picked out the head of the rooster, which he opened with his fingers and held toward me. I picked out the brains—a sweet treat— and ate them with relish. Tony, Angelina and Mike each got a special part in their soup, too: a foot, a heart or a gizzard. My plate was always a small oval dish, and when Mama put it in front of me there were always bits of dandelion and intestine floating in the broth. A grater and a hunk of hard Parmesan were then sent around, and we each waited impatiently to sprinkle a little cheese into our soup.

The pasta came to the table on a large oval platter. Papa served himself and us little kids; we ate whatever was put on our plates. Bread was passed and everyone was expected to break a piece off and fill up on it so there would be enough pasta to go around. After the pasta came the chicken, roasted with potatoes and herbs and served with a salad of escarole and dandelions. Then dessert would arrive—Italian bread dipped in wine. I usually passed on this course but stayed in my seat because soon Mama would bring out homemade *prosciutto*, *salami*, and sausage. Sometimes there would be nuts and fruit as well.

Papa and Tony remained at the table to smoke, drink and continue the dinner conversation, which on this day was mostly about the *mano nera* (the Black Hand). As the afternoon wore on, they felt hungry again and resumed eating—a pattern that might continue for hours. Just before I left the room to go outside and play, I heard Papa say, "Peter Bollo still expects Leonardo's body to come home from the war any day now. He was very sad yesterday when Giovanni and I were there."

"If a body ever arrives, it won't be Leonardo anyway," Tony replied. "There's no knowing whose son will be in that pine box."

Out on the stoop, the Niccoli boys and I watched the people walk by. Suddenly, we heard yelling from the saloon down the street, followed by shots. Shootings were not unusual in our neighborhood. We kids had all witnessed them before, but they still scared us. Before we could get inside, we saw Irish and Slug stagger out of the saloon. Both were wounded. Slug leaned against the doorway, slipped down in slow motion and was dead by the time he reached the sidewalk. Irish lurched across the street toward the police booth on the corner. The cop on duty made a hasty retreat on his bicycle, so he wouldn't learn too much and have to go to court to testify. Irish had killed his best friend and the matter ended there, without the police ever becoming involved.

Chapter 3

TOUGH LOVE

Looking back, those early days appear pretty grim, full of death and dying. But none of that bothered me at the time. I was just a kid and life was what it was. A funeral procession was as much fun as a circus parade; a street shooting as thrilling as a ghost story before bed. There wasn't much other excitement. Mama and Papa were so busy simply trying to make ends meet they had no time to play with us or tell us stories, even if they had been inclined to do so. As an adult, I have been asked to tell school children stories or sing songs from my childhood, but I have had none to offer because such frivolities were not part of my experience growing up.

Nevertheless, it is the nature of children to be bright and full of expectation, and many joyous memories arose for me out of everyday experiences.

One of these occasions was a Monday morning. Monday was always washday, and I would watch and stay out from underfoot as Mama wrapped the dirty laundry in a sheet and carried it down the steps. Then, off we would go together along the street, Mama balancing the laundry perfectly on her head. She was small but strong from hard work in the fields in Italy and the never-ending job of raising a big family. As far as I can recall, she had two dresses, both black, one for washing and one for wearing. She wore her graying black hair puffed out in pompadour around her face and wound into a braided bun in back. Her face was pretty and her blue eyes were quick as a bird's—always alert.

I carried the big bar of Octagon soap, which was used for everything, not just laundry. We washed dishes with it, scrubbed the floor, and scrubbed our faces, too. We took baths with Octagon soap, and used it for shampoo. To this day I can recall the strong antiseptic smell—more potent than Lifebuoy. I also remember Octagon soap bars as being big and heavy, probably because I was so little, but I was proud to be helping Mama, no matter what it took.

On this particular Monday morning, I not only carried the Octagon soap but the washboard as well. It was not easy handling both of these

14

items, but I managed to get them to the basement of the tenement building where Mama did the laundry. All of the neighborhood Italian women came here to wash their clothes and catch up on the latest news from the old country.

When the job was finished, Mama bundled the wet laundry in a sheet and we started home again. Along the way, we met Signora Matti and Signora Grecco and stopped to talk. Like Mama, these women wore long black dresses with black shawls, because they were always mourning someone, and they carried their bulky bundles of laundry comfortably on their heads. Signora Grecco's son Angelo was with them, too. He and I were about the same age, and as our mothers discussed the pressure being put upon their husbands to join the Street Peddlers' Protective Association, we two boys had our own conversation about starting school.

We were balancing on the edge of the curb when I noticed water tinkling down the gutter.

"Look, Angelo," I said, pointing to the small stream and then looking up to check the sky for rain. But the sky was clear.

"Where does the water from?" Angelo and I asked one another.

As the stream continued, we became more and more excited. Here was water welling up like a miracle out of the gutter dust! Unable to contain myself any longer, I pulled on Mama's skirt to get her attention. Mama's response was to pinch my ear firmly between her thumb and forefinger and jerk me painfully around, with an accompanying hiss of *"Silenzio!"* I still didn't know what was happening, but I got the message that I should pay no more attention to the mystery fluid in the gutter. Then I understood its source. Signora Matti was standing close to the curb edge, her skirt pinched out rather elegantly at the crotch, and her legs spread. She was peeing into the gutter, without missing a word of conversation and, probably, without wetting herself with so much as a drop.

The Monday morning laundry schedule resulted in mostly enjoyable outings, but the ritual that took place in our kitchen on Saturday nights was anything but pleasant. Mama was determined to keep us lice-free and healthy, so once a week before bedtime Angelina, Michael and I were ruthlessly shampooed and purged. We never did get lice like most of the other kids, so Mama's prescription obviously worked, but having lice might have been preferable to what we went through to avoid them.

Mike was the oldest of us three young ones, so he was always first. Then it was Angelina's turn. By the time I had watched Mama dunk both their heads in kerosene and shampoo their hair with the Octagon soap I knew their agony would be mine next.

The dreaded basin of kerosene was placed on a chair, and Mama would grab me none-too-gently by the scruff of the neck and immerse my hair in it. She rubbed and scrubbed for only a few minutes, but it seemed like an hour. No matter how hard I closed my eyes, kerosene and soap always got in them, and for the rest of the evening I alternately rubbed my burning eyes and bawled. But this did not deter Mama from her mission of cleaning us thoroughly, inside and out. When she was convinced no louse inhabited my hair, she took to my skin with a wash-rag and the Octagon soap. Indifferent to my misery, she polished my face to a high luster before proceeding. She worked downwards, methodically scouring and scrubbing every inch and every fold of my naked body, until I shone like one of the angels in a church picture. Then she would stand back to admire her work. It didn't matter that my eyes were red and swollen, or that my skin had been all but worn away. Mama cared only that I was clean and without vermin.

But she was not finished yet. Now came the worst part: the inner cleansing! As Mama gave the first cupful of citrate of magnesia to Michael, the bilious green walls of the kitchen began closing in on me. By the time Angelina had been given her dose of laxative, I was beginning to gag in anticipation. But neither gagging nor bawling dented Mama's determination.

She pressed the hated cup to my lips while indicating with her other hand that I had no alternative but to drink. The magnesia slipped into my gullet but always came up again as uncontrollable vomit. I suppose Mama thought it didn't matter that the medicine was regurgitated, just as long as it had been in my stomach for even a brief time

After this came the customary goodnight kiss. I generally accepted these from Mama with pleasure—except on Saturday nights.

My older brother, Pasquali, or Pat as we called him, was about seventeen when he went to work washing dishes and training to become a cook in a restaurant. This job introduced him to tomato ketchup and white American bread. In our household, both were foreign to us because we ate only Italian-style food. We rejected Pat's restaurant bread because it tasted like cotton compared to our hard-crusted Italian loaves. The ketchup was inedible too, because we were unaccustomed to its sweetness. So Pat's early attempts to Americanize our palates were a failure.

Sometime during the early months of 1922, Pat came home and announced that he had been diagnosed with tuberculosis. Mama put him to bed in the room at the end of the flat, as far away from the rest of the family as possible. Mama took him food but none of us kids were allowed to visit him. As far as we were concerned, Pat was a non-person from then on, a vague, tragic, coughing presence who existed on the periphery of our lives.

More trouble came that year when Graziano, known as Harry, came home unexpectedly from his residential Catholic high school wearing a soldier's uniform. Like many Italian parents, Mama and Papa dreamed that one of their sons might become a priest, and our local priest, Father Locksley Appo, had suggested that Harry would make a good candidate. No one had considered Harry's own wishes, however.

Harry spent an hour telling our parents of his dilemma. He had taken up with a married woman and left in a hurry via the bedroom window when her husband came home one night unexpectedly. Harry figured after this that he should get as far away as possible—and since the Army offered a posting in Hawaii, he signed up. There went the hopes of Mama, Papa and Father Appo, and our parents never saw Harry again. They lost track of him entirely, and by the time he contacted me years later Mama and Papa were both dead.

About that same time, Tony brought home another unpleasant surprise. Appearing unexpectedly with a Jewish girl on his arm, he announced, "This is Bessie, my new wife." So now we had a sister-in-law—and she couldn't even speak Italian. Bessie joined Tony in the room where he had kept the mysterious stranger hidden, and it was here that Mama and Papa's first grandchild was born.

Tony had become increasingly involved with the underworld and was not present for the birth. I don't know where Papa was, but I remember Mama bringing in a midwife. Mike, Angie and I were in our bedroom, wide-eyed and a little scared by the commotion. At the height of it all, we heard Mama announce with considerable gusto, *"E una piccola ragazza!"*

Bessie still didn't understand much Italian, so we probably knew before she did that she had given birth to a girl. Little Rosalie was a fine baby, but she was yet another presence in our already crowded apartment. Mama cared for her, even so. About a week after she was born, Mama pierced Rosie's ears with a needle and thread so she could wear earrings. When Rosie was sick from time to time, Mama's remedies included lots of prayer and folk cures such as garlic poultices and hot applications, which were placed upon the baby's bare belly.

In the midst of all these family dramas, something good happened to me. Before I enrolled in kindergarten, Bessie took me to the Board of Health for a smallpox vaccination. I was glad to have someone speak for me in English, and I was excited about my forthcoming adventure, despite the fact that it began with the puncturing of my arm. But I had been hardened by slaps and whacks, by kerosene and citrate of magnesia, and by falls and scrapes that were healed with beatings rather than kisses. I took the shot with equanimity. As the doctor pricked away, he asked Bessie, "Is this brave little man your son?"

"No," she replied. "He is my brother-in-law." I felt proud at being spoken about in English.

At kindergarten, there was the usual playground hubbub, but these calls and shouts came in a mix of foreign languages. We Italians called the kids who spoke English "Protestants," because we knew only three kinds of people: Jews, Catholics, and Protestants. English was the only language taught inside the classroom, and I began adding rapidly to the few words I had learned from Mike, Angie and Bessie.

As kindergarten became a positive addition to my own life, my brother Pat's condition deteriorated to the degree that a Board of Health doctor sent him to a local hospital. Father Appo took all of us in his chauffeur-driven car to visit him. Pat was in a dismal ward with thirty or forty other tubercular patients. Father Appo was obviously as upset by this as we were, and he arranged soon afterwards for Pat to be admitted to a TB sanatorium in Suffern, New York.

Mama, in the meantime, had grown increasingly depressed and was simply not feeling well. Her teeth were giving her a lot of trouble and I began hearing that she had something called "diabetes." Her own troubles probably reinforced her natural tendency to want us younger kids strong enough to survive the tough environment we were growing up in. When I fell down, I got whipped for falling; when I bawled, I got slapped for bawling. The day I fell off Papa's ice wagon and split my head open, she poured wine vinegar into the wash basin and kept dunking my open wound into the acetic antiseptic. Mama believed that if a medicine hurt it, was doing good. She would not have used Mercurochrome, even if we could have afforded it, because it did not hurt when applied to open wounds. We could not afford iodine or peroxide either, so she used the vinegar she had in the cupboard. When she felt certain it had done its work, she wrapped a rag around my head, gave me a couple of whacks for being clumsy, and sat me in the chair to think about it. I didn't mind too much because I expected this response from her. Mama practiced tough love, but at least she was consistent.

Chapter 4

THE EVIL EYE

I was probably the least of Mama's worries at this time. She had one son in the TB sanatorium; another intended for the priesthood who had to drop out of school because he got involved with a married woman; and a third son tangled up with the underworld. Adding to these woes, Papa's income was shrinking as he had to pay the Street Peddlers' Protective Association ever more of his meagre earnings.

At that point Mama decided to do something drastic. I came home from school one day to find her sitting around the kitchen table with Signora Grecco and another of their friends. The jar of leeches that was kept on the shelf beside Mama's home-canned tomatoes sat empty on the table before them. The women had opened the fronts of their dresses and sat contentedly with two or three leeches sucking on each full white bosom. I often saw this scene, because the women believed these sucking creatures were a deterrent against high blood pressure and helped to rid the body of other blood-carried poisons. Soon, they removed the leeches, put them back into the jar, and returned their pale melon breasts to their proper places.

"Someone has put the *malocchio* (evil eye) on our family," I heard Mama telling her friends. "Not only are my three oldest sons in trouble, but now we have two more mouths to feed just when my husband's salary becomes less each week. And my health is not good. I am so tired all of the time, and, lately, my teeth hurt. See, it pains all of the time." She opened her mouth so her friends could look deep inside past the two gold crowns she wore proudly over her eyeteeth.

Signora Grecco made sucking sounds of commiseration with her tongue as she noted the abscesses. "Tich, tich," she said, moving her head sadly from side to side, "but who could have put the evil eye on you?"

"I do not know, but I cannot go on like this," Mama replied wearily. "Bad luck comes again and again to this household. And I grow more and more tired each day." Then she said, "You mentioned that your cousin who just arrived from Italy wears the golden horn and knows about these matters?"

In this way an exorcism was arranged. A day was chosen, and a fee of two dollars was agreed upon. In a matter of days the newcomer to America appeared at our door with her cousin, Signora Grecco. The proceedings were carried out in the kitchen around the table. Mike, Angie and I were sent to our bedroom next to the kitchen, but with the door cracked slightly open we could see the three women working under the dim gas light that hung from the ceiling.

Mama wore a gold cross around her neck. Signora Grecco and her cousin wore gold animal horns. They were all dressed in black, but this was not unusual as they always wore mourning clothes. Mama and Signora Grecco shrank back in fear as they watched the exorcist pull a large black cross out of her dress and hold it before her. The woman began a low chanting that was intended to repel any evil spirits in the neighborhood, and she walked around the kitchen swinging the cross in front of her. She stopped at every corner of the room and spoke her most fierce warnings, each time touching the cross to her heart, then to her forehead, and completing each ritual by kissing the cross. When she began a counterclockwise march and chant around the table where Mama and Signora Grecco sat, Mama cried out in sheer terror and dropped her head to the table.

The exorcism must have been a folk-mixture of pagan and Christian rituals. That would have been fine with Mama, who could not read or write in any language. Though she attended mass she could not understand the spoken Latin either, so her religious understanding probably did not extend far beyond the sign of the cross. We three little kids fell asleep before the evening was over, but in the morning Mama seemed to be in better spirits than usual.

"Life will be easier now that the evil eye is removed from us," she said.

Three days later black handprints appeared mysteriously on a gymnasium wall at my school. The *mano nera!* We kids were scared and I did not dally on my way home that afternoon. The Black Hand was something to be reckoned with. I had heard that in Italy the *brigante* kidnapped poor little boys and sold them into servitude with rich families. Sometimes they took young girls and sold them to rich widowers or older men to be trained as mistresses.

As I ran up 65th Street, I thought of home and Mama as a welcome refuge. I did not even slow down to glance into the candy store window.

"Mama!" I burst into the kitchen, "the *mano nera* was at school!" My voice trailed off when I saw Mama and two of her friends at the kitchen table, holding their heads and weeping.

Their story came out in sobs and moans and great sweeping gestures that seemed to ask, "How can this be?" The three women had been shelling peas in our kitchen when two robbers burst in. One pointed a gun at them while the other took the plain gold wedding bands from their fingers. Oh, the misery of losing your most valued possession, the symbol of marriage which meant you were fulfilling your purpose on earth! And beyond that, the robbers had extracted thirty cents from Mama—all the money she had left in the house for food until Papa's next ice delivery.

"The *malocchio*, the *malocchio*," Mama moaned. *"No e finito."* My story about the black handprints on the gymnasium wall paled to nothing in comparison to what had happened at the flat. The women did not attempt to go to the police booth on the corner. They could not explain in English what had happened, and what could the police do anyway? What *would* the police do? Mama and her friends continued their weeping until it was time to prepare supper for their families.

Mama's sickness worsened. Perhaps the return of the evil eye was too much for her; perhaps it contributed to her physical illness by adding to her depression. But however poorly she felt, she did not go to bed. Angie helped her as best she could, and Mike and I spent a lot of time out on the stoop. Papa continued to bring home a little money. Then one day when Papa had gone to feed the horse, Mama lay down and went into a deep sleep. Bessie summoned a doctor, but Mama was dead by the time he got to our house.

When Papa got home, Bessie sent Mike to get Father Appo, who went straight to Mama's room and prayed in Latin. We three little kids were huddled together on the bed in the room next to Mama's when he came in to comfort us. I can still see that straight handsome figure, so tall that his black curly hair nearly touched the top of the doorway. He stood there for a moment looking at us sadly with large brown eyes. He was an educated man but his kindness was innate rather than something he had learned. It was beyond the boundaries of language or countries.

We jumped to our feet and kissed Father Appo's hand, as we had been taught. Then he did something most unusual for us. He put his arms around us and drew us to him. This was the only real comfort we were to receive when our mother died. I don't remember the words that Father Appo spoke, but I still remember the tenderness and affection with which he spoke them. He spoke softly and slowly, every word gentle as a whisper.

After Father Appo left, another man arrived. Papa had said an embalmer was coming, but I did not understand the term. Mike, Angie, and I were still huddled on the bed as the stranger walked through our room to Mama's. He was carrying a bag and some other equipment. When he re-appeared at our door and inquired, "Where's the toilet?" Angie pulled me to her, turning my eyes away.

"Don't look, Giovanni!" she cried. But it was too late. I had seen the two large jars of blood that the embalmer was carrying.

Mama's funeral was not as grand as Tommy Chevi's. Oh, there was maroon draping in the living room where Mama was laid out on a bier. There was black draping around our apartment entrance and a wreath on the door. But Papa could not afford to hire a band, and when Mama was put into a coffin and carried down the stairs only a few people waited below. When the fine hearse came and started off down the street, I did not follow with everybody else.

I sat down on the curb with the Niccoli boys and watched the cortege disappear around the corner on its way to Saint Rosalie's.

There was one flower-car.

About a week later, Tony appeared at the door with two large vegetable baskets and began breaking our dishes into them. Papa was uncomprehending.

"What are you doing? Have you lost your mind?" he shouted.

"The *malocchio* is on us, and the only way to get rid of it is to destroy everything of Mama's," Tony replied.

Over Papa's protests, he continued smashing all of the dishes into the baskets. Everything went, even my treasured white oval plate. Just to be sure, Tony finished by crashing Pat's bottle of ketchup into Mama's broken dishes.

The red sauce that ran thickly among the shards reminded me of the embalmer in our room on the morning Mama died. For years afterward, I thought she had bled to death, and to this day I don't know what she actually died of—whether diabetes or something else. There was no autopsy, no one even showed interest. She just died.

Chapter 5

LITTLE LORD FAUNTLEROY

Papa stood dejected and downcast, listening to Tony.

"This place has *il malocchio*. Bessie and I are leaving," Tony said. "You'd better get out of here, too. Besides, you can't afford this big flat. You need to find somewhere smaller."

Tony was the boss. Papa knew it was pointless to object.

"The kids are too much for you to take care of. Mike can go live with Father McCarthy, and you can put Angie and Johnny in a home," Tony continued.

Still Papa said nothing. We three little kids hovered anxiously. It seemed that our fate had been decided by our oldest brother. "A home" meant an orphanage. The prospect struck terror in my six-year-old heart. I had seen the tall brick walls topped with shards of glass where the orphans lived under the watchful eye of the nuns.

We did not go to the orphanage right away. Instead, Papa enlisted the aid of a fellow *paesano* and moved our household three blocks, to 62nd Street. Papa's ice wagon was loaded with our meagre possessions. The furniture comprised a table and four chairs, a small marble-top dresser, and two beds, one of which we three kids shared with me sleeping in the middle, my head at the foot end. The luxuries included the Victrola, a picture of Christ with his bleeding heart on the outside of his robe, and a glass containing a candle that was always kept lit in honor of Mama. Papa hand-carried his beloved records of Enrico Caruso and Amelita Galli-Curci, which he played on Sundays after our noon meal. When the voice of Caruso filled our new flat, I remembered the fight between Mama and Papa after he first brought the records home. Mama said we could not afford them, but Papa loved opera, especially when it was sung by Italians.

Our new ground-floor flat was just down the block from the orphanage. I understood what Papa was trying to do. He wanted Angie and me to get used to the idea of being put into a home. I hung around outside the hated building as much as I could so I could learn what was in store for me. What I observed was even worse than I had imagined. The orphans,

25

who ranged in age from four to twelve, were not allowed to come to the fence to talk to us street kids when we called to them, and they had to attend mass all the time. They were prisoners, jailed behind ugly walls that were impossible to scale. Once a week, weather permitting, the nuns would lead them in silence around the block. This was their only outing, and the orphans were disciplined to the point they would not speak to each other on these walks. I would rather have died than live that way. Life on the street had its drawbacks, but it was preferable to prison. I also knew that if orphans were not adopted by the time they were twelve, they became priests or nuns and never got out from behind those fortress-like walls.

The one positive thing about our new apartment was that Father Appo's parish house was directly across the street. If not for that, my despair over the orphanage looming in my future might have overwhelmed me. But just seeing Father Appo gave me a certain comfort.

Father Appo raised Great Danes in a small cage behind his house. The dogs gave birth to puppies that summer, and though the smell was often horrendous, the little animals responded to my attention with wet tongues and soft paws. Inside the back door was a machine that Father Appo's assistant used to stamp Eucharist wafers from thin sheets of bread. I had eaten wafer scraps on previous visits with Papa, and I appreciated them even more that summer because we had less food to eat at home now. Talking with the priests kept me from thinking too much about the orphanage. Father Appo also allowed me to play with his great box of pennies. I stacked these into monetary skyscrapers—an activity that distracted me from loneliness. I missed Mama and the Niccoli boys, and I continued to fear the orphanage. Eventually, the pennies would tumble helter-skelter to the wooden floor, and sadness would crash down upon me once more.

Days went by and Papa did not send me to the orphanage. My spirits improved a little and I started to mingle with some of the 62nd Street kids. Maybe, just maybe, Papa would be able to keep us together, and maybe this new neighborhood wouldn't be so bad after all. Most of the kids were older than me, but I hung around on the edges of the crowd and was beginning to know some names. The 62nd Street kids gave me my first lesson in reproduction that summer.

Geraldo swaggered up to me smoking a butt he had found in the gutter. "Do you know where you come from, kid?"

"What do you mean?" Geraldo knew as well as I that we had come from 65th Street.

"How you wuz born."

Nervous that I had even been noticed, I felt relieved to be able to answer Geraldo's question. "Yeah," I said, "I was born from dust in a corner." Mama herself had imparted this information.

Geraldo spat on the sidewalk. "Ah, shit. You wuz born from your mudder's twat."

Embarrassed and confused, I was unable to reply to this at first, but as the horrible Geraldo hovered over me, I finally managed, "What's a twat?"

"That's how ladies piss," he explained loftily.

Well, I could relate to the body part that pisses, but the rest of the picture was very confusing. I stood speechless and bewildered, trying to imagine how a baby could come out of this part of a grown-up body.

As Geraldo continued berating me as a "dumb shit," I saw something that he did not. A young parish priest was coming up behind him. In those days, priests disciplined street kids whenever and wherever they deemed it necessary. Father Joseph grabbed Geraldo by the neck, gave him a good shaking and then a swift kick, surprising Geraldo so much he almost swallowed his cigarette butt. After this came a dressing-down. The rest of us kids were delighted, but we dared not show our pleasure; Geraldo would still be around long after the priest had gone. Nor would Geraldo have dared to tell his parents that he had been manhandled by a priest. The church was the authority in those matters, and had Geraldo related the story his parents would have given him another kick in the ass.

Father Appo was transferred a couple of months after we moved to 62nd Street, and perhaps for that reason Papa decided we should move again, too, to a smaller apartment on 61st Street. I took it as a good sign that Papa might not put us in the orphanage after all. He was doing the best he could to keep us clean and fed, but it was becoming harder for him as the Street Peddlers' Protective Society demanded ever more of his meagre income. I had one outfit of clothes, which Papa washed occasionally. Then I would sit around in my pants while my BVDs, shirt, and socks dried on the clothes line. Papa sat around in his pants too, because he washed his shirt and union suit at the same time, but he never did our trousers. Mike and Angie had to look out for themselves.

Papa didn't bother about having us bathe. When we washed our faces and hands, we used the faucet in the kitchen sink and simply scrubbed away some of the dirt. Then we would dry off on the heavy cement sack that served as the family towel. But toward the end of summer, Papa decided we needed to do something about our hair, because we would soon start school in our new neighborhood. Angie's hair got a shampooing with Octagon soap, which made it look considerably better. Mike and I did not fare so well. Too poor to pay for haircuts, Papa shaved our heads. As baldies, Mike and I were subjected to taunts and jeers from the kids whose parents could afford to send them to the barber.

This humiliating experience brought Mike and me a little closer together. Before Mama died, Mike had never paid too much attention to me. Now he made me a skullcap. I will never know if his concern now was out of sympathy or embarrassment, but he had a skullcap of his own that partially hid the shame of his shaved head, and somewhere he found or stole an old gray fedora that he used to construct one for me. Removing the brim, he serrated the bottom of the crown with scissors and folded it up until it fit my head, covering as much of my humiliation as possible.

Mike and I wore our caps continuously, even in the house when we could get away with it, though Papa would not allow them at mealtimes. Eating was associated with religion in his mind, and the wearing of hats at the table was not respectful.

Papa went off to work early each morning, and Angie and Mike drifted into street life, so I was alone most of the time. It never occurred to me to go back to see the Niccoli boys, even though they were just a few streets away. In those days, people often passed their whole lives without venturing more than three or four blocks from home. So, I was on my own and always looking for ways to entertain myself.

One day I decided to explore the dingy basement of our new flat. It was dark and unpleasant, so I continued on to the backyard, where I found a small package wrapped in a page of newspaper comics and tied with string. Fascinated with comics, because we never had them in our house, I carefully untied the string. I had not expected the package to contain anything—but inside it were two twenty-dollar bills! I knew what they were because I had learned my numbers at school the previous year. This was wealth beyond imagination, and I ran with it as quickly as possible back to the flat. Of course, there was no one there to tell, but I was unable to suppress the news of my good fortune. Going to the kitchen window that opened on to the airshaft, I called out:

"I have found money! I have found money! Look here, money wrapped in the comics!"

For a time that seemed like an eternity but was probably only a few seconds, there was no response. Then our neighbor, Maria, appeared at the window above.

"Look," I shouted again, this time holding up the money and newspaper. "Look at this money I found."

Maria said nothing at first. Then she called down to me.

"Wait for me, Johnny. I'll be right down. Wait for me now."

Seconds later, Maria appeared at our door, followed by two other women. All were anxious to know where I had found the money.

"In the backyard," I said, "right there in the backyard."

"And your Papa," they asked, "where is your Papa?"

"Selling ice," I informed them, wide-eyed at my incredible find. "Papa will not be home until late tonight. What am I gonna do with this money?"

The three young housewives gathered around me inspecting the bills, trying to determine if it was counterfeit. When they decided it was real, Maria said, "We will help you, little Giovanni. You must give this money to us, and we will go to Macy's and buy something very nice for you."

I was barely six years old and had no one else to advise me, so I gave the three women my treasure.

"Now, you wait right here for us, Giovanni. We will be back soon with your present," they promised as they left the flat.

Two or three hours later they returned, bearing many boxes, one of which was for me. I danced from foot to foot in anticipation, scarcely able to contain myself as they opened my package. Maybe it would be a toy or some candy, I thought hopefully. But when the package was laid bare before me, my heart sank and my face fell. It was a Little Lord Fauntleroy suit. Black velvet short pants and jacket with a white ruffled shirt. The agony of wildest expectation had just been dashed into bitterest disappointment.

The three women were delighted with the suit, however, and insisted that I try it on immediately. I couldn't say no, because adults were not to be refused. As I pulled on the velvet pants I knew I would never wear this ridiculous suit. But the women were insistent. Standing before them in the complete outfit, I must have been a sight because it was too small for me. The pants hiked up in the crotch, and the sleeves of the jacket and shirt ended halfway between my wrists and elbows.

After expressing their profuse admiration, Maria and her friends left, taking the rest of the packages with them. While I was still struggling to get out of the suit, Mike came home. I can only imagine his horror at finding me in short pants and ruffles. He was a little rough as he helped me get the new clothes off, but he didn't demand an explanation until I was dressed normally again in my filthy pants and torn shirt.

"I found two twenty-dollar bills wrapped up in comics in the backyard, and Maria and her two friends helped me," I said, allowing myself to cry because I knew Mike would not beat me for bawling.

Mike confronted Maria and her friends, but they insisted I had found two one-dollar bills and they had spent all of the money on my Little Lord Fauntleroy suit. Mike kindly disposed of the outfit somewhere and I never saw it again—although years later, when I was on my way to fight the war in Europe, the memory of it came back to haunt me. But that's a later story.

Chapter 6

EATING SPARROWS

"Johnny," Mike said one day after school, "Let's go around the corner and see if we can steal some eggs." Neither of us had eaten breakfast or lunch that day, so this sounded like a good idea to me.

"Yeah! If we find some eggs, we can have *fritatta* for supper."

"On the way home from school just now, I saw a truckload of birds pull up in front of the Jewish chicken market," Mike continued. "Maybe they laid eggs in their cages."

As we rounded the corner of the market, Mike explained that he would climb up the side of the truck and search for eggs while I kept lookout.

"If you see anybody coming, holler 'Fox in the bush!' and run for home," he ordered.

I knew how to play Fox in the Bush, because I had been punched in the arm numerous times by kids who spotted rabbis before I did. As far as we were concerned, any man with a beard was a rabbi, and the first kid to spot one would punch the kid next to him until that kid, in turn, saw the rabbi and hollered "Fox in the bush!" and punched somebody else in the arm.

"What does 'Fox in the bush' mean?" I asked Mike.

"It means Jewish rabbis can hide a fox in their long beards."

A rabbi was making the chickens kosher when we arrived at the market. Mike and I watched with fascination as he upwardly stroked the feathers of the neck, chanting a prayer as he did so, then slicing the jugular vein and throwing the dying bird into a barrel to flop and bleed to death.

"What's he saying, Mike?" I asked.

"He's making the *bruchas*."

"What's the *bruchas*?"

"The Yiddish word for prayer," Mike explained patiently. "It'll be easy for you to remember because you know what *auf dein tuchas* is, and *bruchas* rhymes with *tuchas*."

31

Well, I certainly did know what *auf dein tuchas* meant. In fact, I knew how to say "Up your ass," in three languages: Italian, Yiddish and English.

We continued to watch as the rabbi brought chicken after chicken from the truck and went through his gory ritual. At one point, Mike gave me the eye and wandered around to the far side of the truck, where he could climb up to get us our supper. I continued to monitor the rabbi, and when he moved toward the back of the truck, I hollered, "Fox in the bush!" and ran for home as fast as I could.

The signal worked because Mike got away and caught up with me before I reached the flat. We didn't speak until we were safely inside. Breathless and hungry, I asked, "Did you get some eggs?"

Mike had five of them stuffed in his shirt—three small and two large.

"What are those big ones?" I asked.

"Goose eggs."

"What's a goose?" I must have exhausted my brother's patience at that time, but there was no one else to ask.

"A big duck. And the Jews eat goose grease on *matzoh*. You know, 'stitched cardboard'."

Our feast that night was worth all the trouble we had taken to get it. Mike and Angie scrambled the stolen eggs with some cheese, Papa put a loaf of Italian bread on the table, and after dinner we listened to Caruso.

Many of my early memories are related to food because we were hungry so much of the time after Mama died, and this memory is no different. I was sitting on the stoop after school watching sparrows in the street as they picked the undigested oats out of horse manure. The late afternoon was pleasantly warm, and I dozed with my skull-capped head in my hands as the birds fluttered and flew.

An idea came to me out of that place between waking and sleeping where dreams mingle with the everyday world.

"Catch a sparrow and cook it," the dream voice said. By Jesus, for the first time I could be totally responsible for feeding myself. My heart raced at the thought. The rest unfolded like a dream, too, because something hitherto unknown inside me knew exactly what to do. I ran around the corner to the chicken market where I found a wooden apple box and a stick. Back on the street in front of our flat, I put the box over an especially large pile of horse droppings and propped up one end with the stick. From our kitchen I brought string which I tied to the stick. Next, I gathered manure in my bare hands and sprinkled it in a line that led to my trap.

Now there was nothing to do but wait. The sparrows continued to chirp and flit, but it seemed that every time one of them headed toward my trap, a car would pass and startle them. Once the waffle-man went by with his cart and scared a bird that was nearing the box. Then it was a long time before any of them resumed picking oats out of the manure trail. If hunger sharpens the dreams, however, it also sharpens the wits, because at the moment when a bird finally did enter my trap, I had him. With no knife to slit the little creature's throat, and not knowing the *bruchas*, I pulled his head off unceremoniously and started plucking the feathers.

By now, a couple of other kids were interested in what I was doing. "Get matches," I ordered, feeling the situation was mine to command.

The boys ran off, and when they returned, they not only had matches but two mickies (spuds) as well. We broke up the box for firewood and roasted the sparrow and mickies in the coals and ash. The spuds were black on the outside and raw on the inside, but we ate them with relish. The boys declined my offer to share the sparrow. The miniscule mouthful of burned flesh and bones did not look very tempting, but my stomach was empty as usual, so I ate it—and because I had used my wits to provide it for myself, it tasted especially good.

On Sunday afternoons the Italian men of the neighborhood would gather at the truck garden across the street to play *bocchia* ball and cards. The farmer sold wine for five cents a glass and furnished, free-of-charge, salted *lupino* seeds that increased the men's thirst. I got pretty excited about the *lupino* seeds, because I was interested in anything food-related.

This routine came to an end, however, when a steam shovel was brought to the farm and excavation started for the construction of a large macaroni factory. Each afternoon when I came home from school, I watched the digging of the big hole that would become the basement. One particular Saturday, I had gotten up early, no breakfast as usual, and taken up my position at the edge of the hole, watching as the steam shovel operators loaded horse-drawn wagons with dirt.

At noon the shovel crew stopped for lunch, but I stayed on waiting impatiently for them to start work again. About mid-afternoon, the fireman who was also the oiler of the machine came up the bank and said, "Hey kid! Do you want a jelly sandwich?"

I had been taught not to take anything from strangers, including food or money, unless Papa or Mama said it was okay, so I refused. The man explained that it was butter and grape jelly, and that it was good for me. Because Mama was no longer there to say no, I took the sandwich and savored every mouthful of sweetness.

The next Friday afternoon, I went straight from school to the excavation site as usual. As soon as I appeared, the fireman led me to a pile of large pear-shaped cheeses that had been unearthed earlier in the day. I recognized them right away as Provolone. Obviously, they were hot cargo that had been stolen from the docks, abandoned in a hurry, and buried in the empty field.

"Can I have one?" I asked excitedly.

"Kiddo, they're all yours. Take them home."

Wrapped in woven rope carriers, the cheeses weighed fifteen or twenty pounds apiece. I dragged them, two at a time, back to the flat. After telling a neighbor, who told other neighbors about my find, I managed to get two more home before the rest of the pile disappeared. Now, we had cheese to eat with our evening loaf of bread, which we otherwise ate with warm water and olive oil poured over it.

When Papa returned home from work, he told us that the small white maggots we could see in the cheese were good to eat. I took his word for it and they tasted like Provolone. But our good fortune that afternoon did not compensate for Papa's bad luck in being held up at gunpoint. It had happened just down the street, in front of the cement block plant that was a cover for a gang of robbers. A dozen or so men hung around there, and everyone knew that when a likely victim came along the men would come out of the office with their guns. That day it was Papa's turn. The men took all his money, but Papa refused to tell the police for fear of reprisal.

We were always looking for a way to make money. One Saturday morning Mike said, "Johnny, let's go down to Borough Park and see if we can earn some pennies."

"What do we have to do?"

"Well, the Jews aren't allowed to light their gas on Saturdays, so they'll pay us to do it. All the men down there wear little black skullcaps, have whiskers, and are rabbis. The young boys are studying to be rabbis and go to the Jewish school every afternoon to learn Hebrew. Then, when they are thirteen years old, they can be real rabbis."

I always believed every word of my big brother's explanations.

When we got into the Jewish section of town, the appetizing smell of pastrami and corned beef wafted into the street, where it mingled with the pungency of pickled cucumbers, tomatoes, and green apples. Here, customers could buy, along with many other mouth-watering treats, a succulent hot meat sandwich spiced with Jewish mustard, and a two-cent sour pickle.

As we walked along New Utrecht Avenue, a rabbi standing in the door way stopped us and asked, "Will you light the gas for me? I will give you a penny."

Of course! We followed the man up a flight of stairs to the flat above his store. In the kitchen we were shown the matches and the gas lamp, along with a penny which had been placed on the table the day before.

Mike climbed on a chair and lit the lamp, and when he was finished the rabbi said, "Thank you, *kinderla*. There's the penny."

We left happy and rich, but I remained puzzled as to why the man could not light his own lamp or touch the penny. For once, Mike didn't have an answer either, but neither of us were bothered by it for long—and on our way home, we stopped at a candy store and bought a cupful of Indian nuts.

Chapter 7

A NIGHT TO REMEMBER

Papa was cleaning the church after mass when an invitation came from Father Appo for our family to go to his house for Thanksgiving Dinner. My delight was dampened somewhat when I discovered we would have to go to his new parish house in the Williamsburg District by subway. I always suffered from motion sickness on subway trains, and I threw up reliably on this occasion too, but I forgot my illness the moment we reached our destination.

Father Appo opened the door himself and greeted us warmly. After kissing his ring, we three children stood quietly aside and surveyed the scene. There were nine or ten nuns, three street kids whom Father Appo had taken in to live with him, and one other person whom we did not know. She was a tall, beautiful woman who wore lipstick and a wide-brimmed yellow hat and shone like a bright angel beside the monochromatic nuns. Not only did she wear makeup—which as far as we knew was only worn by ladies of the night—she was smoking a cigarette in a long gold holder. Papa didn't say anything, but we knew he must have been horrified to see such a woman in Father Appo's house.

When Father Appo introduced the woman as his sister, Papa was even more shocked. She greeted Papa pleasantly but he could scarcely respond. We had become used to the fact that Father Locksley Appo's exotic lifestyle included chauffeur-driven cars, servants, and lavish dinner parties, but we were not prepared for this: a sister dressed in beautiful clothes, wearing makeup and smoking. Mike, who was the source of most of my information and misinformation, explained to me afterwards that Father Appo and his sister were Algonquin Indians, so it was only natural that both of them had dark skin and smoked. This made sense to me at the time. Years later I discovered that Father Appo's sister was a fashion writer for a Paris newspaper.

Our surprise at finding this worldly woman in a parish house soon gave way to the marvelous smells coming from the kitchen. Mike and I made sure not to speak to the other boys until we sat down to dinner, because we were expected to exhibit our best behavior and knew we should be quiet.

Two tables were set in the large dining room, one for grown-ups and one for us kids. The roast suckling pig that was brought to our table was so far beyond my wildest imagination that I recall nothing else about that Thanksgiving dinner. The pig had an apple in its open mouth and glistened golden with grease.

"The insides are still in it," Mike gasped in wide-eyed disbelief. "It's a whole pig!"

Beyond that there was little conversation at the children's table. We ate what we were served, until I felt a little sick because I was not used to so much or such rich food. Papa evidently found the feast overly generous also, because that evening on the subway he let off a great fart that was heard throughout our half of the car. Breaking wind was quite acceptable in Italy, and Papa smiled broadly. But Angie and Mike knew farting was not socially acceptable in America and felt humiliated.

"Shame on you, Papa," Angie scolded. "You mustn't do that. People don't like it."

The more Angie berated him, the more delighted Papa became, and the more everyone around us laughed in cheerful acknowledgement of Papa's overt flatulence. I had been told not to break wind in school, but, like Papa, I felt it was acceptable to fart anywhere else, and I joined him in celebrating our full stomachs with the occupants of our subway car. That evening as we left the train, Papa led me by the hand, but Mike and Angie, still embarrassed, walked ahead.

Winter was coming and it was a cold evening when Mike and I set out for 65th Street to visit one of his friends who had a crystal set radio. I had never heard a radio before and was very excited. We wore long red sweaters, drew our necks down into the wool of the collars, and walked along briskly until we came upon a lamplighter at work. He was a hunchback, and as he propped the small ladder against the lamppost, I remembered Mama telling us always to be respectful of ill-formed people and never ridicule them. Maybe Mike was remembering this, too, because we both stood there quietly as the old man struck a match and lit the gas lamp.

Around us, people hurried home with their evening groceries. Mike and I followed the lamplighter as he carried the ladder on his shoulder to the next post, watching as he repeated his ritual, fascinated by his work and his misshapen body, feeling sympathy for him. It was as though we formed a trio, the hunchback, Mike and I, a small island of connectedness in the evening rush. Perhaps the lamplighter felt it, too, because he paused to show us how his ladder narrowed at the top so it was just the right size to rest against the horns on the post.

"And when I get to the top, I hang onto the horns, so I don't fall while I strike the match," he explained, pointing upward without looking because it was difficult for him to lift his head out of the hump. "I have to start while it's still day-time so I get all the lamps lit by dark."

Before Mike or I had time to respond, an open touring car with two men in the back seat pulled up to the curb. The men were swearing at each other in Italian. Their driver paid no attention to them, keeping his eyes straight ahead. As the argument escalated, one man called the other a "son of a bitch." Almost casually, they got out of the car and began swinging at each other. The lamplighter moved on, and so did the other people around us, but before Mike and I gathered the sense to leave, one man reached for his back pocket. He pulled out a switchblade, started cutting up the other man, and when the victim slumped to the pavement the attacker got back into the car and issued a command to the driver: "*Presto!*"

Mike and I moved on *presto*, too, and as we looked back, people coming upon the scene seemed to flow around the dead man on the street, in the way that water flows around a log in the river. No one wanted to get involved—and by the time we reached Mike's friend Carlucci's apartment, we had all but forgotten the incident ourselves.

Carlucci had a room of his own where the small, dry-cell crystal set loomed large under the only light. Because he was selective about whom he invited to come and listen to the magic instrument, Mike and I sat quietly and reverently while he tuned it.

"There's a man talking," he said at last, passing the earphones to Mike, who listened for a moment before handing them to me.

At first all I heard was static, but then, slowly, I could make out a voice. Not understanding how those words came through the air, I felt certain Mike and Carlucci were playing a trick on me and had a phonograph connected to this device. It was a pretty impressive trick, even so. In fact, I was awestruck.

The evening's excitement did not end there. When we arrived home, Papa and Angie were in the kitchen, sprucing up. This was surprising in itself, but Mike and I were even more surprised when we, too, were instructed to wash our hands and faces, and comb our hair. "Why are we cleaning up, Papa?" I asked, confused. I had washed my face that morning and did not want to burn my eyes with Octagon soap twice in one day.

"Your new mama is coming tonight," Papa explained. This news further stunned us three kids. We objected, but were overruled as Papa went on, "It's the only chance I have to keep us all together. Signora Yolanda, the go-between, has already met with me, and tonight she brings a woman just off the boat from Italy to marry me."

Angie and I immediately started crying, "We don't want a new Mama!"

"*Silenzio!*" Papa commanded, "They will be here any minute now." True to his prediction, the two women arrived moments later.

As Papa opened the door, Signora Yolanda, a large, imposing woman, pushed the intended bride into the kitchen ahead of her. I could see nothing of her but a dark, pinched face peering out from beneath a black shawl draped over a black dress. The entire scene was dimly-lit and dismal. We three kids stood silently in a row as Papa introduced us to the ladies as "my children." Dispensing with further niceties, Yolanda, all business, immediately began selling the virtues of this stranger to Papa.

"Margarita will make a wonderful wife. As you can see, she is very little and doesn't eat much, so she will not be expensive to support. Also, she worked hard on the farm in Italy and is very strong."

Margarita hung her head demurely and said nothing.

Papa seemed no more impressed than we kids were with the poor woman. She, in turn, must have felt like a chattel as she waited in front of us. Possibly, Papa was considering marrying her more for our sakes than his own, and that was why he turned to us three little ones asking, "Would you like this woman to be your mama?"

We knew that our rejection of her might result in the family having to split up, but we answered in unison with a loud, "No!" We could detect the relief on Papa's face, and our feelings gave him the out he wanted. Turning to Margarita, he gestured sadly with open hands and announced that there would be no wedding.

"I am sorry, but my children still miss their mama too much. I cannot marry you," he said.

Papa's decision meant no money for Yolanda and no husband for Margarita. Even so, the women did not argue.

After they left, we all felt relieved. We knew for sure that we would not have been happy with Margarita—a miserable woman who was willing to sell herself in exchange for food and lodging. But our rejection raised other uncertainties. Once again a family split loomed, and none of us knew what adventures or misadventures lay ahead if we were to break up.

Within a week, our respective fates had been cast to the wind. Father Appo made arrangements for Angie to be placed in a Catholic girls' home. She was crying as she packed her few belongings and kissed us goodbye, not knowing whether she would ever see us again. Waving out the back window of Father Appo's Dodge sedan, she watched us standing on the sidewalk, waving back until the car disappeared around the corner.

Mike was to live with Father McCarthy and study to become a priest. He was looking forward to going, because he still remembered the Thanksgiving dinner with all the food and the other boys at Father Appo's house, and hoped life with Father McCarthy would be similar. But this plan never came to fruition because, within a week of Mike's scheduled move, Father McCarthy died. There was nothing else for Mike to do for now but stay with Papa.

Then it was my turn. Papa didn't say anything until the following Sunday morning, when he announced, "Come on, Johnny. We're gonna visit Pat in Suffern." Having recovered from his tuberculosis, my brother Pat had remained in Suffern and married a local woman after his release from the sanitarium.

I had mixed feelings about going. I wanted to see Pat, but I also knew I would be sick on the train. Papa made sure that I sat next to the window facing the direction we were going, and the forty-mile journey north was an exciting experience for me. I had never been so far from home, and we were traveling on a real train on the main line between New York and Chicago. We passed through heavily industrialized areas, however, and all I saw was the flash of dirty windows in dingy brownstone factories. What I heard was more interesting: the eerie shriek of the train whistle, the rapid clang of the crossing bells, and the syncopated "click-click, click-click" of the wheels on the track.

From the train station in Suffern, it was a short walk to the flat where Pat lived with his new wife, Louisa, and baby. They were surprised to see us because Papa had no way of letting them know we were coming. Nevertheless, they seemed mildly pleased and Louisa started to prepare dinner.

I didn't pay much attention to the conversation because I was absorbed by the view out the window. Tree-covered hills were strange to me. But, suddenly, something Papa said caught my attention.

"Giovanni is a good boy, and I will pay you, of course."

It began to dawn on me. Papa intended to leave me here with Pat and Louisa in these strange surroundings.

"There is a woman in this house, and Giovanni needs a mama," Papa continued.

Pat and his wife said nothing at first. Clearly, they were less than thrilled at the idea of taking me in.

"Are you going to leave me here, Papa?" I got up from the table and went to stand by him.

"Yes, Giovanni, but just for a short while. I will come and get you as soon as I can."

"He will have to mind and do everything just as we tell him," Pat said. "Louisa is busy caring for me and the baby."

No one asked me if I wanted to stay or go, but the others came to an agreement about how much Papa would pay, and when. Then he kissed me goodbye and left. I felt numb inside, like an empty package dropped off on the doorstep of people who did not want it. A little while later Louisa brought me a blanket and showed me the davenport where I could sleep.

Alone at the window that night, long after the others had gone to bed, I thought of Papa and wondered when he would return for me. Eventually I lay down, drew the blanket under my chin, and shuddered in terror as trains screamed back and forth along the nearby rail line. Beginning as far-off wails, the locomotives approached at full-throttle as brutal, belching, bell-ringing monsters that seemed to enter our apartment and obliterated me completely on their way through. They destroyed me, wiped me out for the time it took them to pass, then they faded down the tracks. In the short lulls between trains, I drifted off but I didn't really sleep because soon enough another whistle would begin moaning in the distance.

Chapter 8

A KATHOLIC EDUCATION

Life in Suffern took some getting used to. In Brooklyn, the only dangerous animals we encountered were humans, and I had managed, somehow, to avoid harm from them. In rural Suffern, I had to be on the look-out for more insidious critters: rattlesnakes, copperheads, and water moccasins.

Suffern was different from Brooklyn in other ways as well. The gentle Ramapo Hills, which enclose both the town and the surrounding Ramapo River valley, were veritable mountains compared to the flat slender sandbar of Long Island—and they confined our view. In Brooklyn, we could look from Brighton Beach to the skyscrapers of midtown Manhattan, ten miles away.

Brooklyn had plenty of trees, including a big poplar split by lightning outside the flat where we had lived with Mama, but they had been planted for shade and aesthetics. In Suffern, the trees were native and grew throughout the valley and the hills. They included pines that covered the hills and many varieties of nut trees, including butternut, black walnut, hickory, and pig nut.

Though it may seem surprising, there were more cars in Suffern than in Brooklyn, because people in Suffern had to travel greater distances. In Brooklyn, a horse and wagon still served to get peddlers and business men where they needed to go; only gangsters and the wealthy had automobiles. In Suffern, almost everyone needed a car or truck to get to work or drive to adjoining towns—so the streets were full of Marmons, Fords, Stars, Moons, Durants, Whippets and other early models. Even my brother Pat had a truck, a paneled Chevy that he used in his laundry business.

The greatest changes I experienced had to do with my family life. Suddenly, I was eating three meals a day. These were not bountiful, but they were regular. There was always a piece of buttered toast and coffee for breakfast; boiled beans for lunch; and various pasta dishes for supper. My stomach had to adjust to the increased quantities of food, but the rest of me was grateful. There were drawbacks, however. Papa had paid little attention to our table manners, so Louisa and Pat took it upon themselves to teach me a few. Their methods were direct and based on surprise attack. The first slap, for slurping my spaghetti, took me completely unawares and nearly knocked me off my chair. This shock approach worked, and my manners improved quickly.

Even my name changed when I went to live in Suffern. In Brooklyn, my last name had been Torccio, but Pat enrolled me at school as Tursi, which was the way he spelled his name. I did not question this at the time, because I had learned to do as I was told without asking why. It was not until many years later that I learned from Tony why each of us kids had a different family name.

When each of us was born, the midwife would ask Papa what the new child's name was to be so she could write it on the birth certificate. With great gusto, Papa, would hold up baby and announce its name. The midwife would ask about spelling, but Papa could neither read nor write, so he would just pronounce the name proudly and loudly once again, leaving the poor midwife to spell it as best she could. She would then show the paper to Papa and ask him if she had got was right. Not knowing one letter from another, he would simply agree. A baby could have been named "hot dog" for all he was aware, so it was small wonder that all six of us had different family names on our birth certificates: Torccio, Torrcio, Tursy, Torcci, Turci, and Tursi.

And so I started at my new school with a new name. I was now John Tursi, who lived with his brother in Suffern. The school itself was a big two-story building with a grouchy principal, Beatrice Patchin. Most of us spent recess lined up in the hall waiting to use the lavatory; Miss Patchin did not allow us to talk during this time. A redeeming memory is of the day the straps on her slip broke and undergarment slid—slipped!—down over her shoes as she monitored us in our recess line. After her initial shock, she stepped out of it, swooped it up, and headed like a ship under full sail for the teachers' lounge.

After school and all day Saturdays I worked behind the counter in my brother's laundry, taking in dirty clothes and handing back clean ones. Up front, where I was stationed, there were shelves and a couple of ironing boards. In the back, there was a small, dark room with clotheslines and portable kerosene heaters where items to be ironed—mostly men's shirts—were dried.

Pat picked up laundry in his truck from all around Suffern, and in the nearby towns of Tuxedo Park, Arden and Slotesberg. He then took it to Ramsey, where it was emptied into large perforated wooden cylinders that rotated slowly in troughs of hot soapy water. After this, it was spun dry. These "rough dried" clothes were then delivered back to customers, or brought to the store to be completely dried in the drying room and ironed.

Though the laundry was closed on Sundays, these were work days, too, as I cut and split kindling for the coal fire in the cook-stove. I did this job by candlelight in the basement dungeon, sawing logs of hardwood, usually oak, with a handsaw from which many teeth were missing. Then I split the pieces with a dull hatchet.

After a few weeks I got a paying job, washing dishes at Cerveris' Ice Cream parlor, six evenings a week. For this I was paid two dollars a week. The Cerveris left all the lunch dishes for me, so I arrived as soon as possible after school and worked until seven in the evening. I was never offered any ice cream or candy, and though I was constantly tempted and tantalized by the second-hand smell of chocolate, I never felt able to spend any of my earnings on such a luxury. Instead, I bought clothes and a two-dollar piccolo, which I learned to play well enough that I was asked to play "Barcarole" at a Friday assembly at school. The piccolo disappeared soon after that, and to this day I do not know if it was stolen or used for kindling. Whatever happened, I always blamed it on a less than stellar performance.

It was in Suffern that I became a practicing Catholic, at least for the year or so I lived there. Back in Brooklyn, I had never attended mass or Sunday school. My only tangible connection to the church had been Father Appo's kindly hand on my uncombed hair as he asked, "And how are you, Giovanni, my boy?"

Now, I was glad to follow Pat and Louisa's dictum that I attend church and Sunday school every week. Religious observance gave me a feeling of belonging—which was something I badly needed. Suffern had a population of about three thousand at that time, and the large Catholic Church was so full during the two regular masses that kids had to sit in the balcony and sing in the choir. Apparently I had a good voice, because sometimes the rest of the kids were silent as I sang under the leader's direction. I didn't notice I was singing solos at first, because I was so eager to please that all my attention was focused on the director.

After mass, I went with the other kids to Sunday school in the parochial building. Here, too, I paid attention and was anxious to participate. One morning the teacher asked what we knew about Adam's apple—at least that's what I thought she said.

My hand flew up and the teacher indicated I should answer. "Adam took a bite of the apple, and it got stuck in his throat and that's why men have Adam's apples," I explained proudly. This information presumably had come from my all-knowing brother Mike.

The kids laughed, the nuns frowned, and I was embarrassed because I thought the answer had been correct. Puzzled and hurt, I sat down and hung my head as the jollity continued around me. Then my favorite nun, Sister Carmelina, a young bright-eyed woman full of laughter and enthusiasm, came to my rescue.

"All right, now children, that's enough," she said, coming over to me and putting her hand on my shoulder. "John gave the answer that he thought was right. You must not laugh at him."

In spite of being ridiculed by the others, Sister Carmelina's kindness made me even more eager to study and learn, so I could truly belong to the church. I memorized the first catechism quickly, keeping it with me and studying every spare moment, in anticipation of my first communion. The night before this solemn occasion, I went to confession. I was a little scared in the dark cubicle, as the priest's voice floated out through the wicket quizzing me about my sins. His questions took me by surprise:

"How many times have you taken the name of the Lord in vain?"

"How many times have you lied?"

"How many times have you stolen?"

I was crestfallen. I had no sins to confess, or so it seemed. I would never have taken the name of the Lord in vain. The very worst epithet we could fling was "Madonna," and not even a street kid like me would do that except under the direst of conditions. I knew I had lied and stolen, but those things had occurred in the distant past, in Brooklyn, and did not seem to apply to this situation. So I left my first confession with a feeling of complete failure, determined to do better next time.

I carried my burden of sorrow with me the next day as I marched down the aisle to receive first communion. As much as my perceived failure at confession, the sadness came from loneliness. No-one in the church that morning was there just for me. I wore a tie given me by one of the nuns and thought it might choke me. I missed Mama and Papa and wished they both could have been there.

My best friend in Suffern was a kid named Tony Catanesi (Cat Knees). I worked so much that we couldn't spend a lot of time together, but one Sunday we met up after dinner to take a hike.

"Let's go up the mountain to see King Tut's head," he suggested.

"Who's King Tut?"

"You'll see," he said with an air of mystery.

"Okay, let's go!" My heart raced at the thought of adventure.

The afternoon was warm with sun and bright with fall leaves that rustled and crunched as we climbed.

"Watch out for copperheads," Tony warned as we climbed. "They're the same color as the leaves, and they can rear right up and bite through your pants!"

For a while I wished I was back in Brooklyn, but my fears subsided when we reached King Tut's head. It was a disappointment: nothing but a great granite boulder with a head chiseled into it—a round circle with crude eyes and a nose like kids make when they first begin drawing.

"What's so great about this?" I asked.

"Well, nobody knows how he got here," Tony said. "He's a king from Egypt or someplace." Trying to re-introduce some excitement, he added, "Come on, let's go to the top. Papa said the Ku Kluckers are getting something ready for Election Day."

I vaguely knew about the Ku Kluckers. Mr. Johnson in the flat below ours was one of them. I had seen him leave for KKK meetings wearing his white hood and robes. When I asked Pat about it, he said KKK stood for Koons, Kikes, and Katholics—and Ku Kluckers hated all three.

Tony and I scrambled on upwards and soon found the excitement we were looking for. Coming suddenly upon a large flat outcropping of rock, we stood wide-eyed for a few seconds trying to comprehend what we were seeing. It seemed we had stumbled upon preparations for a KKK burning rite. On the rock before us lay a big Christian cross, three large

"K's" made of wood wrapped in burlap sacks, and several five-gallon cans of kerosene. We knew that one of those Ks stood for "Katholic," and that meant us.

"We've gotta get out of here quick. If the Ku Kluckers find us, they'll kill us!" Tony gasped.

We left in a flurry of fright and leaves, pell-mell down the trail, helter-skelter over fallen trees and rocks. Suddenly Tony stopped and grabbed my arm as I stumbled past.

"Hold it!" he cried. "There's a copperhead!"

Sure enough, a camouflaged snake slithered through the colored leaves at our feet. Tumbling on in increasing terror, we flew by King Tut without so much as doffing our caps.

At the bottom of the hill, walking toward the main street, we tried to appear casual. Safer now among houses and people, we felt embarrassed at having been so scared. Before separating, we agreed to meet downtown on Tuesday evening for the election celebration.

The year was 1926, and the Roman Catholic Al Smith was making his fourth bid to become New York governor against the incumbent, Ogden Mills. I had heard talk about the Ku Kluckers hating Smith but I was not prepared for what happened that election evening. Tony and I were making our way towards the polling booth, enjoying the spectacle of cars driving slowly up and down the streets, horns honking and people waving. It was the next-best thing to a parade. The atmosphere was friendly and festive. Then, a mysterious blast occurred.

Tony and I were among the first to figure out what was happening. Our Sunday adventure was still fresh in our minds, and we immediately cast our eyes upwards towards King Tut. On the hillside above him were the three "K's" and the cross we had seen earlier, now ablaze with fire and hate. The Ku Kluckers must have set them alight with gasoline, drawing the attention of the crowd to their noxious message.

Before people could completely grasp what was going on, shouts echoed from down the street: "The Catholic church is on fire!"

The crowd began running in that direction. Tony and I ran with them. The church was directly across the street from a monument honoring citizens of Suffern who had served in World War I. A yellowish glow reflected in the stained glass windows, and we realized the church itself was not on fire. Instead, out front on the church lawn, a flaming cross burned horribly into the night sky.

As we stood there watching, wondering what terror the Klansmen would unleash next, Police Chief Lenny roared up on his motorcycle. He raced across the grass, knocked over the burning cross with his puttee-covered shoes, and kicked it onto the sidewalk, where it was left to burn out harmlessly.

"Let's get away from here," I whispered to Tony. Though the incident had not been dangerous, we were two scared kids. The Klansmen might know we had discovered their preparations, and if they found us outside the church they might kidnap us and tie us to a burning cross.

Tony agreed we should just go home. We separated, and I worried all the way back to our flat that a passing car would stop, a white-hooded man would grab me, and I would be spirited away. After all, I was a Katholic.

My religious education continued in other ways. One day, in the advanced catechism class, I saw something that puzzled me. I had been given permission to go to the bathroom, and left the room quietly and slowly because, like many kids, I was in no great hurry to get back to the lesson. Walking along dreamily in quiet, rubber-soled sneakers, I paused briefly at the pipe-railed stairwell that led to the basement and happened to look down—and saw my favorite nun, Sister Carmelina, in a most un-nun-like situation.

She stood with eyes closed embracing and kissing the church usher. I was astounded, as I knew that nuns did not kiss men or marry. But there was Carmelina, her habit partially raised exposing white legs that would seldom, if ever, have seen the light of day. The dark, curly-haired usher held her buttocks in his large, powerful hands. They swayed rhythmically together, unaware that anyone was watching.

I did not understand what they were doing, but I knew somehow that it was forbidden, so I slipped away without being heard or seen. When I returned from the bathroom, I gave the stairwell a wide berth, but I could see the two were still kissing. Now, I was more confused about religion than ever before, and it took many years for me to realize that the religious community was as human as any other.

Meanwhile, I continued to go to confession. I even looked forward to this Saturday night ritual because I wanted so much to be a good

Catholic. After my first disappointing experience when I felt I had no sins to confess, I had soon learned to lie to please the priest.

"Have you used the Lord's name in vain?" he asked.

"Yes. Ten or fifteen times," I lied.

"Have you stolen?"

"No, Father," I lied again, not wanting to admit even to myself that I had stolen cherries.

"Have you masturbated?"

"What's that?"

There was a deep silence and Father moved on to the next question without explaining.

"How many times have you lied?"

"I lied ten times, Father," I said, continuing to lie.

All of this sinning resulted in a penance of fifteen "Our Fathers" and twenty-five "Hail Marys." I felt that lying during confession was making me a very good Catholic—though I still remained confused about a heck of a lot of things.

Chapter 9

SUFFERN SUCCOTASH

One of the Suffern's most prominent citizens in those days was a man named Dan Beard. National Boy Scout Commissioner from 1910 to his death in 1941, he lived on an estate outside the town. I never dreamed of becoming a Boy Scout, as the organization was not intended for kids like me who had neither money nor status. I visited Dan Beard's orchard, however, one summer when the Oxheart cherries were ripe.

Tony Cat Knees came with me. He and I scaled the fence, climbed up one of the big trees, and sat enjoying the luscious fruit until Uncle Dan spotted us. He came running across the orchard, shotgun in hand, hollering at us to get out of his tree. We lost no time leaving, so never found out if this fine old humanitarian would actually have shot at us. But it bothers me to this day that his cherries probably went to waste and could just as well have been shared with us.

Not long after this escapade, word got around that the Arctic explorer Captain Robert Bartlett would be showing motion pictures of his recent expedition to the Boy Scouts of Suffern. The event was to take place at the community hall across the street from the church, and several of us non-Scouts decided to try to watch the movies through the window.

We took up our positions and tried to be very quiet so we would not be noticed. One of the Boy Scouts saw our faces at the window, however, and told Uncle Dan, who immediately wanted to shoo us away. Captain Bartlett approached the matter differently. He discussed the matter with the boys and they responded by inviting us in for the program. The only stipulation was that we keep quiet and act like gentlemen. We were happy to do that because the pictures were a rare treat for us and they inspired us to undertake a few Arctic-type adventures of our own.

Usually I had a few free hours on Sunday afternoons, and early in November about seven or eight of us gathered at Lake Antrim to test the ice. We brought with us a long plank liberated from the Ward Company Rock Quarry and slid it out onto the frozen lake. I picked up a large rock and walked to the outer end of the plank with the rest of the boys following. Dropping the rock on the ice, I was shocked to see water boiling up through the test hole that opened at my feet. I yelled for the others to go back, but before I could turn around, we were all in the lake and scrambling over one another to reach the safety of the shore.

We were all safe but terrified and shivering in the sub-zero cold. "Let's go to the asphalt plant and ask if we can warm up there," someone suggested through blue lips. When we appeared at the door of the office, the man who opened it was so shocked to see us, bedraggled and frozen, that he invited us inside immediately. We scrambled atop the steam boiler and stayed there until we were warm and dry. I went home that evening little the worse for wear, happy to be alive even if I would have to explain the soiled clothes.

Later that winter, when the ice had reached a safe thickness, I went ice skating on Lake Antrim using a pair of old clamp-ons that someone had given me. Skating was like nothing else I had ever experienced. At first, when I heard the ice cracking as it expanded, I was afraid it would open and I would be swallowed up again. Gradually I came to trust the frozen waters, and then I would struggle against the prevailing wind to the head of the lake, where I opened my coat and spread out my arms. A winged boy, I would sail downwind through the bitter cold to the other end, swooping and flapping like a large clumsy bird.

On other occasions a group of us kids would form a whip, skate in a circle, and the last person would cut loose and be propelled half-way across the lake. When it was my turn I usually ended up sliding on my back, rather than on the skates, which was sometimes painful but great fun, too.

Some Sunday afternoons I tried fishing through a hole in the ice, but I never caught anything. Other times I would watch as workers sawed great blocks of ice and poled them to a conveyor that moved them into a huge ice house, where they were stored for summer.

Suffern offered other adventures. One day I was greeted by two wild-looking, long-haired men.

"Hee-loo, kid," they said.

"Hello." I tried not to look too surprised at their unusual appearance. Both wore filthy tweed caps stretched down over their ears and dirty brown pullovers that appeared never to have been washed. Each carried a bundle of beaver and muskrat pelts. A father and son, they were on their way to Suffern, where they would sell the furs to buy staples and get their annual haircuts.

I recognized the men as Jackson Whites, members of a local minority group from the Ramapo Hills who were descended from a mixture of British, Blacks and Native Americans. For the most part, they kept to themselves except for annual trips into town with their furs. The most widely accepted story concerning their origin is that during Colonial times, a man named Captain Jackson provided prostitutes for the British forces in New York. Some of these women were white, some were black, and in the beginning they were known as Jackson Blacks as well as Jackson Whites. When the British left New York, the women made their way north and intermarried with white settlers and Indians. Their descendants all eventually came to be known as Jackson Whites.

As a youngster, I knew none of this history, but I still remember my sense of wonder and awe whenever I saw these interesting-looking people. They had high yellow complexions and occasionally coarse features, with prominent cheekbones and wide-spaced teeth. They lived scattered throughout the Eagle and Ramapo valleys and were generally shunned as outcasts because of their mixed blood.

On this particular day, they walked with me along the sidewalk near the railroad spur, but my fascination with them was eclipsed by a locomotive pulling up. As it hissed and puffed to a stop, Mr. Kelly, the engineer who lived in our building, called down to me from the cab and asked if I would like to ride with him into town. He did not invite the Jackson Whites, because they were different from the rest of us.

When I responded with an ecstatic "Yes," Mr. Kelly reached down and pulled me up into the great machine. It seemed unreal that I should be able to ride into Suffern, or anywhere else for that matter, on such a monstrous locomotive, with its huge black wheels and tremendous power. The Jackson Whites were impressed, too, I supposed. They watched wide-eyed as I receded into the distance, waving to them from the cab of what we kids all called the "choo-choo."

Nobody believed me when I told them the story. None of my friends witnessed me riding the locomotive, and it was too improbable that I would have done such a thing. In my heart, however, I felt a secret bond existed between the two Jackson White men, Mr. Kelly and me. They knew, even if no-one else did, that little Johnny Tursi had ridden on a "choo choo."

Suffern was a better place for a kid than Brooklyn, and Louisa and Pat provided for my basic needs, but they were not crazy about having me around. I tried not to be too demanding of them in return. In this period of my childhood, I learned not to ask for anything, because I believed I was not supposed to have things. If I was cold, I did not ask for clothes. If I was hungry, I did not ask for food. Once I saw an erector set in a store window, but a deep sense of resignation kept me from thinking about how much I wanted it.

It seemed to me that my little nephew, Victor, did not like me any more than his parents did. Although he was only two, he took great pleasure in kicking me from his high chair during meals. I complained about this, but Pat and Louisa refused to move Victor to the far end of the table. I imagined they took a covert delight in Victor's kicks, because he was doing to me what they wanted to do themselves.

In fact, I got just as many beatings in Suffern as Mama had given me in Brooklyn, and sometimes my sister-in-law devised other types of punishment. One bitterly cold morning she jerked me out of bed and forced me to stand outside in my long johns because I had forgotten to bring kindling up from the basement. I huddled on the outside landing, barefoot and numb with cold, peering in the window as she built the fire, hoping I would soon be allowed back inside. It was effective punishment, because I never forgot to bring up the kindling again.

The most memorable beating I ever received came about because I refused to eat a plate of beans. It was Wednesday noon, and every Wednesday lunch was the same: lima beans boiled in tomato juice. Louisa called this "succotash," but she was not the cook that my mother had been, and her fancy-sounding dish was tasteless compared to Mama's *pasta fazoola* spiced with garlic, parsley, oregano, rosemary and olive oil. Every Wednesday, when I sat down to Louisa's boring beans, my taste buds rebelled.

On this particular day I just could not get the beans down. I moved them one by one around my plate, stalling in the hope that I would not have to eat them.

"Why aren't you eating?" Louisa asked.

"I don't like the beans," I said, hanging my head.

"Why don't you find another place to eat?"

The courage for my answer came from somewhere deep inside. "Okay! I will!" I got up from the table and left for school.

The next day I had forgotten the incident when I sat down again for lunch.

"I thought you were going to find another place to eat," Louisa said angrily.

I didn't know what to feel. I was embarrassed and angry at myself at the same time. I had not followed through with my threat to eat elsewhere, and I had been called on it. Hungry and dejected, I walked back to school, where I watched the kids kicking a soccer ball around the playground until it was time for afternoon classes to begin.

As I entered the school building, I saw my teacher standing by the door with a look of fear and helplessness on her face. My brother Pat appeared from behind her and grabbed me by the back of the neck.

"What's the matter?" I cried.

"Never mind 'what's the matter'," Pat said, pushing me towards his truck and shoving me inside.

I knew, as my teacher had known, that a beating was coming, and nothing I could say or do would change that inevitability. Neither Pat nor I said a word as he drove us to the laundry, dragged me inside past a horrified employee, and hurried me into the drying room.

"You don't like beans, huh?" he snarled with a half-grin on his face. Then he began beating and kicking me. Each time I fell to the floor, he pulled me up and stood me against the wall, so he could beat me some more.

"I won't say anything about the food anymore. Please stop beating me," I cried.

"You stop crying now, and I'll decide when you've had enough." Pat continued punching and slapping me around. I covered my head with my arms and hands as best I could, trying to save my teeth and ears as the blows continued. When Pat knocked me down yet again, I pulled myself toward the relative protection of a corner of the room, but I soon realized the brutal kicks were more painful than the hand-punches.

I finally knew that I had to stop crying no matter how much it hurt, and when, at last, I managed to quench the tears and swallow my sobs, Pat stopped and walked out—but not until he had delivered one final blow to my head that almost knocked me unconscious. I collapsed into a heap on the floor, emotionally and physically bruised, hurting all over. The only light in the room came from the transom above the door. For a long time I lay in the half-dark, remembering the existence of something called The American Society for Prevention of Cruelty to Animals. I wondered if there was anybody out there who cared about the Prevention of Cruelty to Boys.

Several days later, Pat told me coldly that he had made arrangements for me to ride with a truck driver to Manhattan. He was sending me back to Papa. I had no time to say goodbye to my friends or to check out of school, but I was relieved to be leaving my brother and looked forward to seeing Papa. As I climbed into the cab of the dark-green Reo truck, Pat handed me a slip of paper with an address in Brooklyn scribbled on it. Otherwise, I was empty-handed. I didn't own so much as a toothbrush and had no spare clothes to worry about.

I enjoyed riding in the truck, and I was fascinated with the small towns we passed through on our way. They were dingy, soot-blackened communities on the Jersey side of the Hudson: Hohokus, Ridgewood, Paterson, Passaic, Rutherford and Jersey City. When we reached the Holland tunnel, the driver told me to hide myself in the back of the truck because he could not pay the toll for me. I huddled in a corner where I hoped the police would not see me if they decided to check.

Once safely through the tunnel, the driver stopped and let me off.

"This is the end of the line, kiddo," he said. I stood alone on the street wondering which direction to go. I was nine years old, hungry and with not a nickel to my name, alone in Manhattan with only an address on a small slip of paper.

Chapter 10

A GLORIOUS SUMMER

Since I was out of school on a week day I was hesitant to ask a cop how to get to Papa's, but there was nothing else to be done. I found one who overlooked my truancy and directed me to the Brooklyn Bridge through Chinatown. The smells that rose from the sand on the cobblestone streets of that neighborhood were different from those of Suffern and, to me, pleasantly familiar—a sweet-sour mix of horse urine and manure, fish juice, and all manner of rotten and decaying fruits and vegetables from the commerce of the streets.

Papa and I had once visited his sister in Chinatown, so I vaguely knew about the Tongs—the Chinese equivalent of Brooklyn's criminal gangs. I imagined danger behind every door, trouble lurking around every corner. Distracted by my fears, I inadvertently passed the approach to the Brooklyn Bridge and found myself on the waterfront. There, art students sat beneath the high arches of the bridge, painting the red brick tenements that stretched along the streets in front of them. Admiring their talent, I lingered awhile, watching a woman with a large bandana tied around her head as she recreated the street scene on her canvas. Eventually I decided that I should continue my journey before the warring Chinese Tongs kidnapped me. The woman artist told me, when I asked, that I would have to retrace my steps several blocks to get onto the bridge.

Finding the way at last, I stopped in disbelief at the great structure suspended from cables across the East River. The foot-walk on which I was to cross was high and precarious, and no other people were on it. I wondered if it was the right way to go, and if the cables would actually support me. The decking beneath my feet was constructed of widely-spaced boards set so far apart that I felt I might slip through them to the water below, and the entire cat-walk shook constantly from the vibrations created by the train cars and trucks roaring beneath. Still, my nine year-old-self understood that what lay before me was a test of my ability to survive, because I could not go back. Scared as I was, I knew I had to cross that bridge by myself if I was ever to reach Papa and safety. Even my stomach told me I had to go. The position of the sun overhead told me it was nearly noon, and it had been a long time since breakfast. The delicious fragrance of freshly roasting coffee drifting across from the A & P plant on the Brooklyn side of the river added to my hunger pangs.

Despite my near-blind terror, I was aware as I ventured forth that for the first time in my life I was so high in the air I could look down on the tenement rooftops with all of their pigeon coops. Pigeon-flying was the means of entertainment for many of the men in this stone jungle, and I watched as a man far below me with a long bamboo pole chased his flock into the air, hoping to attract a stray bird. This sight distracted me from my fears, and I somehow managed to keep one foot moving ahead of the other until I reached the high center of the bridge. I realized with relief that the supports were indeed strong enough to hold me, and I could see firm ground at the other end of the span. When at last I made it safely all the way across, I knew I had faced danger and overcome it. This left me with a profound feeling of satisfaction, of a sort I had never experienced before.

It was early evening by the time I arrived at the Banner Avenue address on my paper. I was excited, expecting to see Papa—but my brother Tony answered the door. He was as surprised to see me as I was to see him. He also appeared to have a new wife.

"What are you doing here, Johnny?"

"Pat told me that Papa lived here."

"Papa doesn't live here. I'm not sure where he is." My heart sank.

It was decided that I should stay the night before going on to find Papa, so a bed was made for me on the davenport, and again I found myself at a brother's house where I had not been expected. At least there were no trains wailing outside. Instead, the sirens of emergency vehicles filled the night with their urgent comings and goings. I didn't care. Exhaustion prevailed, and I fell asleep dreaming of dangerous Chinese men in high places.

In the morning, Tony told me that I could stay until he had located Papa, and I could go in the meantime to the new yellow-brick school at Brighton Beach. This was the first of many times to come that I enrolled myself in school. The Brighton Beach principal accepted my word as to what grade I should be in and assigned me to a class. I had scarcely settled in when Tony heard that Papa was working for Cousin LaPoppola who lived at the old Sheepshead Bay racetrack just a couple of miles away.

Papa was not at LaPoppola's, however, and again I found myself on a doorstep where I was not expected. This time seemed different, however, because my cousins were glad to see me and wanted me to stay.

"Little Giovanni!" Cousin LaPoppola exclaimed when he realized who I was. "I have not seen your Papa for months. He was here in the winter, but now he is gone. But you must stay with us. We have a lot of room in this big house."

Wooden and multi-gabled, their house was indeed large, as it was the former hospital facility for the now-defunct Sheepshead Bay racetrack. It was home not only to Cousin LaPoppola and his family, but to his brother Lorenzo, sister-in-law Gianina, and the widowed family matriarch, Serafina. As Cousin Lorenzo and Gianina showed me to my third-floor room they made me feel very welcome and assured me that Papa would soon come to visit. For the first time in my life, I felt wanted—and I had a room to myself.

Lorenzo and Gianina had no children, and they treated me a way that suggested I was filling a void in their lives. Their niece and nephew—LaPoppola's children—may have felt slightly resentful of my presence, as affection in this extended family was now spread among three children. However, it was wonderful for me.

Comare Serafina had a large herd of goats, as well as barnyard chickens, geese, and ducks. Nobody else touched or fed these animals, and Serafina milked the goats every morning, so that I was always awakened to a breakfast of fresh goat milk and bread. Then I would help Cousin Lorenzo clean his stable of thirty draft horses before he went off to his job as a construction contractor.

On Saturdays I occasionally went with him and drove a one-horse roller over the cinder-paved streets that Cousin LaPoppola was building. This compacting work made me feel very important because I drove the horse by myself. I was also accomplishing something, and Cousin Lorenzo trusted me enough to do it without supervision. For the first time in my life, I felt accepted and loved by a family. Nor did they force me to do anything; everything I did, I did of my own volition. I *wanted* to clean the stable, I *wanted* to drive the roller—and having this freedom of choice was a heady experience. I began to develop a sense of being in charge of my own life and destiny.

Most people in Lorenzo's financial position drove cars, but he preferred a horse-drawn buggy. I was a little embarrassed to ride in it, but I was proud to live with him and be known as his helper. One Saturday afternoon, he asked me to go with him to collect some money. On the way home, we stopped at a live-chicken market and bought a beautiful big goose. I held the bird and felt a little more conspicuous than usual riding along in the buggy holding this feathered spectacle in my lap. I asked Lorenzo why he hadn't bought a car.

"I did buy a Dodge touring car a couple of years ago, Johnny, but it didn't work."

"Didn't work! What do you mean?"

"Well, I thought driving a car would be like driving a horse, but on my way home from the garage on the very day I bought it, I found out that it isn't so. That car drove itself right up onto a telephone pole guy wire and rolled over. I walked home and never went back after it. From now on, Johnny, it's just me and horses. Cars are killers as far as I'm concerned."

As Lorenzo told me this story of his first and last driving experience, I noticed my leg was getting very warm. The goose had shit all over my lap, and I felt more conspicuous than ever, driving along in a horse and buggy, imagining everyone we passed on the sidewalk was looking at me.

That summer was glorious. Once school was out, I could do what I liked. Two kids I had come to know at school were helping their father, Donato, bundle radishes and dandelions in his truck garden. I watched them for a time and decided to help them. Every summer, Donato employed a man who came from Italy to help with the garden, and the five of us worked filling the crates with fresh-washed greens. It was pleasant work, and I did it happily without a thought of getting paid. At the end of the season, however, Donato sent for me on a Sunday morning, gave me four half-dollars, and his boys took me to a Hoot Gibson movie at Sheepshead Bay.

Living at LaPoppolas' was the best year of my childhood. I had a loving family, plenty of food, a warm clean bed. Cousin Lorenzo even gave me nickels from time to time—although one of these caused me to be the subject of a beating on my way to school, when about fifteen schoolboys came toward me and one asked for my money.

"I don't have any," I lied, realizing I was about to be robbed.

Each boy had a job to do. One kid kneeled behind me while another shoved me flat on my back. Some boys kicked me; some grabbed my flailing knees and legs; others rifled through my pockets until they found my precious nickel. Though they admonished me not to tell anyone, I told the teacher anyway but nothing was ever done about it.

A short time after this, Papa showed up one day and announced he was taking me to live with him and Mike. He had just rented a new flat above a grocery store. I was glad to see him but sad to leave my new-found family, and they were sad, too, Lorenzo and Gianina especially, because I seemed to make up for the son they never had.

Chapter 11

TALES FROM THE OLD COUNTRY

"*Il Duce* is a *bravo* man," Papa announced, pushing his chair back from the table and indicating the rotogravure picture of Mussolini on the wall of the kitchen. Papa seemed glad to have me back with him, and he was in an expansive mood. It was Easter and we had just eaten our holy day meal alone, since Mike rarely ate at Papa's flat anymore, even on special occasions. Our feast had been only fried potatoes and bread, but there was a little more food than usual, and someone had given Papa a bottle of red wine. Perhaps it was this that made him talkative. He was also enjoying the luxury of being freshly-shaven, having gone the day before to see his friend, Gervasi, who did bootleg barbering at home on weekends. Papa was particular about his appearance, and he was especially proud of his white teeth, which were so strong he could remove a beer bottle cap with them and grind them in anger so fiercely they could be heard fifteen feet away.

"What did Mussolini do, Papa," I asked, gratefully accepting a glass of wine as I gazed at the richly-uniformed man on the wall.

"Mussolini is Italian, Giovanni," was the reply. Since Papa could not read or write in any language, his knowledge of politics amounted to scraps of information he heard on the streets from his equally illiterate friends. Mussolini's picture had appeared in an American paper, and the fact that he was Italian automatically made him a hero to Papa.

"There are three great men in history, Giovanni," Papa continued his lesson. "Mussolini, Giuseppi Garibaldi and King Victor Emmanuel."

Deliciously warmed by the wine, I enjoyed lingering at the table with Papa. I put my foot up on Mike's empty chair to rest my knee, which I had hurt in a cart ride down a steep hill. The pain seemed to ease as I leaned back in my own chair, sipped at my glass, and listened as Papa continued to talk, telling stories now about "the old country."

In those days, the "old country" was nothing but a vague and distant place that was spoken about with nostalgia by immigrant Italians. Papa was never able to show it to me on a map, because he could not read maps. Forty years later I visited my parents' village of Genzano, 125 miles

61

inland from Naples. Located atop one of the mountains in the Matese Range, I found Genzano to be a fortress-like village of white stone buildings and cobblestone streets. Long strings of red peppers and window boxes of colorful geraniums brightened the balconies of the otherwise somber buildings. From the village I could look out across the valley and fields where Mama and Papa had worked hard in the hot Italian sun. Also visible beyond the fields were the black mouths of caves part-way up the rock wall opposite. Some of these caves had been lived in, like houses, for centuries. It must have been one of them that Papa talked about that afternoon.

"We lived in a cave outside Genzano, Giovanni—my mama, my papa, my three sisters and I. It was a fine limestone cave overlooking the fertile valley below. Every day at dawn Papa led us down the cobblestone path to the garden plots where we worked and grazed the burros and goats. I was the official goat-herder and made sure those animals browsed the hillsides and kept out of the vegetables."

"What did you grow, Papa?" Now slightly drunk, I was delighted to have Papa pay so much attention to me.

"Well, we grew zucchini, onions, spicy herbs, and many kinds of greens. I can still smell it, Giovanni—especially the plots of basil that filled the fresh Italian air with their fragrance on hot days. And the lemon trees—the sweet white blossoms, I will never forget. And at the end of the day we turned up the steep path with a basket of greens for supper.

"Sometimes Mama would make *frittata* out of zucchini blossoms stuffed with onions and basil. There would be a great salad of every kind of greens: dandelions, endive, fennel, and lettuce all dressed with olive oil and vinegar and fresh basil. Then there was fresh-baked bread from our own brick oven. And often in the evening we gathered outside with our neighbors to visit before bedtime. Nearly always someone played the concertina or mandolin, and there was singing to go with a glass of wine. It was a good life, Giovanni, my boy—until all of us children began marrying."

"How did you meet Mama?"

"Our marriage was arranged when I was only two years old. It was the day of your Mama Rosina's baptism, two days after her birth. Your Mama's family lived in the cave next to ours, so we joined in the baptismal celebration. My papa and her papa decided that very day that I, Vittorio Torccio, should marry Rosina Caraciano when we were old enough."

"So you grew up with Mama?"

Papa poured more into wine my glass. "No, because a year later the Caracianos loaded their children and their belongings on a two-wheeled cart drawn by their burro and set out for Potenza, fifty to the miles west. Potenza was larger and Papa Caraciano thought it held out hopes for a better life." Papa leaned back in his chair, watching the pictures that formed in his mind as he spoke.

"Then what, Papa?"

"Times became very hard when my three sisters married and their husbands came to live with us in our cave dwelling. Our small plot of land could not support all of us, especially after each of my sisters started having children. By then we were receiving letters from Cousin LaPoppola in America urging us to come, because things were much better in the new country."

"What happened next?" I asked, as much out of desire to keep Papa talking to me as out of interest.

Papa poured yet more wine and sat quietly looking into his glass for a minute. "Next? Next, we tried to make a go of it at home, but at last my three brothers-in-law decided to go to America and leave their wives and children with us until they could send for them. By the time the men wrote from America sending for their families, our Mama and Papa had died, and now my sisters had to think what to do with me, since I was only twelve."

The rest of the story unfolded with the waning afternoon. Papa's sisters reminded him he had been matched with Rosina at her baptism, that the two of them were betrothed, so he should go to Potenza and wait with the Caracianos until he was old enough to get married. With that difficulty settled, the sisters wasted no time getting ready for the trip to America. They gathered their homemade Provolone, *prosciutto*, *salami*, bread and wine, loaded it into the *carretta*, hooked up their little burro, Chico, and with four milk goats in tow, they started out for Potenza fifty miles away. Walking barefoot to save their shoes, each woman carried a bundle of belongings balanced on her head. Their kids rode and slept on top of the *carretta*.

They made frequent stops to allow the goats to feed along the hilly, cobblestoned road. They ate the bread and milk themselves, but saved the dry meat and cheese for the anticipated steamship trip across the Atlantic.

"On the fourth day after leaving Genzano, we arrived at the Caracianos' and I saw your Mama again for the first time in ten years. I was just a boy, but I could see how beautiful she was. She was not as dark-skinned as most of the other girls, and she wore her light brown hair in a thick braid down her back. And your Mama's eyes were as blue as the sky, Giovanni. That summer we walked along the road together gathering wild figs, but we did not speak much. We were both too shy."

As Papa continued with this story, I sensed he was talking to me and not to me. It was as if he was telling the stories to himself as a way of remembering and reliving those bitter-sweet days.

"My sisters sold Chico, their little cart and the four goats to get money for their train tickets to Naples, where they were to board the steamer. I was left behind to work as a goat-herder and grow up enough to marry your Mama."

Papa and Mama married very young, and their three older boys, Antonio, Pasquali and Graziano were born before a letter finally arrived from America. That was in 1905. A professional reader confirmed Vittorio's hopes. Cousin Lorenzo LaPoppola in New York had work for Papa in his excavating business. Lorenzo would finance the trip to America so Vito could drive a team of horses, hauling dirt from the excavations in a bottom-dump wagon.

The young couple's joy and hope were unbridled. In Italy they had been living with Rosina's parents, and the future seemed impossible and bleak. But America meant plenty of food, new ways of doing things, undreamed-of wealth, a house for each family, and land—there would be so much land in the new country.

"I came over first, and after I had saved enough money working for Zio Lorenzo, I sent for your Mama and the boys," Papa said, and then he stopped talking. Perhaps he did not want to recount the disappointments that had come next: the loss of work, Tony's involvement with the underworld, Mama's death, and our current life in which we were dirty and half-starved most of the time. When Papa eventually resumed talking, he complained that his older sons did not support him as they would have done in the old country.

Eventually Papa's head fell forward and he began snoring in his chair. My head had begun to spin. I limped to the toilet and retched up the wine that had fueled the companionship between Papa and me that Easter day—but I still have Papa's stories to this day.

Chapter 12

JOHNNY BANANAS

The Depression was well underway by then and no work was available for uneducated men like Papa. His solution was to buy a pushcart and begin selling bananas on the streets. In this way, Mike became "Bananas" and I became "Little Bananas." We would all go to the banana auction at the waterfront. Papa would buy seventy-five or a hundred stalks and pay a teamster to deliver them to his banana cellar in Brooklyn. An unemployed wino helped load the wagon and rode along with the bananas to assist with the unloading. The green stalks were all hung from hooks in a cellar under a butcher shop, where Papa lit gas heaters to help speed up the ripening process.

Business was good, so Papa decided to expand. He sold bananas from his pushcart, and when I wasn't in school I sold them, too, from a small stand in front of the butcher shop. Mike talked Papa into buying an old converted taxicab with a big box on the back end, with the idea that Mike could drive around the city selling bananas wholesale to stores. I think Mike and Papa must have been very naive to imagine they could buck the protection syndicate by supplying bananas directly to fruit retailers.

Nevertheless, with these expansionist ideas in mind, Papa bought not one but two loads of bananas—about three hundred stalks in all. We were exhausted by the time we had hung the last of them from the ceiling of the cellar, and after Papa lit the gas heaters we closed the doors on our fortune's worth of fruit and went back to the flat to wait for it to ripen. Mike didn't come with us, as he still had enough energy to go joy-riding in the banana taxi with a couple of friends. Papa and I ate peppers and bread for supper and fell asleep that night dreaming of money.

As sometimes happens in New York in late spring, the weather turned very hot overnight and it continued that way for the next couple of days. By the time Papa checked on his bananas the following morning, it was too late. Opening the cellar door he was overwhelmed by the fumes of already over-ripe fruit. No matter that he turned off the gas immediately— the ripening process had begun and could not be stopped.

Mike was nowhere to be found, and without the taxi Papa and I couldn't possibly sell bananas fast enough to recover our investment. Two days later, as the sickeningly sweet smell of not just ripe but rotten bananas wafted up out of our storage cellar and into our neighborhood, Papa and I realized we were financially ruined. Adding insult to injury, Papa had to borrow money to pay to have the spoiled fruit hauled away.

From time to time after that, Papa was able to talk a wholesaler into financing a cartful of bananas, but his credit was gone and we struggled to provide ourselves even with one meal a day. My fruity nickname had stuck, however, and to some old friends I am still known as "Johnny Bananas."

After this episode, Papa would leave the flat every morning before I awoke. I never knew where he went because he didn't tell me, but he didn't seem to work as he rarely brought home money or food. Instead, it fell to me, aged twelve, to support the pair of us.

Weekdays, I continued to go to school. I would check the big clock in the store window downstairs, so I would know when it was time to leave. Breakfast was no problem because I had none. Lunch was the same. Most of the kids bought a bottle of milk as a mid-morning snack. I longed to have one, too, but simply accepted that there was none for me.

No-one at school seemed to be aware that I was starving. They may have noticed I was filthy, and I probably smelled unpleasant. Perhaps the teachers wanted to get me out of the classroom for a while—they may even have considered me reliable—but for whatever reason I was always the kid chosen to run errands. Most days I was sent out to get the teachers' lunches. This was often hot, spicy Oriental food that smelled so good it almost killed me not to eat it. Sometimes I was sent to an old school in Manhattan to pick up supplies. I would be given a note so the truant officer wouldn't question me, and I always found time along the way to watch the firemen at the training building on 62nd Street. They would scale the side of the building with a ladder, and when they were six or eight stories high they would jump down into a net stretched between steel columns far below. I was also sent to teachers' homes with notes because many of them did not have telephones, and, sometimes, I went to the theater district to pick up tickets.

As Christmas approached, we were asked to bring canned goods to school for the "needy." I couldn't contribute anything, but I was asked to help assemble the Christmas boxes. No family could have lived in greater poverty than ours, probably, but I didn't know how to convey this to my teacher, so I just got on with my job. By the end of that day our classroom was piled high with food, but I left feeling utterly depressed. It seemed that someone should have recognized just by looking at me that I was hungry most of the time.

Several days later when I arrived home from school, it seemed that Christmas might happen for us after all. At the foot of my bed—a bare springs mattress with newspapers for a blanket—I saw a large pile of neatly wrapped Christmas presents.

"Maybe brother Pat sent us a bunch of gifts," I thought. I knew better than to touch them and sat down to wait for Mike, knowing he must have something to do with this surprise bonanza. When he finally arrived home, he told me that the boxes had been stolen by one of his friends, who had been hired at the post office to help deal with the seasonal rush. Mike had agreed to store the boxes for him. My hopes for Christmas were dashed again.

As if things could get any worse, we could no longer pay our rent. However, when our landlord went to court to get a dispossession notice, the judge sent someone to investigate. People were being turned out on the streets all over New York for failure to pay rent, and the government was beginning to recognize this as a problem. Papa, Mike and I were fortunate to get a twenty-five dollar rent voucher that allowed us to stay in our flat—even though we still had to come up somehow with five dollars more on our own.

At this time I went to work for Pete Suzzi, the butcher whose shop was above our defunct banana cellar. He agreed that I could deliver orders five mornings a week and all day Saturday for two dollars.

"Can you ride a bike, Johnny Bananas?" he asked the first day.

"Sure, I can," I lied. I had never even tried it, but how hard could it be?

"There's the bike and here is your pouch of change money. Now load these packages in the basket and get on your way."

I did as I was told, but instead of mounting the bike in front of the store, I wheeled it around the corner out of sight. I figured the easiest thing to do was position the bike on the street while I mounted it from the curb.

This worked, but then a new dilemma arose. I was too short to reach the pedals. Fortunately, I had seen little kids riding big bicycles by placing their right leg through the frame, and when I did this myself I was surprised to find I could pump the bike pretty easily. So, off I went on my first assignment delivering packages of meat all around the neighborhood. The job was a good one and sometimes Mr. Suzzi shared with me the pan of pasta that his wife brought down directly from the stove to the shop.

On my first payday, I bought a large beef lung from Mr. Suzzi for five cents. To make the lung look larger than it was, it had been inflated and a knot tied in the windpipe to keep it from collapsing. Mr. Suzzi didn't bother wrapping it for me, and I proudly carried it down the street, looking forward to surprising Papa with lung soup for supper. On my way home I stopped at the vegetable market and asked Cheech for three cents' worth of soup greens. Cheech was glad to accept payment for the half-spoiled trimmings that no one else would buy, and he threw in some badly bruised tomatoes and soft sprouted onions. I picked up a three-cent loaf of bread and headed for the flat with the big lung continuing to expand in the heat of the afternoon.

To prepare supper, I first had to put a quarter in the gas meter, which was located in our dark and dingy basement. Back in the apartment, I cut up the lung and windpipe, being careful not to waste a scrap of it. By the time Papa returned home, a very large kettle of lung soup was simmering on the stove. Papa, who had a keen nose for seasoned food, walked over to the pot, inhaled the aroma, and instead of complimenting me, complained that the soup needed more salt. I longed for praise that night—but I never got it. This bothered me a lot because I was the youngest member of the family and the only one earning money. The least Papa could do was show his appreciation for me and my lung soup. But our supper was a feast, at least, and there was enough left over to feed us the next day as well.

My delivery job did not last, unfortunately. Pete Suzzi decided shortly afterwards to move his shop across the street, and in that location, for reasons unknown to me, he rapidly went broke.

I began coughing at night, for which Papa sometimes gave me *grappa*, an Italian grape brandy. This "medicine" made me feel better so I filled a small bottle with it and took it to school. The teacher never suspected I was drinking brandy. One day, however, when I had eaten nothing for two days but a handful of stolen grapes, I must have passed out in class. When I came to, I found myself in Coney Island Hospital, where I was to remain overnight until the city health doctor diagnosed what was wrong with me.

It turned out I had acute diphtheria, and small wonder. Our flat was infested with roaches and bedbugs, and recently, when checking under the bathtub for the source of a terrible smell, I had found a dead sewer rat. Papa and Mike inquired after me at school when I did not return home, and the next day Mike came on foot and walked me, still wobbly and sick, back to our flat.

After this episode the grocer downstairs offered to give me free milk if I would come for it once a day. The milk came in bulk, and the only kettle I had was a large pot for boiling pasta. The grocer slipped a one-pint dipper into his 10-gallon can and poured the milk into my big container. One pint was barely milk enough to cover the bottom of the pot, but I was grateful because Papa and I could have bread and milk for supper.

I felt lucky also to find a bike near the curb of a deserted street in Manhattan Beach, where all the rich people lived. No matter that the bike had no tires and made a terrible racket as I rode away on it. I was never sure whether the owner was angry or happy that someone took it.

When I was thirteen, I got a job with the Strauss butcher chain, for which I earned four dollars a week. I had to give the money to Papa, of course, but I wanted to keep a little for myself. For ten cents I could go to the Hot Dog Show at Coney Island. Admission cost a dime, and customers were given the choice of a hot dog or a piece of pie with coffee in a large smoke-filled room where movies were shown.

On one occasion I held back twenty-five cents from my wages because I had made up my mind to go to Coney Island. I was pretty strong by then, so Papa couldn't force me to give him the extra quarter, but the struggle over it was so unpleasant that after that I would give him all my money, then steal some of it back while he was sleeping. He would put his change on the chair beside his bed and once he was snoring loudly I would take eleven or twelve cents. Papa never suspected because he couldn't count very well, and I reflected that it was probably not just the hot weather that caused him to fail at the banana business.

In any case, just when things were looking up a little because of my job, I lost it. One Saturday night about nine o'clock a well-dressed man came up to me as I was washing the white enameled meat trays.

"How old are you?" he asked politely.

"Thirteen," I answered eagerly, proud to have such a job at my age.

"And when did you start work today?"

"I come in at eight o'clock every Saturday and work until nine. On school days I can't get here until one o'clock," I said, volunteering even more than I was asked.

The nice man thanked me, went up front to the manager, presented him with a summons, and I was fired on the spot because I was too young. What did age have to do with it, I wondered, if my boss was satisfied with my work? Here I was willing to work, but society wouldn't allow it. This must be the reason people started stealing.

Papa was mostly getting by panhandling and borrowing from friends. Then he thought if he could just get his citizenship papers he might have an easier time finding work. He had been told of people who, for a fee of fifteen dollars, would make arrangements with the right officials to get him his papers. Whether or not he could read or write; they would take care of it. Papa eventually saved enough money to do it, but he never got his final papers.

Meanwhile, my eighth-grade graduation was coming up. I asked the teacher ahead of time if I was going to graduate because I would need to obtain a pair of pants for the occasion. My shoes would do because the tops were pretty good—though I had to carry folded newspaper in my pockets and replace it in the soles several times a day to cover the holes. My teacher hesitated but said after some thought that I would graduate.

Brother Mike came through for me on this occasion. He bought me a new pair of pants and an autograph album. My friends Moishe and Charlie signed the book, addressing me as either Johnny Bananas or Louie Ricarno, the name of the actor who played Capone in a movie. In the space after "My hero" I wrote "Al 'Scarface' Capone."

Graduation night arrived, but no member of my family was present. No one applauded as I walked up to receive the district diploma. Then, suddenly, a lone person who probably felt sorry for me gave a couple of claps.

The only prize I ever won at school, incidentally, was for a drawing of a small, sick-looking dog walking up the sidewalk toward the door of a big building labeled The American Society for the Prevention of Cruelty to

Animals. I suppose I had drawn it as a way of expressing the anguish I felt at the beating brother Pat had given me in Suffern. It hung for a while in the Metropolitan Museum of Art in a collection of school drawings, but I have no idea what became of it after that.

Chapter 13

QUITTING SCHOOL, QUITTING PAPA

Heady with importance at having graduated from elementary school, Moishe, Charlie and I decided to strike out on our own. In those days, kids who wanted to run away went down to Greenwich Market and helped the drivers load their trucks in exchange for a ride out of New York City. We three arrived early in the morning, loaded a truck with empty wooden boxes, and got a ride to western Pennsylvania.

There was no work to be had except occasional odd jobs that got us meals, so we lived by our wits, stealing milk from doorsteps. Sometimes we were able to take pastries from small Ma and Pa stores, but we were desperate by the time we reached central Pennsylvania. Then, late one afternoon as we walked along a country lane, we came upon two men—farmers—speaking broken English.

"Do you have any work for us?" I asked, speaking for the others as well as myself even though I was the youngest.

"You kids from the city?" the man with the Italian accent asked. "Things are getting worse and worse in the city. We got no money either, but we got food." I felt a wave of relief wash through me because I was pretty sure we would get work here.

The Italian said I could go home with him, and the other man, a Pole, took Charlie because his parents were from Poland. That left Moishe, but the two farmers knew a childless Irish couple, and they agreed to take him. We would not be paid any money for our work—just room and board—but we were grateful as we climbed aboard the men's horse-drawn wagon.

Hoeing spuds and learning to milk cows, I felt productive and contented. Not so Charlie and Moishe. Their families in Brooklyn may have been better-off than mine; they came to me complaining they were homesick. With the irrepressible optimism of children, we set off early one morning to go back to New York. My Italian boss gave us a fruit jar full of milk, and by eight o'clock that evening, hungry and tired, we had made it as far as the Philadelphia market. No rides were available from there at that hour, so we spent the night walking and hitching, stealing milk from doorsteps as we went. Afraid to be caught by the police with milk bottles in our hands, we drank as much from each one as we could and then left them half-empty on the curb.

Rides were scarce, so we waited at a stoplight and climbed onto the back of a large van. This had just enough room on its open tailgate for the three of us to stand holding on to the ropes that secured the cargo. Because we had not slept, we took turns keeping each other awake. Finally, a car pulled up to the cab of the truck and alerted the driver, who chased us off. When we arrived at last in Brooklyn, Moishe's mother wanted to have me arrested for leading the other two kids astray. Papa, on the other hand, had not been concerned with my disappearance at all.

Several months of summer remained before I started high school, so I went to work for Toni Monti's brother-in-law, Bill, scrapping old cars for a sandwich a day. One of my first jobs was to dismantle an almost-new Chrysler that a detective friend of Bill had arranged to have Bill steal, so the detective could collect the insurance. Toni and I worked in an old shed and quickly took out the engine, which Bill sold, along with the wheels and tires, to some rum runners. Those old cars had a lot of wood in them, so it was relatively easy for Toni and me to winch the body into the empty lot next door and set it afire. By the time two detectives arrived on the scene, not a trace of the Chrysler remained.

As the Depression deepened, the unemployment lines grew longer and longer. Once a week that summer I went to Manhattan and joined lines of men hoping for work, but older men were always chosen instead of me. Bill found me useful, however, and he put Toni and me to work for a short time digging a basement under a building at Brighton Beach for a dollar a day.

The most interesting job Toni and I did that summer was hauling ashes out of the basement of a house of prostitution. Our employer in this instance was one of our neighbors, a man named Ibrahim. He was a Turk who worked as barker at an exotic dancer side-show in Coney Island. He was very dark with tattooed temples and hands, and he told fascinating stories about jumping ship as a sailor with the Turkish Navy. To me, he looked about eighty years old and his deeply wrinkled face was accentuated by a toothless grin. He had a shiny bold pate and usually went hatless, though when he went to work he wore a white turban on his head, bright red Turkish pantaloons and a satin shirt.

In addition to being a barker, Ibrahim was landlord for several of the girls from the sideshow who used his rooms for prostitution. In the basement below, Toni and I worked hard all morning, hauling several years' accumulation of cinders up the steps to the alley. About noon one of the girls appeared with a pitcher of homebrew. To our amazement she was wearing nothing but a long black veil and a G-string. I had never seen a woman's bare breasts before, except when leeches had been applied to them or they were used for nursing. For some reason this didn't look the same to me. The girl left us with the pitcher of beer and the receding vision of her body beneath the scanty clothes.

"Johnny, did you see her tits through that veil?" fifteen-year-old Toni exclaimed.

"Boy, did I. And were they big!" I enthused. "How would you like to nuzzle them?"

"I wonder how much whores charge."

"Two dollars," I said, demonstrating my worldly knowledge. "All whores charge two dollars."

Toni looked away dreamily and asked, "I wonder if a guy could buy a dollar's worth." He was undoubtedly considering how to spend his hard-earned buck.

"I know what I'm gonna do with my buck," I said. "There's a hot dog and hamburger war going on in Coney Island. They cost three cents each. I'm gonna go down there and buy a big stack of them." At fourteen, I was much more interested in food than sex—though my priorities would eventually change.

September came, and I started the ninth grade at the Abraham Lincoln High School annex. I was still just as hungry and dirty as I had been in grade school and, to add to my unhappiness, the gym teacher told me to bring soap and a towel for his class. I was unable to comply as we had no soap at home and our only towel was a cotton cement sack, used for all purposes. Regardless, all students, including me, were herded after gym into a large shower room. The custodian controlled the water temperature and when he felt we had enough hot water he would turn it to icy cold. Pandemonium ensued because we could not escape the shower until the custodian unlocked the door to let us out. To further add to this misery, I had to pull my dirty clothes onto my shivering wet body and wait for them to dry during the next class.

Another distraction presented itself during these first few days of high school: I had three abscessed teeth that hurt constantly. Sitting in class, I kept a finger in my mouth most of the time, trying to loosen them. After many hours, one tooth yielded to all the pushing and pulling. As it shifted, the abscess broke and the pain eased a bit. This encouraged me to keep on until, two days later, I pushed the tooth all the way out. This felt so good that I continued the same treatment on the other two and in another week all three teeth were out.

About a month had gone by when Miss Goetches, my elderly biology teacher, asked me to stay after school to explain my drawing of an onion cell. Even at the time it seemed ironic that I was expected to study onions when I would have been much happier having them at home for supper. I did not say this to Miss Goetches, however, but defended my work, as I felt I had done the assignment rather well. Miss Goetches had other thoughts.

"Johnny, I think you should quit school," she said bluntly.

"Can I really do that?" I asked, excited at the possibility.

"Yes. You've finished the eighth grade, you're fourteen years old, and you can get your working papers."

My head was swimming with the joyous thought that I was finished with school. Now, I could go out into the adult world and work. My elation persisted, even though Mike and Papa showed no enthusiasm for my new-found status. Perhaps they figured that since they couldn't find work, there was little chance of my finding it either, whether I had working papers or not.

Mike and Papa were right. Though I looked for work, I couldn't find any and had to go back to wrecking cars for Bill for the same meager midday sandwich. I was out in the lot cutting up old chassis with a hammer and chisel late one afternoon when Papa appeared and ordered me to go home. I could see from the look on his face that he was furious. I dropped my tools in the dirt and started for the flat with Papa close behind me, muttering Italian cuss words.

"What's wrong, Papa?" I asked as we mounted the stairs.

"Why didn't you cook supper?" he shouted, grinding his teeth as he always did when he was angry.

"You didn't leave me any money, Papa," I defended myself.

"When I got up this morning, I woke you up and told you to get fifteen cents' credit at the butcher shop, but you did not obey your Papa."

I had no memory of that, but when I tried to tell him that he began kicking and punching me, becoming insane with rage as he continued his attack. I could not hit back—he was my Papa—so I turned and escaped from him, flying down the stairs and scarcely touching a step as I went.

I stopped at the doorway to the street, hoping that would be the end of it, but Papa called down the stairs after me.

"Get back up here," he shouted in Italian.

"Are you through beating me, Papa?"

"Get back up here," he shouted again. Believing for some reason that his anger must have dissipated, I obediently climbed back up the stairs. When I got to the kitchen, he immediately slapped me again, then reached over to the drain-board, picked up a butcher knife, and came towards me with it. I dodged him and sailed back down the stairs, knowing I would never sleep under Papa's roof again, as I was sure he was capable of killing me.

Fearing that he might follow me, I ducked down into the subway and then left the city the same way I had done earlier the same, by hitching a ride on a truck out of Greenwich Market.

I was only to see Papa once again in my lifetime. About a year after my spontaneous departure, I saw him walking towards me on the street. I turned up a side-street to avoid him. I figured his inability to find work and his bad luck had driven him half-mad. But he had never learned how to discipline me, either. That had been Mama's job, and Papa didn't know how to handle what he perceived to be my disobedience. In any case, I continued on to new adventures, and heard many years later that Papa had died alone and unhappy.

Chapter 14

BLUE SOCK GANGRENE

I hitchhiked as far as West Virginia, growing more desperate by the day for work and food. The only thing to do was to keep going until I found one, or the other, or, preferably, both. No matter which direction I headed, there always seemed to be more traffic going the opposite way. I had no particular destination in mind, so I would sometimes cross the road and started thumbing the other way if I saw a car coming along. Finally a farmer picked me up and dropped me off near a farmhouse. Too hungry to be shy, I knocked on the door to ask for help.

A kind looking woman with shoulder-length gray hair appeared and asked what I wanted. She was neatly attired in a clean house dress and apron. I felt nervous but hopeful.

"Ma'am, do you have some work for me to do in exchange for a sandwich? Any kind of work," I pleaded. "I'll do anything."

"No!" The kindness I thought I had seen in her face disappeared as she frowned down at me.

"Do you have any bread or food that you are going to throw away? I don't care what it is," I begged quickly before she could say more.

"No! And get off my property immediately." She slammed the door in my face.

As I walked down the lane toward the highway, bitter tears came to my eyes. It wasn't so much that the woman wouldn't give me food, but she wouldn't let me work for it. A terrible anger welled up in me, and I felt, however irrationally, that if I had a gun I would use it if it would help me get food.

Having no other idea of what to do, I decided to go back to Suffern to see if brother Pat might be more receptive towards me. Several years had passed since I had left there, and I thought Pat might have mellowed and could maybe help me find work. I arrived late at night. No lights were on in Pat and Louisa's apartment, so I slept on the floor in the hallway until the next morning.

There I was again—the phantom kid, always showing up unannounced. Pat and Louisa were surprised, but they didn't appear to be angry at me.

"I quit school and am looking for work," I hastened to explain, lest they think I planned just to mooch off them.

They fixed me breakfast and I told Pat that Papa had beaten me. I did not add that he had tried to kill me. Pat said there was little work around Suffern, but I could iron shirts at his laundry in return for room and board. He also said that Angie was coming out of the orphanage to live with them in a month, and that I would have to leave at that time. This was better than nothing. I had a month's reprieve before I would be homeless again.

At the laundry, one of our customers, Mr. Williams, told me he was an executive at the California Perfume Company, the predecessor to Avon. I asked him if there was work at his factory. He replied that I should report to his secretary. He was very encouraging and I felt confident that I would get a job. The interview proceeded well until the question of my age came up.

"I am fourteen," I answered proudly, "and I have working papers."

"You are too young to work in this plant," the secretary said with finality.

In that instant, I decided instantly to become eighteen.

By this time my month with Pat was almost up. Angie was due in a couple of days, so I found myself on the road again. After hitching back to Brooklyn, I spent a night on a bench in Prospect Park, considering my options. I knew I would never go back to Papa. Cousin Lorenzo came to mind, but perhaps because theirs was a more distant branch of the family, I felt unable to impose myself on them. That left brother Tony as the only person I could turn to.

I arrived at Tony's the next day. His in-laws were living with them, but I was made to feel welcome and Tony said I could sleep on the sunporch.

That first night as I sat on the edge of my wicker couch bed, pulling off my socks, I felt a furious itching in my right big toe. On closer examination I found a large open blister discolored by the blue dye of the ten-cent pair of socks. With all my travels of the past two months, my socks had never been washed and they had caked to my feet. I had been too concerned with other matters to worry about my disintegrating footwear, but now my leg was swelling so I was forced to pay attention.

All night long the itching persisted uncontrollably, moving from my foot up my leg until by morning it had reached beyond my knee. In the daylight I could see that my leg was not only swollen but discolored, and when I tried to bend my knee, I couldn't because the skin was stretched so tight across it. Now, it was beginning to get painful, and I knew I was in trouble. Minnie, Tony's second wife—or perhaps she was his third—told me to go to Coney Island Hospital. With no cane, no crutch, I hobbled and hopped the mile to get there, dragging my sick leg along the best I could. In the receiving room, I joined about seventy-five people, mostly pregnant women, waiting their turn for attention.

When I was finally taken into an examining room, the two young interns took one look at my swollen blue foot and decided something had to be done immediately.

"It looks like gangrene to me," the first young doctor said.

Even though I didn't know exactly what "gangrene" was, the prospect terrified me. I had heard of countless soldiers in World War I dying of it. Without bothering to explain, the doctor directed a nurse to bring him an instrument, and when she re-appeared it was with something that looked like a carpenter's twenty-penny spike, polished to a shine. I thought it was truly an instrument of torture. Without benefit of anesthetic, the doctor took the spike and pushed it through the all-but-bursting skin of my ankle. The pain that resulted was so excruciating I almost blacked out. My suffering was partially relieved, however, by the encircling arms of two nurses who held and comforted me as the doctor did his work. He continued to pierce my foot, pushing the instrument ever deeper until the point came out on the opposite side. The nurses squeezed tighter and reassured me that everything would be all right. Having experienced very little mothering in my life, I wanted it to continue now, but finally I could bear the pain no longer and cried for the doctor to stop.

After a few more piercings, he did so. When I looked down at my foot I expected to see blood oozing. Instead, I was surprised to find my foot and leg completely dry.

"You must go home, now, and soak your foot in very hot water with Epsom salts. Soak it for twenty minutes and remove it for twenty minutes all night long. And tomorrow, bring in a legal guardian to sign so we can amputate your leg," he said casually.

At this point the pain was so bad I could scarcely comprehend his words. The two nurses squeezed my arm sympathetically as they left the room, and one came back with a cane to help me make the trip home.

"I don't have a legal guardian," I whispered feebly.

"Bring somebody," the doctor ordered curtly.

As I limped home, the physical pain and the thought of impending amputation made me realize why Coney Island Hospital was dubbed "the butcher shop." The prospect of losing my leg was overwhelming, but I supposed it was better than dying from gangrene. Stumbling on homeward, I envisioned myself with a crutch and peg leg, like the many war amputees in Brooklyn at that time.

The pain and my depression were about equal as I eased my nearly-exploding foot into a tub of hot water and salts. I could not sit because my leg was so swollen that my knee would not bend.

Watching the agonizingly slow movements of Tony's clock, I wondered what good this treatment could possibly do for me. Twenty minutes in the steaming water, twenty minutes out. Repeat. Five minutes into the second bath, pus began oozing out of the punctures that the intern had made in my foot. This was a nausea-inducing sight, but it got worse. As I watched, the yellowish-green drainage congealed in the hot water, turning into long wormlike creatures that writhed as if alive. What made this horror bearable was that the pain began to subside, and I knew from this that if I continued the salt bath regimen through the night, I would probably be all right by morning and my leg would not have to be amputated after all. I took it as another good sign that, after all the bathing, my foot was no longer blue.

Chapter 15

CONEY ISLAND COWBOY

My leg healed and I went to Manhattan each day looking for work. I really didn't know how to go about getting a job, but whenever I saw older men standing in line I would join them. The older men were always hired over me. I was merely an inexperienced fourteen-year-old kid claiming to be eighteen.

I knew there were soup lines on the waterfront near the Fulton Fish Market, and I made sure I to get there about noon. The homeless and jobless milled around cooking hobo stew in milk cans that bubbled away over fires made of produce crates.

"What do I have to do to get some soup?" I inquired of one grimy chef on my first day.

"Do you see that garbage scow tied over there, kid?" he said. "Go find yourself a can, wash it in one of the fish markets, and come back."

When I returned with a relatively clean tomato can, the man asked if I had brought anything for the pot. At that moment, a horse-drawn wagon loaded with celery happened to be passing by. I reached into a crate and pulled out a celery head as my contribution. The cook chopped it up immediately, adding it to the boiling pot.

Though I was almost constantly looking for work, I was still just a kid, too. Sometimes a group of us played dice on the street in Gerrard Court, a short block of white stucco bungalows separating Sheepshead Bay Creek from Banner Avenue. A girl named Gloria Cohen lived in the court with her divorced mother, a woman whose radiant beauty caused sinful thoughts to run through our minds. Young as we were, we appreciated that thirteen-year-old Gloria was destined to blossom like her mother into a classic Jewish beauty. But we did not anticipate what was to happen one warm summer evening before then.

Irish Flicker, who always carried a pair of dice, had organized a group of us to shoot craps for pennies. We were vaguely aware during the game that Gloria was watching us from her porch steps. When the game broke up, we stood in a circle discussing what we would do for the rest of the evening. Then Gloria appeared and squeezed in between Moishe and me. For a moment she just stood there, not saying a word as we gaped at her long dark curls and the modest swell of her young breasts beneath her light summer dress. Then, to our complete surprise and amazement, she lifted her skirt up to her belly button. She wasn't wearing anything underneath. "Look!" she exclaimed proudly pointing at her crotch, "I'm grown up now. See, I have hair."

Too stunned to utter a word, we all found our eyes riveted to Gloria's pubic area with its fascinating crop of fuzz. Then it must have dawned on each of us at the same moment that we boys would be jail bait if any adults came upon the scene. In one simultaneous action, we sprinted off in different directions, leaving Gloria standing with her dress still raised and a look of bewilderment on her face as if to say, "Did I do something wrong?"

Since I had been unsuccessful in finding a job by myself, Tony found work for me at his plumbing shop. Rules prohibited relatives from working together, so I was assigned to a temporary apprenticeship with an Irishman—a master plumber who was refurbishing some old sandstone tenements in south Brooklyn. The tenements had recently been purchased by a Mr. Bommer, a wealthy, distinguished-looking man who had a neatly-trimmed white goatee and dressed very formally in an Oxford gray suit and Stetson hat. Mr. Bommer considered the master plumber an artist, and each morning he would arrive in a chauffeur-driven car to watch the man at work.

In those days, houses were piped with lead, with the plumbing joints made of molten solder. To make the joints, a liquid mixture of tin and lead was poured from a ladle onto the pipe ends. With canvas-gloved hands, the plumber would allow the solder to run around and down the joint, wiping and shaping it as it hardened. He would control the slowly-cooling metal by spitting into a wiping pad, using the saliva to cool the bottom of the joint. This was where the craftsmanship came in—and if a building inspector was mean, a plumber could get back at him by not cooling the solder properly, so that a sharp needle of metal would be left hanging and the unsuspecting official would cut himself as he ran his hand along the bottom of the pipe.

Mr. Bommer, in any case, would watch in awe for an hour or more at a time as the Irishman sculpted perfect elliptical shapes from the flowing metal.

"That man is truly an artist," he would remark. "People don't realize that men who do such work are really professionals."

My brother Tony was an excellent craftsman, too, but he was always looking for easier ways to make money. Occasionally he was hired by would-be plumbers to take the proficiency test in their place. A person who wanted a plumbing license would buy off the proper officials in city hall and pay Tony fifty dollars.

When my temporary plumbing apprenticeship ended, I found new employment in a shoe factory. The work was repetitive and tedious, but I looked forward to my first weekly paycheck. This was supposed to be seven dollars for six days' work. However, when the paymaster brought the small yellow pay envelopes around in a shoebox, and handed me one with my name on it, it contained only six dollars and thirty cents.

"Where's my other seventy cents?"

"Ten-percent of everybody's wages is held out for union dues. And if you don't want to pay it, you're out of work."

Tony charged me five dollars a week for room and board, so I was left with sixty cents for carfare and seventy cents for clothing and entertainment. This wasn't much and it galled me that I should pay ten percent to a non-existent union to protect my job. Eventually I quit.

My next job paid seven dollars for seven days a week of work, but I didn't have to pay the kickback money and the work was much more enjoyable. In fact, I was working with horses at the track at Coney Island, exercising my inner fantasy of being a cowboy.

Part of the job was to attract people and entice them to ride the horses. I quickly learned how to hold onto the pommel so I could dismount and mount a three-quarter Indian piebald at full gallop. When things got slow, the boss would order in his broken Italian, "Johnny, do tricks." This gave me an excuse to ride and show off to the people on the boardwalk. I soon became known as "The Coney Island Cowboy."

Not all of the work was exciting, however. Starting early in the morning, I had to clean the stalls, wash the horses with soap and water, and brush them until they were ready for the track. Other boys did this too, and we would each ride a big horse along the bridle path to Coney Island with six other horses in train behind us. Once there, our main task was to walk alongside people taking pony rides, keeping the horses calm and holding kids on saddles so they wouldn't be thrown off.

My friend Hymie always seemed to have lots of spending money, and when I asked him "how come?" he shared the secret of his wealth.

"Johnny, you can do it too. When a kid pockets his change, watch which pocket it goes into, gallop the pony, and when the kid is bouncing along get his money. If the kid comes back complaining he's lost his change, pretend to look for it in the sand. It's easy."

So, that was how Hymie was able to buy so many hot dogs. From time to time, I had even helped look for change "lost" by some of his victims. But I could never bring myself to pick the pockets of my own clients, because it never seemed right.

One day a very attractive, well-dressed woman came to the ticket booth. She had been watching a large chestnut stallion and wanted to hire him, not to ride sedately around the track but to take the animal out on the bridle path. The boss finally agreed that if she came back on a slow day, she could hire the horse for a couple of hours. The following Wednesday, much to our surprise, she appeared in full riding habit—derby, riding crop, and shiny boots—carrying a bag of apples and carrots.

"Johnny, you go with her and see that she doesn't gallop or whip the horse," the boss instructed me.

As we trotted along together on Ocean Parkway, I asked about her work. I figured she had to have a pretty good job because she was so well-dressed.

"I'm the society editor for the *New York Times*," she confided. "I go to lots of swanky affairs to get my news."

I didn't know what "swanky" meant but I agreed with her that those were the affairs to go to. An hour later we turned back, me lagging behind because I was feeling increasingly ashamed of my own awful clothes. At the end of the ride the woman gave me a fifty-cent tip and thanked us profusely for letting her ride the horse.

Later that summer, I had another encounter with a woman that was much more intimate. It was not uncommon for girls to watch us as we took the horses back to the stable in the evenings, and sometimes we would pick up them up and give them a ride. One warm night, a woman I knew as Pauline was watching the horses from the sidewalk, as she had done many other nights after her nursing shift was over.

"Can I have a ride with you to the stable, Johnny?" she called.

"Okay," I said quietly. "Meet me up the street so the boss doesn't see."

Pauline was an attractive brunette with hair bobbed in the fashion of the day. Unmarried and well-built, she wore a light cotton summer dress with flowers printed on it in shades of yellow and green.

"Hold on to the pommel real tight," I said. "I'll control the horses as we go under the 'El', and let's hope there isn't a train rumbling overhead that will startle them."

As I helped her on the horse, her dress slipped up above her knees, but she didn't attempt to cover herself.

"I'm exposing my thighs to the world, Johnny!" she laughed.

I couldn't help noticing that she was exposing other parts of herself as well, since she wasn't wearing underpants.

As we rode along, in and out of the pools of light shining down from the standards, I continued to glance at the white flesh of her legs. All along the wooded path, I allowed my sexual imagination to roam freely, but then quickly dismissed my fantasies because Pauline was a mature woman and I was merely a fifteen-year-old kid. Besides, I had no experience with women. With the exception of Gloria, who barely counted, I had never even been close to one.

At the stable I fed and bedded down the horses. When I had finished these chores, I found Pauline lying seductively on a park bench inside the exercise ring. A large oak tree grew in the center of the ring, and the area was surrounded by a tall board fence that gave us complete seclusion. A full August moon shone overhead and a bare bulb gave off dim light just inside the stable door. Surveying the romantic scene, I noted that it included a large pile of horse manure—but clearly this didn't bother Pauline.

She motioned me to sit beside her, and then, unbelievably, she drew me toward her and touched her lips to mine in a way that I could never have imagined possible. We continued to kiss, and then she began unveiling to me the mysteries of the female body. She was a nurse, a woman of the world. I was one wildly excited kid.

Had we been someplace else, we might have continued these delightful explorations for a while longer. But the park bench wasn't comfortable, and it didn't occur to me to suggest that we move into the hayloft. Instead, I walked Pauline to the trolley car and said, casually, "so long," as she boarded her ride to Brighton Beach. My head and heart were still racing, however, and had I but known how I would have begged her for another date. Instead, unable to afford a trolley ride myself, I turned away and walked home.

Brighton Beach, 1933

Chapter 16

THE BLUE DIAMOND SOCIAL CLUB

Freddie and Tom were close friends of mine, and I often went to their house. They had learned how to make a few nickels by buying punchboards and suckering kids to spend money on them. Big Tom, their father, was a counterfeiter. He specialized in dollar bills, which were easier to pass in those days than larger denominations. One batch was badly printed, however, and needed to be destroyed. But instead of burning them in a furnace, Big Tom stupidly built a fire in an empty lot across the street. He didn't bother to ensure that all of the bills were completely burned, and the neighborhood kids gathered up the undamaged remainders and took them to their parents.

Inevitably, somebody's parents informed the police. Big Tom was taken into custody, but his associates posted bail and got him out in a hurry. Several weeks later, as he walked to the subway on his way to stand trial, he was gunned down two blocks from his house by men in a speeding car. That was the end of the family, because the boys' mother was already dead. Young Tom vowed that he would avenge the killers even if it took him the rest of his life, and both boys disappeared into the underworld.

In our neighborhood, bootlegging was more common than counterfeiting. Brother Tony, who was involved in both bootlegging and gambling, often brought loads of raw alcohol into the basement of our house to be stored until he was able to distribute it to "cutters," who would dilute and flavor it. This liquor was then bottled, labeled "Canadian Club," and sold to saloons.

The bootleg alcohol was made in two huge auto storage garages, a block from our house. I could look through the windows of these buildings and clearly see the fermenting mash cooking in gigantic vats. The odor from this process permeated the neighborhood and was so strong that it would have been impossible for the police to ignore it, unless they were "being taken care of."

On Sunday afternoons, Tony ran a dice game in his basement. About twenty gamblers would arrive on foot, so there would be no tell-tale cars parked outside, and they would go directly to a blanket-covered table that was set up downstairs near the steam boiler. A large porcelain light fixture shaded the single bulb that lit the room. Tony raked twenty-five cents a pass, and Max banked the game, paying Tony five dollars for the privilege. It was understood that if there was a police raid, Tony would provide bail for the players. My job was to take care of the door, admitting only those who wanted to gamble. Tony's wife and child went to movie matinees, so they would not be in the house while the game was going on.

One Sunday afternoon, at about two o'clock, there was a knock on the door. Peering through the glass, I could see two policemen on the stoop.

Taking my time to answer the door, I shouted a warning down to the gamblers: "The cops are here!"

"We have a complaint of a disturbance at 1112 Banner Avenue," the first cop said.

"There is no 1112 Banner Avenue," I told him. "Our house is 1110 Banner, and the house next door is 1114. And I've been sitting here all afternoon reading the comics, and haven't seen or heard anything unusual."

I was lying, but the cops appeared to buy my story and went on their way. When I reported the encounter to Tony, my brother Mike, who was also on hand, asked me if one of the cops had been Joe Espozito. Yes, one of them was Joe. Mike convinced Tony to let him go and fix things up, because Joe was a friend of his.

Mike caught up with the cops several hundred feet down the street. When he returned, he assured everyone that the matter had been taken care of. Fifteen minutes after the precinct shift change, however, six radio-equipped Ford roadsters arrived and surrounded the house. A dozen officers and one sergeant covered the windows and doors, twirling their night sticks. I issued another warning to the gamblers in the basement, then turned back towards the door. Pulling open the curtain over the adjacent window, I found myself eye to eye with the sergeant.

Pounding on the door, the sergeant shouted: "Open up! This is a raid!"

Tony had come up the stairs and was standing behind me as I opened the door. "What's going on?" he demanded. "We're just having a social dice game with a bunch of friends."

"We have proof that you're running a gambling house here," the sergeant said.

"What would it take for you to forget about it?" Tony asked, inviting the sergeant and two other officers into the dining room. He and the sergeant sat down at opposite ends of the long table as Mike and I and the two cops stood watching. The rest of the officers guarded the windows and doors to prevent any of the gamblers from escaping.

"How much is this gonna cost me?" Tony asked, knowing that he was responsible for protecting the gamblers.

"Ten dollars for each officer and twenty-five for me," the sergeant responded without blinking an eye.

"Bullshit," Tony hollered. "I can bail them out of jail cheaper than that, and you know it. I ain't making that kind of money."

The sergeant kept insisting, until Tony said, "Forget it! Just take us all to jail, goddammit." The sergeant hesitated, and Tony knew it was time to make his last offer. "Fifteen bucks for you and five bucks for each of your men. That's it! Take it or lock us up!"

The sergeant didn't take long to make up his mind. Tony shelled out seventy-five dollars on the spot and agreed to meet with the sergeant again later. As the dark green roadsters disappeared down the street and around the corner, the gamblers resumed their game in the basement, confident that they would not be disturbed again.

I had watched with wide-eyed surprise at the business-like negotiations between Tony and the law-enforcement officer. Through most of the proceedings I had been convinced that we were all going to go to jail—but Tony saved the day and I learned that there were ways to circumvent the law.

Brother Mike also taught me useful lessons. He was now married, but when he was single he had belonged to a social club comprised of neighborhood men. He suggested that I and other unmarried young men in the area start a club of our own. It would be a way to meet girls and we would have a place to dance that wouldn't cost us very much. Acting on this advice, about fifteen of us rented a basement in Brighton Beach for five dollars a month. We painted the walls blue and decorated the ceiling to look like a night sky adorned with stars, comets, moons and planets that Mike had come across in his work in the theatrical district of Times Square.

Completing our handiwork, we called our organization The Blue Diamond Social Club. We furnished it with cast-off davenports and chairs and a record player. A few of my buddies had girlfriends, who brought other girls with them to the club. Word spread fast among them that the Blue Diamond was a good place to dance and have fun, be out of the weather, and meet boys. Within a few weeks, we were overwhelmed with young women from Brighton Beach and Coney Island—and the Blue Diamond became a passion pit.

Partitioned off from the main dance floor was the furnace room, where we installed a davenport for attendees who wanted to have sex. The furnace room soon became more popular than the dance floor, with couples waiting anxiously for their turn. Those who couldn't wait availed themselves of an overstuffed chair in a dimly lit corner of the dance floor.

I had told brother Mike about my night with Pauline, and after that he kept me supplied with rubbers. One Saturday night, when I was about to leave for the club and he had omitted to give me my usual safeties, I signaled across the room to him, miming rolling something along my index finger. Mike caught on immediately, disappeared into the bedroom, and returned with a couple of rubbers, which he palmed to me.

"What are you doing?" Mike's wife asked angrily, knowing full well what he had just given me.

"Nothing," Mike lied.

She started crying. "Johnny is just a kid. You men are all alike."

I was surprised at her reaction. I had always assumed sex was okay. No one had ever suggested to me that it wasn't. Not wanting to get into a family feud, I pocketed the rubbers and left.

Our favorite record that winter was Hoagy Carmichael's "Stardust." It was a slow waltz, and I was enjoying it on the dancefloor with the luscious Clara Stein in my arms when I noticed Abie Schwartz in a dark corner. Abie and Shirley Greenfield were engaged in some heavy loving, and I became anxious for him because he was noted for premature ejaculation. This night was no different. Abie suddenly got up leaving his confused girl, and started towards me with bowed legs and a look of disgust on his face.

"Abie," I said, trying to make light of it, "it happened again, huh?"

"Yeah," he said, close to tears, "I don't think I'll ever get into a woman."

"Maybe you just need more practice," I said.

It wasn't all sex and dancing that winter, however. One Saturday night a group of Greek boys from Coney Island came to the Blue Diamond

Club to avenge a fight. This had started the previous summer over a simple flirtation between a girlfriend of one of the Greeks and one of our boys. We Blue Diamond boys answered the challenge by going into the street to fight—but the bloodshed we anticipated never happened. In the previous few days there had been snow, then a thaw, then another freeze, so that glare ice covered the sidewalks and streets. Every time one guy swung on somebody else, he fell to the ice. If two grappled in their anger, both would fall down. The whole thing became a slapstick comedy, and, at last, we all laughed and shook hands. Shaking hands was customary in those days, win or lose. There were a few black eyes and bruised faces among us, but no one was hurt badly.

Winter continued and grew colder still. I was without work and the snow that fell incessantly on the city only made me feel more miserable. Few people braved the streets, except a few half-frozen chestnut vendors who huddled near their fires, or the occasional brave teamster trying to control his wild-eyed horse as it tried to find traction on the glaze beneath its hooves.

Momentary relief came from George Terra, a well-known local boxer known as the Georgia Terror, though he had never been out of New York. A precinct committeeman had given him ten work tickets to distribute to his friends for snow removal. George gave me one of the tickets, instructing me to be at the hiring hall in Coney Island at seven o'clock that night if I wanted to be hired the next morning. I wrapped my legs with burlap bags and arrived at the scene thirteen hours early—only to find myself fifth in line. By eight o'clock there must have been a thousand men hoping to be hired.

The weather was bitterly cold—eight or ten degrees below zero—and like most of the other men, I was inadequately dressed to spend the night outdoors. I held my hands under my arms for warmth, huddling against the building with the other men, sharing body heat in the hope of surviving. George brought a paraffin-coated cardboard container of hot coffee which he shared with me, but that was all that went into my stomach that night.

Morning and the hiring boss arrived. "Only the first fifty will be hired today," he announced.

As the word passed back, some of the men seemed relieved that they would not have to stay and work in the ice and snow all day, but others were dejected because they had starving families at home, and the anticipated pay of fifty cents an hour was much more than the usual dollar a day paid to casual laborers.

I was assigned the miserable and tedious job of chopping ice and making a path from the curb to the trolley stop. When the noon hour arrived, I sheltered in a recessed doorway. The proprietor of a nearby delicatessen saw me there and asked if I had anything to eat.

"I've been watching you work hard all morning," he said. "You need something in your stomach. Come with me and I'll give you a sandwich."

My frozen spirits warmed a little, and I responded eagerly. "I sure appreciate that, and I will pay you as soon as I get paid myself."

I worked until five o'clock, walked home, had supper and went right back to wait the night in line again for the next day's work.

I stuck to this schedule for three days and nights, but by the fourth evening I hurt so badly from cold and fatigue that I didn't return, other than to ask for my earnings and pay the shopkeeper. I gave the rest of my money to Minnie for board. She gave me three dollars back to buy some shoes, warning me not to mention it to Tony.

The night of Franklin D. Roosevelt's first inauguration, March 4, 1933, my buddy Tony Monti and I visited the local pool hall. This was a large upstairs room containing twenty-six tables. Our table was in the back of the room, and I didn't realize, at first, that an armed man was holding the other players against the wall at the far end of the hall. "If you little bastards don't get up here in a hurry, I'm coming after you," a second man shouted, directing us with the barrel of his revolver.

Tony and I obeyed immediately, raising our hands above our head, and joined the line against the wall. I took a position next to Walter, an elderly black man whom I knew to be a kindly gentleman. He always dressed in a suit and tie, and carried a flashlight because he had to walk through an unlighted garbage dump to get back home from the pool hall.

A third armed man stood at the top of the stairs to prevent anyone from escaping. Eventually I realized the gunmen were not robbers but police detectives looking for hoodlums who had committed a robbery in the neighborhood. One detective frisked everybody, and when he got to Walter he found the flashlight. These, along with screwdrivers, pliers, and jackknives, were considered to be burglary tools, so the detective accused the old man of being involved in the crime.

Poor old Walter was shaking with fright, and though the pool hall proprietor convinced the detective of Walter's innocence, the plainclothesman confiscated his flashlight. Then he moved on to me. "How old are you," he demanded. I answered that I was twenty-one. "Twenty-one!" he scoffed, "You're not twenty-one!" Grabbing me by the shoulder, he pulled me out of the line, booted me in the ass and told me to get the hell out and never come back. It was cold out but I didn't even think to grab my jacket. As I ran past the policeman guarding the stairs, he hit me with his open hand on the back of my neck throwing me off balance, so that I stumbled and rolled the rest of the way down.

After this, life seemed more bleak and hopeless with every passing day. Not only was there no work, there was no place to hang out now, either. The pool hall was off-limits, and the city had shut down the Blue Diamond Social Club after placing a large red sign on the door which read: "Closed by the Board of Health—Do not enter these premises."

When a friend of mine enlisted in the army, I tried to do the same, but at sixteen I was too young. Then I tried applying to the CCCs—the Civilian Conservation Corps, a program started by the new Roosevelt Administration to provide work for young men on welfare—but I was too young for that, too.

Out of desperation I decided to ask the principal at my former elementary school to write a note saying I was eighteen. She was horrified. "How dare you ask me to perjure myself!" I had never heard the word "perjure" before, but I could see from the look on her face that I should leave, *presto*.

"I am just trying to find a job," I apologized as I backed out the door and ran down the hall.

My despair lifted slightly when Mayor Fiorello LaGuardia obtained a crime prevention quota from the CCCs to clean New York City streets of incorrigibles. By then it was spring, 1934, and on a sunny day in April the bright thought occurred to me to go to Canarsie to ask Father Appo, whom I had not seen since I was six, if he could help some of us get into the Cs.

Moishe, Charlie and I arrived at his house after lunch. We had not given Father Appo advance notice of our visit, and he was busy with a group of mothers and their daughters as they practiced for their confirmation. Clearly we had caught him at a bad time, but he sent us into the kitchen to be fed because we admitted that we had not eaten lunch. Having fed us, Father Appo gave us a note introducing us to the desk sergeant at the police station and requesting that we be accepted into the CCC program.

"Don't you kids have jobs?" the sergeant asked.

"No," we all answered in unison.

"How would you like to go into the three Cs?"

"Great," I answered for all three of us.

I could scarcely contain my excitement as we proceeded to fill out the forms. I decided to tell them I was twenty-one because I wouldn't need a legal guardian to sign the papers. No matter that I was just sixteen and looked it.

The officer who helped me fill out the application didn't question my age—and that was it, I was in the Cs! Shocked and jubilant, I could scarcely believe that I would now have steady work. The Depression had caused me a huge amount of grief and suffering—but it was also the driving force behind a government work relief program that would completely change my life.

PART II

THE PACIFIC NORTHWEST

1934-1941

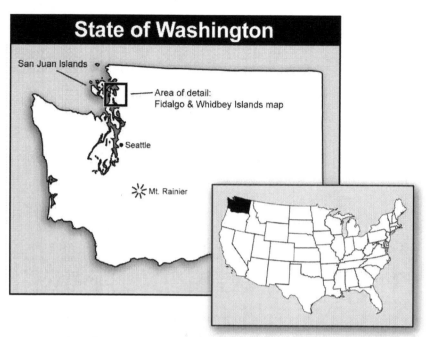

State of Washington

San Juan Islands

Area of detail:
Fidalgo & Whidbey Islands map

Seattle

Mt. Rainier

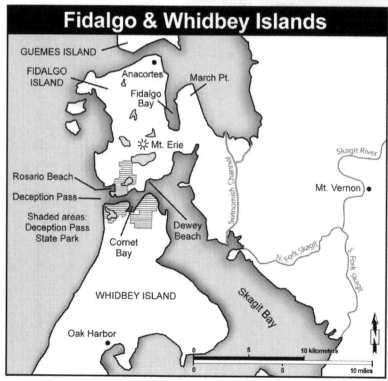

Fidalgo & Whidbey Islands

GUEMES ISLAND

FIDALGO
ISLAND

Anacortes

Fidalgo
Bay

March Pt.

Mt. Erie

Skagit River

Rosario Beach

Mt. Vernon

Deception Pass

Swinomish Channel

Shaded areas:
Deception Pass
State Park

Cornet
Bay

Dewey
Beach

N. Fork Skagit

S. Fork Skagit

WHIDBEY ISLAND

Skagit Bay

Oak Harbor

0   5   10 kilometers
0   5   10 miles

N

Chapter 17

POWDER MONKEY

"Wait'll you get the hook! Wait'll you get the hook!" chanted the "old-timers." They had been inducted into the CCCs a mere twenty-four hours earlier and watched as we newcomers marched to the dispensary. Although we were incorrigibles from the streets of Brooklyn who thought we were tough, many of us succumbed to the scare tactics of the kids who had already received their immunizations. Dozens of young men raised in an environment of crime and fear passed out on the steps of the dispensary at the thought of getting a jab.

The shots were our initiation into the Civilian Conservation Corps. This program had come into being by act of Congress the previous year (1933) as one of the Roosevelt Administration's New Deal measures to address unemployment. At that time, twenty-five percent of the labor force was without jobs, and the Emergency Conservation Work Act was passed to put unmarried, unemployed young men between the ages of 18 and 25 to work on public projects associated with natural resource conservation. Food, clothing, housing and transport would be provided by the military; the work projects were devised and supervised by the Departments of Agriculture and the Interior. Three hundred thousand men were inducted into the CCCs within the first couple of months; my own induction came the following year. We were all paid a dollar a day, of which five dollars per month was given out as spending money and the remainder was sent home—in my case, to my brother Tony—and either deducted from the family welfare payments or (supposedly) saved for the young man when he got out of the Corps. Knowing Tony's gambling habits, I wasn't sure how much of my money I was eventually going to see, but I was happy for now just to have work, food and somewhere safe to sleep for the foreseeable future.

The CCCs had projects all over the country, and none of us new inductees knew where we were going until we were delivered to the train station two days later. Scrawled on the side of our Pullman car were the words "Anacortes, Washington." Few of us knew much geography. We assumed a word had been misspelled and we were going to Anaconda, an airfield outside of Washington, D.C. To our amazement, the train headed due west across Pennsylvania.

I was already enjoying this new adventure. In New York, I had been self-conscious about my background because the slurs against Italians were constant. Even though I knew that many Italians excelled in art, science and athletics, I had become reluctant to admit my heritage because we were all considered to be gangsters and ditch-diggers. It didn't help that my Italian parents were rustics from the south of the country. In New York it was commonly held that the illiterate Italians, Irish, and Blacks were good for nothing except common labor. I was determined to escape this fate. My education was limited, but I had dreams of advancing myself.

About seventy-five of us CCC kids were heading west. Keen to distinguish myself, I volunteered to do KP duty on the train. An army mess-sergeant was in charge of cooking, which was done on two legless wood-burning stoves set in a bed of sand. My job was to peel potatoes and help serve, carrying large kettles of vegetables and salmon up and down the aisles.

As we were rattling through Montana on the third day of our journey, a well-dressed man boarded the train and told us we were going to a small town in the northwest corner of the state of Washington. This meant little or nothing to most of us because our experience had been limited primarily to New York and its environs.

The next morning, when the train stopped at Spokane, we expected to see cowboys and Indians and were surprised when we saw none. Starting our climb into the heavily timbered mountains beyond Leavenworth, I anticipated seeing burly lumberjacks like those I had seen in geography books. Though no loggers were visible, I was elated at the sight of the vast conifer forests on the west side of the Cascades. I had never seen such massive trees, and they were growing in an environment seemingly undisturbed by humans. The Suffern woods seemed parklike by comparison.

Until then, the weather had been hot and clear for our entire journey across the country, but when we arrived in Anacortes we were greeted by a heavy overcast sky with drizzle. In spite of the weather, my spirits were high. I had the feeling that this was going to be the best thing that ever happened to me.

Anacortes was a small town located on Fidalgo Island, part of the San Juan archipelago but connected to the mainland by a bridge. From the train station we were driven in open trucks along a hilly, winding road past small family farms hacked out of dense woods along the edge of a beautiful lake with a small island in its center. This was Campbell Lake, and I was to learn later that it had been popularized by Ripley's Believe It Or Not because it contained an island on an island.

At a place called Dewey Beach, we boarded a five-car ferry. This vessel was so far removed from the huge ferries plying the New York harbor we feared it might sink under the weight of our trucks. It took us across the swirling green waters of Deception Pass—so-named by the explorer Captain George Vancouver because he thought it was either a river estuary or the opening to a bay, and that the rocky bluffs to the south of it were part of the mainland. In fact, the bluffs belonged to yet another island, which Vancouver named after his ship's master, Joseph Whidbey.

I loved every minute of the ferry ride across the water from Fidalgo Island to Whidbey, so I didn't even think about getting sea sick. Arriving at a place called Hoypus Point, our trucks debarked onto a small wooden dock leading to a gravel road that wound through dense conifer woods to our camp at Cornet Bay. The drizzle persisted, but the closer we got to our destination, the more elated I became. Not only would I have work, food and shelter in this beautiful place, I felt confident that I would be able to do whatever was asked of me. Deep down I knew somehow that I had abilities and skills that were simply waiting to be discovered.

Unlike many of the CCC kids, I had no feelings of homesickness. I had lived in so many houses and with so many people that I had no close bonds to anyone or any place. I accepted things for what they were, and I didn't take shit from anyone. I was on the defensive, willing to fight for what I felt was right.

Dropping down a narrow steep road we came to a flat clearing that had once been an Indian campsite. Now it was home to a number of wooden barracks-type buildings that had been designated by the military as the 266 Company CCC camp. I was assigned to Roosevelt Hall, a basic bunkhouse that was simply a long room filled with double-tier beds and two large wood-burning stoves. My bunk had a straw-filled mattress and was adjacent to the cubby hole, a small open room that was home to two men charged with keeping discipline.

Toilet facilities were located in a smelly, open-ended shed that could accommodate about fifteen kids at a time. Trooping to the crapper *en masse* that first night was a new experience for us city kids. As we did our business, we agreed that we would surely not work the next day because of the rain. In New York, nobody worked outside when it was raining. The next morning, however, even as the rain continued, we were called out and issued with a set of raingear because, as we were about to learn, in the Pacific Northwest outdoor work goes on, rain or not. Otherwise, nothing would ever get done!

Our new canvas clothing protected us not only from wetness, but from thorns and nettles as we walked the mile or so through the woods to our work site. Our first job was to build a road that would connect existing Whidbey Island roads to a partially completed bridge across Deception Pass. Workers from another CCC camp located at Rosario Beach, on the north side of the Pass, would do the same for Fidalgo Island.

Most of us were handed picks and shovels. I was assigned to Isaac Love, the "powder" man.

"You going to be a man, you got to have some snoose," Isaac said in a heavy Swedish accent. "Like this," he continued, proffering a small round can of Copenhagen tobacco and showing me how to place a pinch between my gum and lower lip.

Isaac and the other local men we had met were all tough and strong, and I was eager to do whatever it took to be like them. I sucked on the snoose and then watched for Isaac to spit, because I needed to spit. He didn't spit, so I didn't either. Instead, I saw him swallow and followed suit. Over the next half hour I felt increasingly nauseated, and then I began vomiting and running from the rear end simultaneously. A month or two passed before I dared to take another chew of snoose.

Isaac left the job three weeks after I started work with him, but in that time he taught me all about the powder trade. Not only did I learn how to drill, blast, and chew snoose, but Isaac explained to me how dynamite could make a powder man sick. As you peeled dynamite sticks and split them with a jackknife before tamping them down in the drill holes, the nitroglycerin could get on your skin. From there it would be absorbed into the body, resulting in a massive headache. I expected this to happen to me occasionally, but I got headaches every day I worked with the dynamite.

100

They were so bad I often had to go to bed right after work without eating supper. But I never complained. I was glad to have the opportunity to work and wanted to do a good job. Besides that, blasting gave me a feeling of importance because of the danger connected with it and the sense of accomplishment that came with actually building a road.

After Isaac's departure, I became the new "powder monkey." One day a U.S. Department of the Interior cameraman came to photograph our crew at work, and I felt proud and a little cocky as I set off my largest charge yet. More than a ton of dynamite had been placed in holes drilled into the road we were building. I told the photographer to shelter with me behind a huge Douglas fir, from which he would have an unobstructed view of the blast. Before pushing the plunger that would set off the charge, I hollered "Fire in the hole!" three times, so as to warn everyone around of the impending explosion. Then I let go of the plunger and hugged the tree, confident the seven-foot diameter trunk would protect the photographer and me from the blast. What I hadn't anticipated was the debris that cascaded down upon us from above. We were showered with small rocks and branches. This was long before the days of safety hats and we were fortunate to escape with bruises and minor scratches.

The road was to be the bridgehead of two spans across Deception Pass that would connect three islands—Fidalgo, Whidbey, and the small rocky crag of Pass Island in the middle—and put the little Dewey Beach ferry out of business. Our work site was high above the turbulent waters of the Pass. From the Whidbey side I could see snowcapped Mount Baker with its glistening glaciers and green foothills. A deserted prison camp clung to the sheer rock wall of Canoe Pass on Fidalgo Island, and I often thought of the prisoners who had worked there, suspended halfway between the top of the cliff and the wild waters below. Imagining the conditions under which these men had lived and worked as they crushed rock for the early highways of Washington State made me even more thankful for my job and my freedom.

On headache-free evenings I often hiked back to the work site to watch eagles fishing the waters far below. I marveled at the strength of those beautiful birds as they snatched up large cod and salmon and flew with them back to their nests, which were always built in the highest trees around. To me, the adults always looked very proud as their young ones feasted on the prey. I felt extremely fortunate to be watching them, and had divorced myself from Brooklyn so completely that all I thought about now was my work and enjoying every bit of scenery and wildlife that I could.

Going to sleep at night I would listen to the sound of rolling waves, funneled from West Beach through Deception Pass into our bay. On very still nights, I could hear the distant chugging of tugboats straining to move their log rafts across Rosario Strait, the relatively open stretch of water to the west. The sounds of the city had disappeared completely from my mind and I decided I never wanted to hear sirens or traffic again. More than this, I was so taken by the beauty and silence of the Pacific Northwest that I wanted to be identified with the area. I started by deliberately losing my Brooklyn accent. I also incorporated local idioms and commonly-used Indian words into my speech. We CCC kids were called *cheechakos*, which is Salish for "newcomer." I also learned to say *skookum chuck* for "strong running water," *mowich* for "deer," and *squaw* or *klootch* for "woman." "A couple a three weeks" or "a couple a three days" were measures of time, and directions were often given as "this a way" or "that a way."

When the powder work finished, I became a high rigger and added yet more words to my Northwestern vocabulary. Our foreman, Earl Lamphear, taught me everything he knew about tree climbing. Our task was to remove the "widow makers," or hung-up broken branches, suspended over the newly constructed road. I had to learn how to splice cable, and this involved a "bull prick," used to separate the wire strands of a cable so they could be easily woven. Another new term was "Molly Hogan"—an eye splice that could be accomplished without a bull prick. When I questioned Earl about this, he explained, "Molly Hogan was the most famous of all the whores on Seattle's Skid Road. She was reputed to have the biggest pussy in town." I looked down at the Molly Hogan I had just completed and, sure as hell, it resembled that part of a woman's anatomy exactly, complete with frayed wires that looked like pubic hair.

Other logging lingo included "hanging a guy," which meant to make a guywire fast from the top of a spar to a stump; "choking a log," or putting a wire strap around a log to be skidded out; and "the bull cook," who was the head cook.

In addition to expanding my vocabulary, cable and rope splicing were to prove invaluable in my later life as I worked in the Pacific Northwest logging industry and in Europe during World War II. In fact, the CCCs were preparing me for adult life in ways I could not yet imagine.

Chapter 18

FIST FIGHTS AND FOOD FIGHTS

About half of the New York and New Jersey unit in Cornet Bay was made up of kids on probation or parole. Their case workers had given them assumed names when they entered the CCC program, but mail always came to them via their legal names. Thus, a guy we knew as John O'Brien might get a letter addressed to Stan Kowalski, which would tip us off that he was a felon. The kids with assumed names hated mail call not only because their co-workers would discover they were outlaws, but because their caseworkers were always pressuring them by mail to get promotions, and there were almost none of these to be had.

The non-felons among us always looked forward to mail call, however. My brothers never wrote, but I received letters regularly from Minnie, Tony's wife. One letter made me especially happy to be thousands of miles from Brooklyn. I had asked Minnie to send me five dollars from the twenty-five-dollar monthly CCC allotment that she and Tony were supposed to be saving for me. She sent the money, together with some startling news:

Dear Johnny,

Enclosed find the five dollars that you asked for from your account.
Everything is going well with us, and you are lucky that you are out there where you are. Your gang got into a fight with the Greeks again, and one was killed and one had an ear cut off and wound up in the hospital.

Your sister-in-law, Minnie

I wished she had included a few more details, such as who was killed and who lost the ear. I also felt a little remorseful because the five dollars had come out of my savings. In retrospect, however, I should have asked Minnie for money more often. After my two years of hard work with the CCCs, she and Tony never sent me a penny of what should have been my accumulated allotment. I am almost certain Tony played the ponies with the money and lost it all.

For entertainment we went to movies or dances. The first few times we went to Oak Harbor, a town of about four hundred inhabitants ten miles south of our Cornet Bay camp. When fifty or sixty CCC boys arrived in Oak Harbor for an evening, it seemed to the resentful locals that we were over-running the place. They were largely Dutch, church-going types, and we were a noisy rabble in comparison. The dances were held at the community hall, a large wooden building that never seemed to warm up, perhaps because only a few of the Dutch girls were more adventurous enough to risk criticism from their parents and peers and dance with us.

One night the Oak Harbor American Legion hosted a boxing match between the CCC kids and the local boys. Everything was going smoothly until about halfway into the program, when the Oak Harbor referee made what we considered to be a bad call. This caused a riot to break out. We CCC kids were outnumbered ten to one as folding chairs sailed through the air and everybody's fists flew. Even some of the supposedly demure Dutch girls entered the fray, knowing we would not hit them. I turned at one point just in time to see a cute blonde swing a chair at me from behind. I deflected the blow with my wrist and arm, and took the chair from her. This spirited young woman eventually married the camp doctor.

Eventually our camp commander, Harry Liebe, an ex-football player from the University of Washington who weighed at least three hundred pounds, started pulling people apart. I was a CCC policeman, and though I had no real authority, I felt a responsibility to help calm the crowd and set about helping him.

"Calm down," Harry shouted in his loud authoritarian voice. Then he ordered all the Cs to leave the building and report to the truck.

"Don't come back! Don't come back!" the Oak Harborites shouted as we left.

"We won't come back! We won't come back!" we chanted in return.

And we didn't. We chose instead to make Anacortes our new recreational headquarters, although it meant having to take the ferry to get there and returning to camp afterwards at an earlier time than most of us energetic young men would have liked.

Other forms of recreation presented themselves to us occasionally. On Labor Day weekend some of us decided to climb Mount Rainier, the massive white-domed volcano south-east of Seattle. Bouncing along in the back of the army truck, we sang "Silent Night" and "Sweet Adeline" to help pass the miles. Our group included the camp education director, his assistant, and two supposedly experienced mountain climbers from the Tacoma Ski Club.

Arriving at the base of the mountain we set off along a burro trail, each of us carrying a number ten can of food under our arms as none of us had thought to bring backpacks. Hiking for hours in the rain, we crossed Emmons Glacier after dark and arrived at last, exhausted and with arms almost paralyzed, at a rustic bunkhouse. This had originally been constructed to accommodate workers at an adjacent silver mine. Years earlier, the lumber for the building, the large cast iron stove, and the beds had been carried by pack mules up the same precarious trail we had just hiked. The mattresses had long since disappeared—though, as it happened, the mystery of their fate would be solved before our weekend on the mountain was over.

After a midnight supper of pork and beans, we were sent upstairs to bed. Soon after that the flatulence started. The beans, combined with the low atmospheric pressure associated with the high altitude, had turned us into gas chambers. We farted and laughed with equal helplessness—and there was no relief from the fumes because the single window did not open.

Snow fell lightly during the night and we awoke to a white camp. Going downstairs, none of the adults were awake. We tried to open the door of the bedroom where the education director, his assistant, and the two mountain climbers were sleeping, but they had barricaded themselves in. We were puzzled by this, and the men were unresponsive to our demands for breakfast, so we youngsters set about lighting the stove ourselves. Eventually the four older men roused themselves, stumbled sleepy-eyed out of their room, and fixed a hearty meal of hot mush and stewed fruit. We then set off to ascend the majestic mountain. Snow was still falling lightly and it was difficult to see very far ahead, but we were able to follow a trail. When we arrived at the 10,000 foot level, the snow was falling more heavily, and the decision was made to abort the attempt for the top.

By the time we arrived back at the miners' lodge we were wet, cold and tired. We kids went to bed right after supper, leaving the four men to themselves. Before sleep came, we smelled smoke. Exhausted, we hoped it would go away, but it didn't. Something had to be done. Ripping the boards off the boxed-in chimney, we discovered that sparks from a crack in the bricks had set fire to an old mattress that had been disassembled and stuffed piece by piece into the wall space around the chimney—the work of pack rats.

The next morning we awoke to a terrific blizzard. The snow outside our lodge was now up to our hips and continuing to deepen. We left as quickly as we could, and though the snowfall lessened as we made our down the burro trail, the wind increased alarmingly. Boarding the truck, we felt we were safe, but we hadn't driven more than a mile or two before we came to a tree across the road. After this was another. And so it was all the way back to Tacoma. We would drive a few miles, then have to climb out of the truck and buck fallen trees before continuing. But we made it to Tacoma eventually, dropped off the two mountain climbers—who had turned out to be not so experienced after all—and headed home to Cornet Bay.

A couple of months passed, and the education director arranged a weekend beach party, to which he invited his two friends from the Tacoma Ski Club. Tents were set up on North Beach and a lot of whiskey was consumed—in the course of which the education director's assistant concluded that his boss and the two climbers were gay. He informed the camp commander, the camp commander called in the sheriff, and the sheriff called in the FBI.

The party was well underway when the law arrived. We kids never knew what transpired, but we also never saw or heard of that particular education director again. Meanwhile, his morally upstanding—or perhaps just ambitious—assistant was promoted to take his place.

The hopelessness and poverty of Brooklyn now seemed far behind me, and I resolved never to go back there. I loved the forests, the water and clean air of the Pacific Northwest. The unharried, unhurried lifestyle of the locals suited me just fine also. They cooperated in cutting and hauling wood or putting up a building, and they shared their garden and orchard abundance. They weren't bothered if they didn't have a car to drive ten or fifteen miles—they just set out and walked. This rustic simplicity probably reflected the fact that the local economy wasn't any healthier than anywhere else in America in those years—but the Pacific Northwest seemed a better place than Brooklyn to be poor.

The three Cs didn't give us much money to spend, but I felt as rich as I'd ever been in my life, as the Corps provided us with food, housing, healthcare and clothing. These met our basic needs, though we improved on them when we could. The pants originally issued to us were World War I surplus "ankle chokers," so tight we couldn't pull them on over our shoes. As soon as we could save enough of our five dollars per month spending money, we all bought cream colored corduroys to wear instead.

The food was all-you-could-eat, and some kids had no trouble putting away twenty hotcakes and a dozen eggs at breakfast. Not all meals were palatable, however. Our first mess sergeant was an Oak Harborite and former logging-camp cook. He was allowed sixty-six cents per day per person to feed us, so he was always looking for bargains. Once, when someone offered him a good deal on eggs, he purchased more than could be used before they spoiled. The CCC boys who did the actual cooking lacked the experience to know a good egg from a bad one, and one Sunday morning they unwittingly served up soft-boiled rotten eggs. One by one the eggs cracked open, exploding their pent-up sulfurous stink into the mess hall.

I had been looking forward to a good breakfast and this unpleasant surprise prompted me to offer an egg to my bunk mate, Moko, halfway across the room.

"Hey, Moko, try this. It's a good one." I threw the egg toward him before he had a chance to refuse. Moko reached out to catch the fragile-shelled missile and it crushed in his hands, the foul odorous liquid splattering over his hands and face and onto the table.

Returning my generosity, Moko fired an egg back. It missed me and hit little Di Nunzio, triggering a full-blown food fight that we kids thought was hilarious. Rotten eggs and cantaloupe flew through the mess hall and rained down from the open trusses of the ceiling. We had eggshells and juice in our hair, on our faces, and running down our chests, until eventually we ran out of ammunition.

We headed for the shower room to clean up but were stopped by the bugler blowing assembly. Surprised, we lined up in formation before a very red-faced, angry captain.

"There'll be no more of this," he shouted. "If it happens again, I'll send you home!" He dressed us down in no uncertain terms, but also promised to bring in an army cook from Fort Lewis to oversee the kitchen.

"And now, you get back to the mess hall and clean it up until I am satisfied that it is done right," he ordered.

A new, Lithuanian sergeant took over the mess, and from then on the food was not only ample but gourmet. We had a different kind of soup for every day of the week, always with home-made, freshly toasted croutons. There was roast meat every noon hour except Friday, when we had fresh salmon, halibut, or oysters. In those days, it was possible to buy a hundred-pound sack of oysters freshly harvested from Padilla Bay for a dollar, so the whole camp could be fed for five bucks.

So it was really no wonder that, in spite of all our hard physical labors, nearly everyone in camp gained at least twenty-five pounds—including me.

Deception Pass, 1935

Chapter 19

DORIS

Anacortes was a fishing and lumbering town and the locals were mostly tolerant of transients and *cheechakos* like us. Salmon fishing was seasonal, with men coming from all over the west coast to fish Puget Sound and Alaska. In summer, the town was a mecca for salmon processing on Puget Sound and out-of-towners arrived to work in the canneries—Farwest Fisheries, Sebastian-Stewart, Western Fisheries and Anacortes Canning Company.

There were also many lumber mills—Morrison Mill, Fidalgo Lumber and Box, Anacortes Lumber and Box and E. K. Wood Lumber— and nine shingle mills. Shingle weavers and sawyers were tramp workers who moved from one mill to another, wherever the grass looked greenest, whether upriver or down south. Sometimes dissension arose between a weaver and a sawyer if the sawyer wasn't cutting a good grade of shingle. Since the weaver's job was to weave the shingles, he would walk off the job because he wasn't making enough money. Shingle weavers and sawyers came and went accordingly. They were easy to recognize because none of them had ten fingers. Working close to the saws, they inevitably lost fingers or parts of their hands to the dangerous rotating blades.

Feeling at home in Anacortes, where we CCCers were more readily accepted than in Oak Harbor, I went to Saturday night dances at the IOOF and Eagles halls and to movies at the Empire Theater. As a CCC policeman, I got into these places for free. The dances were run by a man named Shorty Cavanaugh, and the city required that he hire a special cop, Lawrence Pollard, to keep the peace at these events. Pollard was the first person I met in Anacortes, and often he would turn unruly CCC kids over to me to make sure I kept them out of trouble and got them safely back to camp.

On the Fourth of July, 1935, at a dance at the Eagles Hall, I met two sisters, Doris and Phyllis Anderson. They had the same hairdo and were dressed alike in white sailor dresses. As Pat Anderson's band struck up the first notes of "Paper Doll," I approached Doris.

"May I have the pleasure of this dance, Miss?" I asked politely, as I had been instructed to do by the Camp Commander in our Wednesday night Social Ethics class. Doris said yes, so I placed a white handkerchief in the palm of my right hand—as I had also been taught to do, in order not to soil my partner's dress with perspiration—and steered her on to the dance floor.

"Are you a CCC boy?" she asked.

"Yes," I replied. "I'm Johnny Bananas from Brooklyn." Doris laughed, and I supposed "Bananas" must have sounded funny to her. At least it was a name she would remember.

Afterward, I returned her to the chair against the wall where she had been sitting. Thanking her, I bowed politely—again following the commander's instructions—and complimented her on being a good dancer. This was true. She was also very attractive and I was keen to dance with her again.

I waited out the next number or two, then went once more in the subdued light of the rotating mirrored ball toward the attractive girl sitting alone in her white dress.

"May I have the pleasure of this dance, Miss?" I asked again, and again she accepted.

As we waltzed around the floor, she asked, "Are you a CCC boy?"

I was surprised, but I again answered, "Yes, I'm from Brooklyn."

I didn't add my name, thinking she would at least have remembered Bananas.

Many dances later, I realized I had been dancing with both Doris and Phyllis, and that the sisters delighted in puzzling me as to who was who. Though they were very much alike, I was more attracted to Doris. She was the older one and was more outgoing and lively. Her rich brown hair was pulled back from her forehead and ended in soft curls about her face. She was slender, with beautiful long legs that caught my attention. At five foot five, she was what I considered the right height for my five-foot-eight-inch frame.

I hoped Doris thought I was right height for her, too. I wondered what she thought about my straight brown hair, slicked straight back in the style of the day. And what about my eyes? They were pale blue compared to hers, which deep enough to drown in. As we danced I wondered what it would be like to hold her properly, and how she would respond if I kissed her.

Three or four of us CCC kids stayed until the end of the dance, missing the last truck that returned by ferry to Whidbey Island. There was just one way to get back to camp that night. We walked the nine miles to Deception Pass. The bridge that would soon link Fidalgo and Whidbey Island was almost complete. The steel had been riveted together to form an arch one hundred eighty-five feet above the swirling waters of Deception Pass. The road decking had yet to be put in place, but a temporary two-by-twelve catwalk had been placed on the steel beams for workers' access. I thought back to the day I had crossed the Brooklyn Bridge as a youngster, and told my buddies that if the construction guys could walk the Deception Pass planks, we could walk them—never mind that it was dark and we were unaccustomed to such heights.

Perhaps we started across this narrow walkway partly to show our bravado, but if we could cross the bridge safely, it would mean we could spend a couple of extra hours in Anacortes on future dance nights—even if it took us another four hours after that to get back. Relying on our dubious night vision, we each placed one foot firmly ahead of the other in the darkness high above the treacherous waters. No one uttered a word and the walk seemed endless. When at last we reached safety on the Whidbey side, we gloated over our winning gamble, knowing the kids back in camp would be greatly impressed by it.

One Saturday, we stayed overnight in Anacortes in comparative luxury at the old Vendome Hotel, on the corner of Sixth and Commercial. Earlier that day, Lou and I had "broken the dice game" at camp and we decided to celebrate by going to town for a steak dinner and spending the night there. When we informed the rest of the guys of our plans, three of them decided to pitch in five cents apiece and join us. Rooms at the Vendome cost twenty-five cents for one person. I would check in at the front desk, and when I had gotten settled in for the night the others would sneak up the back stairs.

With our winnings of three dollars apiece, Lou and I walked the nine miles into town in the afternoon, arriving at the Marine Club with very big appetites. We ordered the thirty-five-cent steak special, which included French fries, toast and coffee. After polishing that off, we ordered the same meal again. The waitress was disbelieving, and when we both requested a third dinner, she almost refused to order it. Either she couldn't believe we were serious, or she thought we had no money and planned to leave without paying. But Lou and I indeed ate—and paid for—three dinners that night. Then we pooled our change and bought a bottle of sloe gin.

Because we were under drinking age, we hid the bottle beneath a bush in nearby Causland Park. When our friends arrived on the recreation truck, we took some of them there for a drink, then went on to the dance hall. All the while I was anticipating a good night's sleep in a real hotel bed. When I finally arrived at the Vendome, I found the door to my room open and a couple of kids already sleeping in the bed. At one o'clock in the morning the suspicious hotel owner appeared at the door to find a room meant for one occupied by nine half-drunk kids. She ordered all of us to leave, but I argued that I had paid for the room so she acquiesced: I could stay, but everybody else had to go. As soon as she settled back down at her desk, the boys drifted back upstairs, one by one.

In the morning we all shared one towel and a bowlful of water, and disappeared quickly through the rear exit.

In addition to being the powder-monkey and a high-rigger, I had learned to drive the camp truck and often acted as chauffeur on the recreation runs into town. I also became something of an electrician, mechanic, carpenter, blacksmith and plumber. One job that required my jack-of-all-trades skills was the building of a "modern" latrine. This comprised ten seats back-to-back above a rectangular, thousand-gallon sewage tank. The system included a large cantilevered dump bucket at one end that, when full, automatically emptied into a trough, flushing all the effluent out into the drain pipe.

When the system failed, I was asked to find the trouble and remedy it. This meant hauling hundreds of buckets of crap down to the bay. A grapefruit, stuck in the outlet, proved to be the source of our trouble, and after several hours of work the toilets were operating normally and everybody was happy again.

Two days later, to my surprise, I was called out of the morning formation and asked to join the officers standing in front of the group. I assumed that I was going to be reprimanded, although I couldn't think why. Suddenly the company commander, holding a large roll of toilet paper, began reading a commendation that had been signed by everyone in the company.

"We knew this was a nasty job, and you did it diligently without objecting or complaining. We all want to thank you for relieving us of our problems."

As I received the scroll, I wondered to myself if it was truly an honor to be recognized on a roll of toilet paper. But then the whole company applauded and I realized that for the first time in my life (except for the dog drawing I had done in elementary school) I was being complimented and appreciated for something I had done.

I was dating Doris Anderson quite regularly by this time, and we always went to the Saturday night dances. These were family affairs with mothers, fathers, and kids in attendance. Women got in free; men had to pay twenty-five cents.

The Anderson family didn't have a car at that time, so I devised a way to disconnect the speedometer of the recreation truck after dropping my fellow CCCers off in town. Then I would pick up the five Andersons. Doris, Phyllis, and their mother rode up front with me; father and brother rode under the canvas canopy in the back. They were especially glad of the ride on rainy nights, and I was happy to ingratiate myself with the family any way I could.

As a truck driver, I was able to help the Andersons when I was called to haul kitchen supplies from Anacortes to a CCC camp on Orcas Island, in the San Juans. A troop train had arrived with a contingent of replacement kids destined for Orcas, and the mess sergeant helped me load all of the surplus food from the train onto the truck. He also had a load of split wood that he was going to throw out of the kitchen car, and when I told him I knew a family in Anacortes that could use it, he said I could have it.

When Mr. Anderson and I finished unloading the wood, I looked at the food. I figured it was surplus too, just like the wood. "Can you use some eggs?" I asked.

"Sure," he replied, eagerly accepting the crate I pushed toward him.

"How about some butter and ham?"

"Great!"

"What about meat?" I went on, eyeing a quarter of beef that had been sent with me.

"Of course!"

"Well, go get a butcher knife!"

When he returned, I cut the round, the sirloin, rump, and T-bones leaving a miserable string of leg and backbones lying on the truck bed.

The look of satisfaction on his face and his profuse thanks let me know that I was appreciated. Excusing myself because I had a ferry to catch, I left with him still shouting his thanks.

Late that night, I arrived at Olga, on Orcas Island, and the remaining supplies were unloaded at Camp Moran. I stayed there overnight, and in the kitchen the next morning I heard the cooks discussing the whereabouts of the supplies that were to have been sent over from the train. I was horrified to realize I had given away food that was meant for the one hundred eighty-five kids at Camp Moran. But the few crates in my truck would never have fed that many people. Nor could I understand why the camp did not have more supplies already on hand, since the camp managers would have known well beforehand that a large group was coming in.

They asked, "Did you bring all of the food over?"

"Yeah," I lied. "What's in the truck is what they gave me."

The next Friday, when I went to pick up Doris, the Andersons told how they had canned the meat and baked hotcakes with the flour and eggs. I sheepishly confessed that the food had not been surplus and was intended to be used for supper and breakfast on Orcas. But I never felt too sorry about what had happened, because in my courtship of Doris I seemed to be courting her entire family. If I wanted to win her, I would have to woo them all—and then, perhaps someday, they would become my family too.

Doris, 1942

Chapter 20

PREPARATION FOR LIFE

For me, the Cs were also a family of sorts, and as in most families, fights were common. One that I particularly remember occurred one evening in the mess hall. Benny and Lou got into an argument in the mess line that might have broken into a fist fight, except that Lou escaped Benny's attack by running into the mess hall. He stopped just inside the door at the bread case, where he picked up a large French knife and waited for Benny to come through the door. Fortunately, Benny stopped outside for some reason and a short kid named Di came through the door instead. Di was about four foot ten, so when Lou made a roundhouse swing with the knife, he missed the top of Di's head and embedded the knife in the door casing. Di turned paper white, while Lou thought it a huge joke that he had scared the shit out of the kid. Benny, for his part, thanks God to this day that he did not go straight into the dining room that evening. Otherwise, he would have been decapitated.

Though I worked hard and was happy with my circumstances, I got in a number of fights myself. One Saturday night at the dance with Doris, two of our boys came to find me. They reported, breathlessly, that a big kid named Angelo was going to beat up little Di. I ran to the corner of 6th and N Streets, where, sure enough, Angelo was threatening his much smaller opponent.

"Knock it off, you guys," I said, "You'll get arrested, and anyway Di's too little for you, Angelo."

"If I want to hit Di, I'll hit him, and if I want to hit you, I'll hit you," Angelo retorted.

I could not let this go by unchallenged, so I put up my own fists and knocked Angelo down, leaving him bleeding on the sidewalk, his lip and chin split open. Leaving Di and the other two guys to take care of him, I then went back to the dance.

"What happened?" Doris asked.

"I knocked out a guy," I said. "But he deserved it."

"But your hair isn't even ruffled."

"No, and he's the camp boxing champ." To heck with modesty; I wanted to impress my girl!

The next morning at breakfast Angelo appeared with his chin and lip bandaged. I apologized to him, and he apologized in return. "I had it coming," he said as we shook hands. Several months later when Angelo went back to New York, he still bore the scar, and for all I know he has it still.

When not fighting each other we fought other things, such as forest fires. Called down to Freeland, on the South end of Whidbey, we arrived to find a fire raging across three or four acres of second-growth forest and brush. I was the truck driver, not one of the fire crew, but I was asked to carry a back pump and patrol the fire break, putting out sparks that jumped the trail. Through dense smoke I saw a glow and went in to quench what I assumed was the start of a new fire. Instead, I discovered Charlie Burelli, a fellow CCCer, passed out on the ground in a pair of smoldering denims.

I called for help and we dragged Charlie out into fresh air where he began to recover. At some point he vomited, which he said made him feel more uncomfortable than the slight burn on his stomach.

By the end of the day the fire was contained, and a grateful local farmer invited us to help ourselves to strawberries in his nearby field. We had not yet eaten fresh berries that season, so we gorged ourselves on the delicious red fruit before heading back to camp. Supper had been held for us, and when we finished our main meal the cooks announced dessert. To our dismay, this turned out to be a huge dishpan of beautiful fresh strawberries. Any other evening, we would have eaten them with relish, and the cooks could not understand our lack of appetite.

The CCC projects completed at Deception Pass State Park between 1934 and 1936—the years of my tenure—are still enjoyed by thousands of local people and tourists each year. We built sturdy log houses for the park superintendents at Bowman's Bay and Cranberry Lake; public restrooms in those locations and at Rosario Beach; and attractive public kitchens with fine wood burning stoves and huge fireplaces, around which families still gather for hotdog or marshmallow roasts or for warmth on cool misty days. We also constructed the beautiful stone and log guard rails enjoyed by millions to this day along Highway 20 in the Deception Pass areas of both Whidbey and Fidalgo Islands.

All of these structures were designed and built according to National Park Service guidelines, which emphasized both practical and aesthetic principles, including non-intrusiveness and the use of natural materials. The results were rustic but sturdy, and while it took a lot of work to turn greenhorn kids into competent tradesmen, the excellent condition of the CCC buildings and fences at Deception Pass eight decades later attests to their quality. Most of our work was overseen by skilled local people including foreign-born stone masons, who were paid $45 a month. We also handcrafted the hardware and hinges for the doors, and these, too, remain in good condition to this day.

In addition to the practical crafts that we CCC kids learned during the day, we were encouraged to study at night with the camp education director. The first of these—before he was "outed" as gay—was a licensed teacher who taught us mathematics, English and typing. Many of us had no education beyond the eighth grade, and some kids needed to learn such basic things as how to write a letter.

The camp doctor taught first-aid one night a week, and his classes were so comprehensive we felt by the end that we could perform surgery if necessary. Add to this the social education provided by our camp commander ("May I have the pleasure of this dance, Miss?"), and the case can be made that the Corps supplied much of what we street-raised kids needed to take our places as useful citizens in the outside world.

We were grateful to be paid, too. Each month our sergeant would strap on his .45 revolver and go to the bank in Anacortes for the payroll. Our five dollars of spending money was given out in silver, so money for a hundred kids was quite a bag full.

With our monthly allowance, we bought soap, toothpaste and cigarettes. Most of us smoked roll-your-owns and if we saved the ends we could get by for a month for less than a dollar. Once in a while I would buy a five-cent candy bar, and we were all eager to buy civilian clothing, whether from stores or from each other. My friend Benny Colacino from Bayonne, New Jersey, was a good source of clothes. Benny's family back home seemed to be well off, so he always had his entire thirty dollars to spend each month. His problem was that he usually gambled it away, and then he would have to sell his much-admired brushed wool sweaters, suede jackets and cream-colored corduroys to pay his gambling debts. I bought many items of Benny's clothing for as little as two-bits.

Not everyone took to the CCCs the way I did. Many kids went back to the city afterwards. But the program was a life-saver for me. It took me away from the iniquities of Brooklyn, where my last home had been on a street that had two houses of prostitution, one counterfeiting operation, three bootlegging establishments, and one gambling house—my brother's. Had I remained there I would almost certainly have been forced by circumstance into a life of crime as the only means of survival.

The Pacific Northwest, by contrast, offered life anew—work, food, shelter, security, a family of sorts (the CCCs), a girl I loved, and a sense of place. The climate was gentle, the winters never bitterly cold or the summers insufferably hot. Even the rain was okay.

And so, even when federal appropriations for the CCC program dried up in 1936, I stayed on in Cornet Bay. A lot of other kids did too. We were no longer paid our monthly allowances, but we continued to receive food, lodging, and the promise of a Pullman ticket if we changed our minds and decided to go home after all. There was also the possibility that if the government did renew CCC funding, we would get back pay. This happened eventually, but by that time I had decided to get out. I knew I wanted to make the Pacific Northwest my home. I also wanted to marry Doris. The CCCs had given me the skills, work-wise and otherwise, for adult life. Now it was time to get a real job and settle down.

Chapter 21

UNION MAN

I was eighteen and had nine dollars in my pocket when I was honorably discharged from the Cs in late spring of 1936. I got a room in a boarding house in Anacortes and would go early each morning to Morrison Mill, at the bottom of 15th Street, and hang around the office with the other men looking for work. When everyone else packed up and left about eight-thirty a.m., I stayed on. The weather might be a little soggy, but it was nothing like the bitter cold I had endured in Brooklyn waiting in line overnight for a job.

I was down to my last fifteen cents the morning I ordered coffee in Curly's Café.

"Aren't you gonna have any breakfast?" Curly asked.

"No, I'm not hungry."

"What's the matter? You out of money?"

"Yup!" I admitted, somewhat reluctantly.

"I'll stake you breakfast," Curly offered. "Staking" was a common practice in those days to tide over miners and loggers who were down on their luck. When I told Curly I would pay him back as soon as I could, both of us hoped my perseverance at the mill would pay off sooner or later. Neither of us expected it to happen that very morning.

Fortified by Curly's coffee, I returned to the mill and was still there at 10 a.m. when Dewey McFaddan, the yard boss, came out.

"I've got some work for you for the rest of the day," he said.

In those days nobody asked what the work was, or what the pay would be. I just followed Dewey as he took me over and introduced me to Walter Wagner, foreman of the chip storage bin. Walt told me to scoop the chips away from the conveyor and throw them as high as I could against the side of the building. When the conveyor shut down at noon, I stayed on site because I didn't have any money for lunch. Later in the afternoon the boss came and told me to slow down. "No need to work so hard," he said. I didn't slow down, because I was working at a pace that suited me. Perhaps that's why I was taken on again the following Monday.

At the end of two weeks I was made boom man. This meant working with the flotillas of logs anchored in the waters off the mill. They were brought by tugboat from wherever they had been cut, and my job required that I leap around on top of the logs to maneuver them towards the mill. My experience in the Cs came in handy, because I was able to sort the different species of logs. But boom work was hazardous; every year six or eight boom men drowned in the Pacific Northwest. One day, I almost became one of them. I was spreading logs with a pike pole when the pole broke and I fell headfirst into the water between the logs, which then closed together and trapped me by my ankles. Suspended upside down in black water polluted with sulfite pulp liquor, I swallowed some of it as I tried to free myself from the log vise above. All I could think of was that I would die a murky death—but then, with my last bit of energy I finally spread the logs.

As my head burst up from the water my co-workers arrived, shoving their pike poles toward me and helping me out of the water. I coughed and spat out what I could of the water. Small bullheads and other fish floated belly up around us. No one cared about pollution in those days, so all mill wastes, including pulp liquors, sawdust and bark were dumped into the water, fouling the bay and killing marine life. In retrospect, I probably stood as much chance of being poisoned as drowning.

In spite of the dangers, I felt fortunate to get a job at Morrison Mill. It was the steadiest mill in town, and—though I couldn't know the future—it was to outlast all the others. The next step was to establish credit at Allen's Mercantile, as was the custom. Everyone charged whatever they needed and paid their bills on payday. I lived as cheaply as I could and even managed to set aside a little from my earnings.

Within a couple of months I had saved the great sum of twenty-four dollars, and my employment future felt secure. My physical future seemed a little less certain—I was a boom man, after all, and had nearly drowned once already—but perhaps because of this Doris and I decided to get married. Her Scottish-Protestant parents weren't too crazy about having me as their son-in-law, in spite of all my efforts to ingratiate myself with them. Because of my Italian heritage the Andersons assumed I was Catholic, though I assured them that my youthful religious inclinations had long-since lapsed—so they agreed to go with us to Mount Vernon for the wedding.

After getting the license from the court house, Doris's father drove us around town in his green Dodge to find a more hallowed place for the ceremony. At the Baptist church, we came upon the minister mowing the lawn out front. He said he would need to change his clothes, but he would be happy to marry us as soon as he had done that.

As the minister disappeared into the parsonage next door to the church, I mentally recalculated my finances. Doris had set her heart on a seven dollar ring. We had spent another twelve dollars for the first month's rent of an apartment, although this included all the wood we could burn. The marriage license had cost us two dollars, and I was planning to give the preacher the accustomed two dollars for the ceremony. That would leave us with one dollar until next week's payday. Then the minister reappeared, freshly shaved and dressed in a fine suit, and I was so impressed and grateful that I decided to pay him three dollars—and then we were broke.

Our wedding, on July 11, 1936, was as unpretentious as our pocketbook. No flowers, no special clothes. Doris wore her best dress, I my cream-colored corduroys. Nervous and anxious for the ceremony to be over with, I said "I do" before I was supposed to. Doris's younger brother and sister burst into giggles.

There was no celebration afterwards. Either the Andersons' lack of enthusiasm for having me as part of the family, or their inability to pay for anything special, or both, made a party out of the question. Rather than lingering at their house, Doris and I walked over to our new apartment, where I served up a wedding supper of spaghetti and meatballs. The wood cook-stove snapped and popped as we discussed plans for our future.

"As soon as we get enough money, I'll buy a fresh ham and make Italian *prosciutto*," I said.

"And I'll can tomatoes, corn, peas and beans," Doris said. "There'll be lots of peaches, pears and plums, too."

Like a couple of squirrels preparing for a long winter, we continued to make plans. I was eager to get our married life started in another way, but we held off going to bed as some of my co-workers had promised a charivari. Still, I was content for now. Snuggling with my new wife beside a warm fire in our own place, I felt certain that although Tony may have gambled away my CCC money, Doris and I could take care of ourselves.

Eventually, when it became clear that no one would be banging pots and pans outside our window, we went off to bed in our sparse surroundings—and for me, one of the many pleasures of that night was that I did not have to get Doris home by midnight.

The very next day we began scrounging jars that could be used for canning. Crescent coffee jars were especially desirable for peaches and pears, as the wide mouth and square shape allowed the fruit to be arranged in an eye-appealing display. We also used the jars for preserving an old cow that I bought for seven dollars. The meat from this animal was so tough that canning was the only way to tenderize it. Doris and I labored all day, and when the last jar of meat was finished, we tossed the remaining bones and yellow fat into the large copper boiler. We added every kind of vegetable and seasoning, making enough delicious-smelling minestrone soup to keep us going all winter. Exhausted by then, we decided to wait till the next day to can the stuff—but we had left it too late. When we awoke in the morning, our noses told us that our great kettle of soup had spoiled in the night. We both felt like crying, but there was nothing else to be done but flush our hard-earned winter's sustenance down the toilet.

Doris had been training as a beautician, and after completing her apprenticeship she borrowed eight hundred dollars from People's Bank to set herself up in business, with her uncle Fred Fisher co-signing the loan. From a strictly financial point of view, the Kulshan Beauty Shop was not a great success as it only brought in enough money to make the loan payments, pay the rent, buy supplies for the shop, and keep Doris in clothes. But there were side benefits. Mrs. Massey, who had a ranch on March Point, traded fruit and vegetables for Doris's services, and a Dutch lady whose family had a turkey ranch on Whidbey Island bartered a turkey every Thanksgiving. This was fine with me, though I drew the line when Doris came home one evening with two bartered squabs, still in their down, for me to butcher for supper. They were too much like the sparrow I had trapped and eaten as a starving kid in Brooklyn.

About this time we bought our first house. At four hundred dollars—five dollars down and five dollars plus interest per month—we considered it a real bargain. It had hot and cold running water, an inside toilet and bath, and the price included the wood-burning cook-stove in the kitchen. We felt like we were in heaven, and not just in a metaphorical sense. As we lay in bed on our first night, we could see all the way through the wide cracks of the dry shiplap ceiling and the missing shingles of the roof to the starry sky above.

Certainly, the house needed work. That first winter, we nailed a blanket between the kitchen and bedroom because there was no door to close, and the only heat we had was the cook-stove. It was bitterly cold outside, and before going to bed I set a kindling fire, so I could jump out of bed in the morning, quickly light it, and return to bed until the kitchen warmed up. I also let the water run in the sink so the plumbing wouldn't freeze up. One morning I friskily jumped out of bed, dashed into the kitchen and went sliding on my ass across the floor. The drain trap had frozen under the sink, causing the trickling water to spill onto the floor and freeze into a miniature ice rink.

When spring came, I started a vegetable garden. I didn't know much about growing things but planted pole beans in circles, placing willow saplings in the center for the plants to climb up. A few mornings after this, on my way to the woodshed, I noticed the beans I had planted sticking up above the ground. Assuming that rain had washed the soil off them, I stopped to poke them back in. I did this for another four or five mornings until, one day, Doris called out to me, "What's taking you so long to bring in the wood?"

"The goddam beans won't stay in the ground, and I'm pushing them back in."

"They're not supposed to stay underground. That's the way they grow, silly."

A week later, I realized that I had killed most of the bean seedlings—and the willow poles were sprouting into a dense forest.

I had grown up with hunger and poverty, and I had always managed somehow to survive, but marriage meant I was responsible for Doris as well. Strikes and jurisdictional disputes often made it difficult to get a full week's work at the mill, and Doris's beauty shop was barely breaking even, so I was always on the lookout for ways to supplement our household income. When Doris's Uncle Fred gave me a magazine advertising that we could get rich by raising mushrooms at home, I fell for it. Borrowing ten dollars from Uncle Fred, I sent away to Seattle for a bag of soil that was supposed to contain mushroom spore, and I converted the garage into a mushroom cave. Weeks passed with no sign of a mushroom. After several months, realizing that I had been bilked, wrote back to the scam artist who had sold me the worthless block of clay. I called him every name I could think of, adding that if I ever got to Seattle I would work him over so he would never forget it. Several months later I received a letter from the postal inspector and feared I was going to be prosecuted for threatening a man's life. I learned instead that I was not the only sucker to have fallen into the mushroom trap. The postal service had indicted the con-man, and they were seeking evidence that he had used the mail to commit fraud.

The Depression was still upon us when my buddy Harold Springer asked me if I thought we could bag a deer at Deception Pass State Park. I assured him we could. The hunt would be illegal, but we decided to declare our intentions to Judge Al Sallenthin at City Hall. Harold Hinshaw, the Anacortes police chief, was with the judge when we arrived at his chambers.

"Things are getting tough," we told them. "It's hard to get a full week's work because of the strike situation, and we can't get welfare because technically we're employed, so we've decided go out to the Park to get a deer." I laid it on the line. "You can either arrest us now or wait until later, but we are going out to the Park to shoot a deer."

The judge and chief looked at each other in surprise, and neither uttered a word as Springer and I turned and left.

I didn't own a gun, but Springer had several. With some hesitation he handed me a rifle and asked, "Are you sure you can shoot this?"

"I've shot a .22 lots of times." This statement wasn't true; I could only hope shooting a rifle was like riding a bicycle.

"This ain't a .22," Harold said. "Be careful, and make sure you only shoot at the deer."

Within two hours we had bagged our quarry. Some people dismissed the little Whidbey Island deer as overgrown jackrabbits, and ours was certainly small, but it was still a deer. We never heard from the law, but when the last of the animal had been consumed, we were relieved because the evidence was gone.

On our hunting trip Harold and I had discussed the need to put our energies into longer term remedies to our situation, instead of relying on stopgap measures like poaching deer.

Harold said, "The union leaders at the mill want us to change affiliation from the AFL (American Federation of Labor) to the CIO (Congress of Industrial Organizations)."

"I'm willing," I said. "Maybe it will stop all of the jurisdictional disputes, and we can get a full week's work."

Under the AFL, the different trades would decide independently to go on strike, but each expected support from everyone else in the mill. The workers all honored the picket line, so our work was very unsteady. We felt that if we could all join the CIO and be represented by one union, problems could be resolved more easily—one contract would cover everybody.

A dozen or so of us took the job of organizing the timber workers into the CIO—among them Paul Kreuger, Bill McNutt, Wes Collins, Harold Springer, Merton Perkins, Vern Sumey and myself. A number of men at the forefront of this movement were avowed Communists, but they were not looking to overthrow the government; they had joined the Party simply because it promised more for workers. They wanted steadier work with some kind of job security and better pay. As things were, it was well known that one of the mill bosses liked wine, so some of the local fishermen kept him supplied with "Dago Red" to ensure he would hire them at the mill when they returned from fishing in Alaska in the fall. Exhibiting a total lack of conscience, the boss would fire good workers at this time and replace them with his fishermen buddies, leaving the other men without work for the winter. The saying around the mill was, "If you don't part your hair right, you'll get fired when the fishermen come back."

It took us several months to persuade a majority of our fellow workers to vote for a switch to the CIO. This outcome caused the AFL to bring goon squads up from Seattle and throw jurisdictional picket lines around the mill. Hearing that district AFL president Joe Skovich intended to visit Anacortes, we knew yet another picket line would ensue. The whole town was suffering from the effects of these strikes. When mill workers did not get paid, the merchants who staked them did not get paid either. Harold Springer and I decided to take matters into our own hands.

As soon as word got around town that Skovich had parked his Dodge sedan in front of the new Wilson Hotel and taken a room in that establishment with his wife, Springer and I paid a call on Mayor J. George, who was equally fed up with all the loss of work.

"We're gonna give Skovich until nine o'clock tonight to get out of town, or we will run him out," I said. The time then was about 5.30 p.m.

"Yeah," Springer agreed. "We're gonna run him out of town, and we would like the police to be busy elsewhere when we do it."

"No problem, boys," the Mayor said. He picked up the phone and asked the operator to connect him with the police station. "Chief, I want you to see to it that none of our police are available for the next few hours. A few CIO boys are here, and they plan to encourage Skovich to leave town around nine o'clock tonight—before he can strike the mill tomorrow." When the mayor put down the phone, he turned to us saying, "Funny thing! It seems no one knows where any of our police are, and there's no chance they can be found until well after nine tonight."

Having secured official support, we went back to the hotel and had a talk with Skovich in the doorway of his hotel room. His wife peeked around from behind with a yapping pet poodle in her arms.

I said, "We're sick and tired of jurisdictional lines, Skovich. We want you to leave town by nine o'clock tonight, or we will drag you out behind a car."

He bristled. "Listen here, I'm a citizen and have every right to be in this town for as long as I want."

"And we are citizens who have the right to work without your interference," Springer snapped back at him.

Skovich went into his room, slamming the door behind him. We retired to the lobby to wait. Outside, a crowd was gathering in the street, blocking traffic and forcing cars to detour around the block. When seven o'clock rolled around, and there was no sign that Skovich was making a move to leave, we started for the stairs to go back up to his room again, but the hotel management would not allow it.

"He's been making phone calls," the desk clerk said. "He couldn't get hold of any of our local police and when he tried to get the sheriff to come over, the sheriff said he couldn't because he hasn't been called by the city cops. Skovich is on the line now to the state patrol, but they won't come because they haven't been called by the Anacortes police for assistance, either."

When the line was clear, I phoned Skovich, observed to him that it was after seven o'clock, and advised him to start packing. He remained adamant that he would not be run out of town by any number of toughs. The crowd outside continued to grow, and by eight o'clock there was a lot of fist shaking and hollering. Springer and I began to worry that things could get out of hand.

Another call to Skovich warned him that the folks in the street were growing unruly, and he had better get out while the getting was good.

By a quarter of nine, just when we were really beginning to feel apprehensive, Skovich and his wife came down the stairs. We held back the townspeople as he got into his car and drove off. As far as I know, he never visited Anacortes again.

Our own dispute was settled for now, but there was still trouble in other places. Loggers in Lyman, forty miles up the Skagit River, had voted for CIO affiliation because the organization was opposed to the current practice in which the men were paid according to the number of board feet of timber they fell and bucked. This was called "busheling"—a slave type of operation in which a man could kill himself trying to make a living. Loggers might spend half a day to fall a tree that turned out to be "punky" or "conky," and was graded so low they wouldn't get paid for it.

The main aim of the CIO was to replace this kind of piece work with negotiated hourly wages and better working conditions. The AFL threw jurisdictional picket lines around the Lyman operation, however, and, as in Anacortes, the workers respected the picket lines. The lines were illegal but nobody wanted to be labeled a "scab." Fed up with the picketing and logging operators resorted to locking out everybody, including the district CIO president, Karly Larson, an avowed radical. Karly called us in Anacortes and invited us to help with the dispute.

Two carloads of us arrived at the dingy Lyman union hall, where Karly greeted us with a cud of snoose tucked in his lower lip. The rest of the Lyman boys were huddled around the wood burning heater, arguing the merits of the CIO versus the AFL because a few diehards had not yet switched their allegiance to the former. Karly called the meeting to order and, without spitting snoose once, talked for thirty minutes trying to convince the AFL holdouts to swing over.

Then we Anacortes mill guys took turns trying to convince our Lyman brethren to pull together and eliminate most of their troubles. As the evening wore on, tempers began to flare. Some of the resisters announced they were going to go back to work and start falling trees, lockout or not, picket line or not. We pointed out to them that they would probably not be paid if they did, and they could even be arrested for trespassing. Finally, we calmed them down and convinced them to settle their differences—and all joined the CIO.

Chapter 22

PITCHING FISH

Even after I began enjoying regular full-weeks of work, Doris and were still in the hole financially because we bought everything on credit, and—like everybody else—we had overextended ourselves. I did not shoot any more deer, but resorted to other measures. Tony Campano's stepsons, the three Allen boys, and I often launched a rowboat at the Swinomish Slough bridge and went out to raid the unclaimed oyster beds in Padilla Bay. I also cut wood on shares with Roy Mesersmith and his brother-in-law Don Toogood on Widow Douglas Almond's land at Alexander Beach. Mrs Almond was beautiful and she took a shine to handsome Don. One day when she came to inspect our wood cutting operation, she pretended to slip. Falling to her knees, she reached up to Don in her most coquettish and appealing manner and asked him to help her. We ribbed Don that he missed the chance of a lifetime by not taking up with the wealthy widow, but he was virtuous and true to the young lady he was going to marry.

I tried another woodcutting venture as a means to earn a bit of cash. Frank Giesler, who owned an eighty-acre ranch near Campbell Lake, heard that Roy Mesersmith and I were willing workers. He offered us some huge old-growth windfall fir, seven and eight feet in diameter, if we would help him build a road into the woods with his team of horses. The trees had blown over as much as a century before and had settled a foot deep into the soil. The wood was preserved in excellent condition, however, because a fire prior to their falling had burned off the bark, seering the sap and encasing the trunks in a protective shell. We could never earn more than eighty-five cents a day bucking and splitting those logs, but we at least got our own firewood—though it seems unthinkable in this day and age that we used beautiful old-growth fir merely for cooking and heating.

To transport the wood, Roy and I used a little box trailer that I towed behind my Chevy coupe. John Weir, who lived on Heart Lake Road, noticed when I drove past that I did not have a license for it. John was also selling wood and reported me to the local cop, Marvin Beebe. Marvin lay in wait for me and told me that I would have to get a license for the trailer or stop hauling wood.

"Marv, I don't have the money for a license—I'm barely eating—and I'm not about to stop what I'm doing. If you arrest me, I'll have to stay in jail. I don't have the money to pay any fine," I said angrily.

Marv repeated that I could not drive the vehicle without a license. I told him I was tired of listening to his bullshit.

"Take me in and lock me up now because I'm not going to quit otherwise," I said. Marv walked off mumbling, but fate was on his side because shortly after this my Chevy succumbed to all the abuse it had taken up in the woods.

Catching and selling crab was another sideline. After my car pooped out, I would strap two large crab hoops to my back and hike the two and a half miles out of town to the railroad trestle that ran across Fidalgo Bay. Baiting the traps with free meat scraps from Guy Hurd's butcher shop in Allen's Mercantile, I would set them out beneath the trestle, build a driftwood fire under a boiler full of sea water, and sit down to wait.

The wait was never boring because I found it meditative to be sitting on the tracks surrounded by the peaceful waters of the bay, with snowcapped Mount Baker in the distance and the gentle farms of March Point right in front of me. A small peninsula, March Point was shown on early maps as Marsh Point; later it became March's Point after Fred March, an early settler. In those days it was completely pastoral, with a few stump ranches where some the mill workers lived and supplemented their income with milk cows, chickens, pigs and a garden. As I sat contemplating this panorama and daydreaming, it seemed like no time before my traps were ready to be pulled up again, so full that I could barely lift them onto the trestle. When I had caught about fifty legal crab I cooked them, put them in a burlap sack and toted them into town. I got five cents apiece for them in the beer taverns—until somebody informed the game warden that I was selling crab without a license.

I also practiced illegal beach-seining with Frank Voyvodich in a twenty foot open skiff powered by a Star engine that had been cut in half to make it a two-cylinder power unit. Neither of us had any experience with boats and we ran this one twice onto a reef. Another time we were so loaded with dog fish that the tide carried us out into the strait; only when the tide turned in our favor were we able to get back to the fertilizer plant with our catch. Frank and I soon realized we weren't making any money, and if we continued with the work it might just kill us. Before that happened, we decided to do away with the boat. We chopped a hole in the bottom, pushed it off the beach into Guemes Channel, and watched it slowly disappear beneath the waves.

When the salmon started running in a big way, my buddies Bill and Chet and I looked for work with Western Fisheries. The cannery boss, Bill Parks, offered us a job pitching fish. This work was usually done by Indians, as it was considered too dirty and menial for Caucasians. We would also be expected to stick at it around the clock until all the fish were unloaded—but the pay was good, so we accepted gratefully. Bill and I pitched the salmon out of the hold onto the deck of a fishing boat called the *Kasaan*. Chet relayed the fish from there onto a conveyor belt that carried them up into the cannery. Sometime after midnight, Bill and I realized we were up to our knees in fish gurry—fish slime, blood and seawater— and Bill yelled with alarm, "Hell, this boat is sinking!"

"Chet," I called up anxiously, "look over the side and see if this boat is sinking."

"It sure as hell is," he called down to us. "The goddam water is up to the gunnels."

The *Kasaan*'s elderly engineer was called out of bed, and one look down into the engine room told him he had forgotten to close the sea cock. As he scrambled down into the flooded compartment, we untied the boat from the dock and began pulling her around to the beach to prevent her from sinking in the deep water. When the *Kasaan* settled on the sand, we expected the engineer to appear. When he didn't, we looked down the companion way to discover that a five-gallon can of gasoline had spilled below and filled the engine room with asphyxiating fumes.

Leaving Bill and Chet to muscle the old man up onto the deck, I ran to the office to call the fire department—six blocks away—to come with a resuscitator. Fireman Shorty Strom responded immediately, driving the city's fire truck at full-speed downhill towards the dock. Fireman Milton Cookston cranked the hand-operated siren. Watching them careen through the empty streets towards me, I knew they were going too fast to stop. Afraid for my life, I waved my arms wildly, jumping out of the way as Shorty slammed on the brakes and the truck skidded out of control across the wet wooden dock. The front wheels leaped the heavy timber bulkhead, and the truck came to a tenuous halt, teetering precariously above the icy waters of Guemes Channel. The two firemen—still seated in the truck—started blaming each other for their predicament.

"Knock it off,'" I hollered. "Get the resuscitator and follow me. There's a man dying out on the boat."

Fortunately, the engineer had regained consciousness by this time, and we took comfort in the fact that he was going to live.

The excitement over, Bill, Chet and I went back to work. Our grueling fish-pitching job lasted for forty-eight non-stop hours, and when we were finished we were paid the unheard-of amount of seventy-eight dollars. This was enough for Doris and me to square up all of our bills, and we vowed never to go in hock again.

North Cascades, 1940

Chapter 23

SURRENDERING MY RIFLES

By 1939, the US economy had improved and ripple effects from the rumblings of war in Europe were being felt even in faraway Anacortes. Hitler had embarked on his conquests of the countries bordering Germany and the Luftwaffe was ordering great quantities of Sitka spruce for building aircraft. Italy was trying to expand out of Italian Somaliland, and she, too, was buying Pacific Northwest timber to build planes in her fight against Haile Selassie in Ethiopia. In anticipation of a larger conflict, Britain, France, Belgium and Holland began expanding their air forces also, which created an even bigger demand for our strong lightweight woods.

I was still working at Morrison Mill when an extra shift was added just to cut airplane lumber. Some of the spruce logs were so huge—thirteen feet or more in diameter—that they had to be drilled and blasted with black powder in order to pass through the throat (guides) of the head saw. The finest grades of this wood were sawed into flitches or rough-sawn timbers and shipped to Europe. The leftovers went into making refrigerator frames, piano sounding boards and box shooks (parts).

It was a welcome sight to see Model-T Ford jitneys driving down Commercial Avenue towing ten or twelve wagon loads of box shooks in tandem like a trackless train. Commercial Avenue is the town's main street, and the trucks were headed to the port dock at the northern end. There, the shooks would be stacked in warehouses to await a tramp freighter. Most were shipped to Shell and Texaco refineries in Mombasa, Africa, where they were assembled into boxes, packed with two five-gallon cans of lube oil, and re-shipped throughout the world. The demand for shooks and other timber products created steady employment in Anacortes and was a great lift for a town that was all but dead a few years earlier.

Doris and I relaxed a bit as our own economic position improved, and I managed to buy a Model-A Ford for twenty-five dollars. Owning a car allowed us to travel around the northwest part of the state with our friends Roy and Mabel Mesersmith, and do some gold prospecting. We would split the cost of gas and drive into the mountains until the tank gauge showed half-full, so we would be sure to have enough gas left to get us home again. When we reached our destination, Doris and Mabel would build a fire and prepare a picnic lunch, while Roy and I prospected in the creek. At times, a good show of gold in the Cascade River would excite us enough to talk of giving up our weekday jobs, but I always remembered what an old prospector had told me years earlier. While I was still in the Cs, I met an old man with a bushy white beard and crumpled felt hat leading a heavily laden burro down Burpee Hill, near the upriver settlement of Concrete. He could have just come out of Death Valley.

"Have you found any gold?" I asked.

"Yup, there's gold everywhere in these creeks and streams," he said, "but it's very fine and very scarce."

"I'd like to do some prospecting myself," I told him.

The old man obviously recognized me for the greenhorn city kid that I was. "Son," he warned, "if you find anything don't take it seriously, because there's more money lost in the search for the yellow stuff than anyone ever makes. If you've got a job, stay with it."

So, although Roy and I prospected every creek in the Skagit and Skykomish Rivers basins, we never allowed ourselves to fall prey to "gold fever."

As our circumstances continued to get better, I saved enough money to buy a nice little Jersey cow for twenty dollars. Roy agreed to take care of the cow on his fifteen-acre lot, and we would share the butter, cream and milk between the two families. I also bought weaner pigs which Roy and Mabel raised on the skim milk, so we would have meat as well as dairy products.

The cow's name was Daisy, and she was as gentle as her name. Once it became obvious that her hormones were flowing, Roy and I walked her the couple of miles up the road to the Duranceau Dairy to be bred. Lorene Duranceau had us turn Daisy loose in a small electric-fenced enclosure while he brought his prize bull, Pierre, to the farmyard boudoir. Closing the fence behind Pierre, Lorene held onto the bull's lead chain, holding it high above the electric fence. The three of us watched intently as the two animals became acquainted. When Pierre began making moves on Daisy, Lorene became so excited he dropped the chain onto the electric fence.

"Goddam!" he screamed as the jolt hit him, throwing him to the ground.

Lorene was not the only one shocked. The electricity hit Pierre and Daisy through the chain, causing both animals to fall to their haunches, bellowing and snorting. Wild-eyed and frantic, each must have thought this the most incredible sexual encounter ever, but not in a good way. Daisy scrambled to get out and away from under Pierre, and Pierre was just as happy to let her go.

It soon became obvious that the two animals had lost interest in the project, so we opened the gate expecting to put the chain on Daisy and lead her back home. The little cow had other ideas. Apparently blaming us for her painful and embarrassing experience, she bolted past us and headed for Roy's on her own.

During her next heat, Roy and I again took Daisy up to the Duranceau farm to see Pierre. But both animals had been indelibly imprinted with the earlier encounter and would have nothing to do with each other. Not wanting to waste any more time, we headed immediately down the hill to the Dixon Farm. Bob Dixon assured us his fine bull, Buck, could breed our cow and the fee would be "two dollars, just like it would be in any sporting house." (Apparently the rates hadn't gone up since I was a fourteen year-old kid in Brooklyn!)

I winced at the sight of Buck, a big old Holstein at least twice the size of our little family cow, but he was our only hope unless we wanted to take Daisy five miles out to Summit Park.

Buck and Daisy were led into a small board enclosure that looked like a rodeo chute. Little Daisy appeared calm and expectant, and she looked lovingly at Buck with her large brown eyes. But the ancient bull didn't excite very easily in spite of his owner's claims. Bob felt compelled to assist in the matter by rubbing Buck's protruding vertebrae with his cane.

"Maybe you should rub someplace else," I suggested.

But Bob apparently knew what he was doing, because Buck decided at that moment to get on with the job. We paid the two dollars and took Daisy back home with Bob's final words ringing in our ears: "I guarantee Buck's potency. If it doesn't take, bring her back—no charge."

Nine and a half months later, Daisy presented us with a little bull calf, Henry. Roy turned him into a steer and when the time came we had him butchered. This was hard to do as Henry had been our little pet, but hunger took precedent over sentiment. The meat was shared between the two families and canned—and we continued to think of Henry as we ate him.

Having decided by that time that the house we were living in was beyond repair, and with my work situation stable and my income continuing to increase, Doris and I bid on two adjoining lots that had been Henry's pasture and were now up for tax-title sale. I offered ten dollars for each lot, but Charlie Dean, the clerk in the treasurer's office, turned us down. He demanded a twenty-dollar minimum for each to cover the cost of advertising the sale. I grudgingly accepted and paid this amount as an advance deposit. Our funds beyond this were limited, so before the auction I contacted Wallace Sharpe, the county commissioner, to ask if we would have any trouble winning the bid at forty dollars. Wallace assured me that there would be no opposition, and made sure of this by explaining the situation to Mike Demopoulis and Emil Schreiber, two local businessmen who always bid on every piece of tax-title property. They held off in this instance, and my forty-dollar bid was accepted, unopposed, in less than a minute. Doris and I were elated and immediately began making plans to build a new home on our now-expanded property.

I spent fifteen dollars at Tucker Lumber to buy a set of blueprints for a five-room house, and a further two hundred dollars on twelve thousand feet of shiplap and structural lumber. Over the next year I happily put all my spare time and money into building our new home. Watching it take shape was a dream come true.

One Sunday morning I was shingling the roof when Doris came out of the old house next door and called up to me that Pearl Harbor had been attacked by the Japanese.

"I don't believe it," I shouted down to her.

"Well, it's true," she said. "Come on down. President Roosevelt is on the radio now."

I got into the house just in time to hear Roosevelt say something about "this dastardly attack by the Japanese."

Doris and I talked about what this would mean for us. Watching as Europe was engulfed by war, the Roosevelt Administration had introduced a draft system in 1940, but I had been given a deferral because lumber milling was deemed a critical industry. (We had to supply the Axis powers with lumber for the air forces, after all!) This direct attack on the U.S. was sure to change things, however. We were now a country at war and I felt sure that sooner or later I would be conscripted—if I didn't volunteer first.

I was not anticipating having to make a decision right away, but an incident occurred the very next day that settled the matter for me.

A couple of years earlier, after having to borrow one of Harold Springer's guns for the Deception Pass deer hunt, I had bought two rifles of my own. One was a lever-action Winchester carbine that had notches on the stock commemorating each of the deer and elk that had been shot by its previous owner, Dr. Frost. The other rifle was a 30.06 sport model Winchester. My co-worker, Len Lobdell, had sold it to me along with eight hundred rounds of World War I ammunition which I intended to use for deer hunting.

The day after Pearl Harbor—Monday, December 8—Marvin Beebe, now promoted to assistant chief of police, tentatively made his way towards the log boom where I was working.

"Come over here," he called gruffly, not addressing me by name, though he knew very well who I was. "I want to talk to you."

I felt a surge of panic as I leapt from one log to the other before arriving to face Marv on a solid float. His serious, excited manner suggested he had brought news of an accident to Doris, or some other mishap.

"What's wrong?" I asked.

Marv looked at me without a smile. "We, that is, the police department, have been told that you have two rifles and a lot of ammunition, and we want you to hand them over."

For a moment I couldn't answer. What bastard would have informed on me for having legitimate hunting rifles and ammunition which I intended to use for sport? It made no sense. I could only figure that perhaps, because of my union activity, someone held a grudge against me. Then I decided I was being discriminated against because of my heritage. Even in Anacortes, I heard plenty of anti-Italian slurs. That must be it. The police were taking my rifles because I was Italian.

"And what if I don't give them to you?" I said angrily.

"We'll come and take them," Marv replied simply. He gave me a vengeful smirk, knowing this was one time that I couldn't challenge his authority.

I thought of Doris, knowing that if I refused to hand over the rifles things could get worse. I had heard talk of Americans of German, Japanese, and Italian backgrounds being moved inland, away from the sensitive coasts.

"Okay," I said reluctantly, "Come and get the goddam things at home, after I get through with work."

When Beebe came by that night, I insisted he give me a receipt for the guns and ammunition so I could reclaim them after the war.

When I ran into Tony Campano, a fellow Italian, a week or so after this incident, I inquired after his three stepsons, the Allen boys with whom I had gathered oysters. I knew they were stationed with the U.S. army in the Philippines, and Tony was always happy to talk with me because I spoke Italian. He told me he and his wife hadn't heard from the boys. But he said that the police had been to see him, too, warning him that he might have to move to someplace inland. Tony lived a very meagre existence, supporting himself and his family with a small truck garden. He had been badly wounded as a soldier in the American Army in World War I, but local "patriots" had threatened him when he came home. Fortunately, a veteran's group came to his defense and later saw to it that Tony got a disability pension, albeit more than twenty years late. Subsequently, Tony's three stepsons all lost their lives in the Philippines—so it could be said that Italian-American Tony Campano paid his dues in full to his adopted country.

As Japan allied itself with the Axis powers, anti-Italian sentiments in Anacortes became so vehement that I decided to quit my job at the mill and volunteer for the army engineers. I would prove to the self-proclaimed "patriots" that I was a loyal American who would do a good job defending our country. So I boarded up the windows and doors of the unfinished house and said my farewells to both Doris and the small town I had come to love. Then I climbed aboard a bus to Fort Lewis, wondering if I would ever return.

PART III

THE WAR

1941-1945

Chapter 24

DOGFACE

At Fort Lewis, as ten of us filled chuck-holes with gravel, anti-Italian sentiments resurfaced.

"Those goddam Dagos can't be trusted. They're nothing but gangsters and gandy dancers," one guy said.

"Yeah, we've got to get over there and clean 'em out," another said.

I listened for some time, getting madder and madder, until finally I declared that I was of Italian parentage—"and I'm as good an American as you guys."

That ended the conversation. Ten minutes later, the guy who had been most antagonistic swung his pick and shattered a small rock, part of which flew up and smashed his eyeglasses into needle-like shards. Slivers of glass were embedded in his eyeball, and I warned him not to close his eyelid or touch his eye. After assisting him to the first-aid station, I never saw him again, but I was certain that this unfortunate incident finished his army career.

At lunch we were surprised to see Sally Rand seated at one of the tables. She was a burlesque dancer who had made her name at the Chicago World's Fair for her "artistry" with fans and feathers. Word got around that she had come to visit her husband Tuck Greenough, an inductee waiting to be shipped out. The two of them sat together eating in the mess hall, while the rest of us joked about scarcely recognizing Sally with clothes on.

Fort Lewis was south of Tacoma, Washington, and functioned as a sorting station. Though I only stayed there two days, I saw how men avoided being transferred to combat units. A sergeant would ask if any of the recruits had experience in tailoring or pressing. Those who volunteered were put to work in his barrack tailor shop, pressing and altering the poorly fitting class-A uniforms that were issued to us. The recruit helpers received no pay; the money went to the entrepreneurial sergeant, who in turn probably paid off his superiors.

The second day, as a group of us non-tailors climbed aboard a covered army truck with our barrack bags and orders, we became victims of another sort of quick-buck operation. While the truck driver revved up the engine, signaling us to hurry because the train was waiting at Nisqually, a GI from finance quickly handed us some money and asked us to sign a receipt for it. Before we had a chance to count the bills the GI waved the driver on. The money was to be used for meals, but we had been sent off with only a dollar a day each. Since most of us would be traveling by train, and meals in the dining car cost several dollars each, this allowance was grossly inadequate. Obviously we had been ripped off, and we were already cynical enough to believe that this kind of racketeering occurred at military posts all over the country.

At Camp Claiborne, in Louisiana, I was assigned to the 342nd Engineer General Service Regiment. We new arrivals were placed in quarantine and began six weeks of basic training in a desolate, snake-infested swamp. There weren't enough rifles to go around, so we were issued with tent stakes. One night I was assigned to guard duty with Les Wilder, who was also from the Pacific Northwest. About one in the morning Les began yelling: "Corporal of the Guards! Corporal of the Guards! Help! Post number one."

Fortunately for us, armed only with our wooden stakes, the infiltrators were not spies, but emaciated wild pigs trying to make their way to the garbage cans by the mess hall.

Eventually we were issued our personal gear and rifles and began infantry training. This included a series of twenty-five-mile hikes, one of which ended in a torrential rainstorm. Arriving back at camp exhausted, hungry and wet, we found not a single tent standing. The guy ropes had shrunk in the steaming downpour, pulling all the tent stakes out of the wet sand. "Damn stakes ain't good for anything," Wilder said.

When not hiking all day, we were sent on "problems." We always had to carry a full field pack for these, including four blankets, although we knew we were not going to sleep out, and we would have been unlikely to use the blankets even if we did because it was so hot. We were also ordered to carry cumbersome gas masks, although we knew there would be no gas attacks.

One particular morning, the order of the day did not require that we bring gas masks. Our "problem" was to assault a hill, behind which was the second battalion of our regiment. Advancing in a skirmish line, we formed just below the crest and were ordered to attack. As soon as we went over the hill, we were surprised by the would-be enemy who stopped us dead in our tracks with smoke grenades and shells. With no gas masks for protection we made a hasty retreat, gasping for fresh air and struggling to see out of tear-blinded eyes.

As soon as we were able to clear our throats and eyes, we began demanding, "Who the hell fucked up on this one?"

"If we're gonna fight Germans, we'll never win the goddam war this way," I said.

"This is typical of the Army," another voice complained. "Situation normal, all fucked up." The voice belonged to a Private Walt Cramoga, and the look of agreement that passed between us was the beginning of a long and close-working partnership.

Our officers had all been recruited from Coulee Dam, in Washington State, and were construction experts who had been given commissions without any military training. These men didn't know how to wear their hats or even make up a pack, and they looked pretty ridiculous. Some of the enlisted men with us in Louisiana were Pennsylvania National Guardsmen, and they helped the new officers shape up. These experienced cadre-men were elevated as leaders and given stripes, and they took advantage of their newly assigned authority to make it as miserable for us new recruits as possible. A number of us became very angry with them, boasting that when we were aboard ship, we would throw them over the side if they ever came above deck.

When our six-week quarantine was over, we moved on to Fort Dix, New Jersey. Our work here consisted of post security and practicing boarding ship on a simulated gangplank, so we assumed time was short before we shipped out. As unofficial confirmation, we were told that if we wanted to visit nearby family or visit New York City we had better get on with it. I decided to pay brother Tony and Minnie a visit, and got a pass to Brooklyn.

Minnie was surprised and happy to see me. "Your brother is at the Coney Island Legion Club, gambling," she said. "Come, get in my car, and we'll go find him."

Tony was playing poker in the far end of a room on the second floor of the club. Minnie beckoned to him from the landing and when his hand was finished, he came over, impatient because we were interrupting the card game.

"What the hell are you doing here?" he snapped at me. "Didja eat?"

"No," I said.

"Not much has changed, then," Tony said. "Take the kid out for something to eat," he ordered Minnie.

That was it: a short, none-too-sweet farewell from my oldest brother as I headed off to war.

I did not see Tony again for another sixty years. Eventually his daughter got in contact with me and arranged for us to get together. But it was clear to me that Tony was still a crook, even then, and our reunion was an unpleasant one.

After Fort Dix, our home for the next ten days was a former luxury liner, *Duchess of Bedford,* on board which we were to sail across the Atlantic. Alongside her at the dock was the French liner *Normandie,* which had burned during repairs and now lay helpless on her side. She was eventually raised, re-named the *Lafayette,* and became our largest troop ship.

The *Duchess* came to New York from Singapore, where she had taken a bomb on the stern. Repaired and converted to accommodate five thousand GIs instead of seven hundred well-off passengers, she was anything but luxurious for us. The officers got the best quarters, sleeping on cots in the dry covered swimming pool. We dogfaces were assigned rope hammocks in unimaginably cramped quarters below decks. The cabins were stifling hot and smelled strongly of sweaty woolen uniforms and body odor. Still prone to motion seasickness, I knew that sleeping was going to be almost impossible. The toilet was a wooden shed built on the fantail of the ship that accommodated about forty or fifty men at a time, with a steady stream of water flushing the effluent directly overboard.

I was happy to pull guard duty the first night aboard because it took me out of the foul smelling hold. I watched from the deck as tugs quietly eased us out of the slip into lower New York harbor. There were no lights or whistles, and aboard the *Duchess* it was my duty as Corporal of the Guard to keep the decks clear and enforce total blackout.

Making the rounds, I noticed a light coming out of the skipper's cabin door, which had been left ajar in the heat.

"Turn off these lights and keep this door closed," I shouted gruffly.

My jaw dropped as an emaciated old man in short black pants and white ruffled blouse came scurrying out of the shadows toward me. He was obviously quite alarmed.

"Shhh! You'll disturb me Master," he whispered in a strong Cockney accent, wagging his index finger back and forth in front of pursed lips.

"Jesus Christ, what is this?" I said, incredulous. Then I realized the old man was a prat boy—one of a vanishing breed that dated back to the days of sailing ships when parents would sell a nine- or ten-year-old boy to a ship's captain. The lad would be paid a few dollars a month to perform household and sexual duties, as required, for the master of the ship.

This prat boy was in his sixties, but he still dressed as a child. In fact, he looked just as I must have done in my Little Lord Fauntleroy get-up twenty years before. He wore black patent leather pumps with large silver buckles and sagging white stockings that climbed his skinny calves and disappeared just below the knee of his velvet knickers. His blouse, scruffy and in obvious need of a wash, was in keeping with the pale gray skin of his wrinkled face.

As soon as I gained my composure, I repeated my order, though I spoke more quietly and added "please," so that it sounded more like a request than a command. I remained shocked at the sight of a prat boy grown old, however, and continued to think about him for the rest of the night.

We had left in dense fog but this cleared around noon on our first day, revealing the flagship *Texas* off our bow. She was towing a paravane, a floating tube that was used by the lead ship in a convoy to indicate speed or direction change. A British Marine was posted twenty-four hours a day on the bow of our ship to observe the paravane and keep in telephone contact with the pilot house. This method of communication was necessary because of the total blackout and complete radio silence.

A column of destroyers on each side of us made our troop ship and accompanying freighters almost impenetrable to the wolf-pack of German submarines that were patrolling the North Atlantic at that time. On our starboard flank, the battleship *Nebraska* mothered us like an old hen protecting her little chicks. It was very comforting to know that a huge armada of both British and American naval ships were escorting us—the largest troop and cargo convoy to that date.

Five days out of New York, the cargo ships headed northeast toward Murmansk, Russia. We continued southeasterly toward what we suspected would be England. Several months later, we learned that our departing ships had become part of an ill-fated convoy that lost 24 of its 35 merchant vessels to U-boats and the Luftwaffe. Unchallenged, the German aircraft—for which I had undoubtedly helped provide Sitka spruce—picked the ships off like sitting ducks as they made their way into the Arctic Ocean.

The troops aboard our ship included advanced cadres who would arrange for their parent units to follow at a later date. Among them were about fifty men of the Fourth Ranger Battalion. They were the most elite, rugged group that I have ever seen in the military. Of the five thousand men aboard, these volunteers were the only gung-ho soldiers. The rest of us were merely following orders and generally felt anxious about going overseas.

Daily exercise helped to keep our spirits up, and on one of my walks around the deck, I encountered a familiar face.

"Weren't you the commander at the CCC camp at Deception Pass?" I asked.

"Yes, and now I can place you," he said. "You were there too, weren't you?"

"I sure was. You probably remember me as Johnny Bananas."

We talked for about half an hour. Robert Brown was now a Major and an aide to Colonel Kermit Roosevelt of the First Infantry Division.

"Johnny," he said, "do you want to come into my unit? If you do, I guarantee you a commission when we get where we're going. I can make arrangements for the transfer."

I was pleased at the offer, but after thinking about it for a few minutes, I decided I should stay with the group for which I had volunteered. Somehow, I felt fate had relegated me to the engineers, and I should stick with them. I was pretty sure I had more useful skills to offer as an engineer than an infantryman. At least part of me figured I might live longer that way, also.

As the ship sailed ever closer to the war zone, Colonel Roosevelt assembled the troops on the deck for a pep talk. He was a small man, not at all like his husky father, Teddy. Kermit Roosevelt was known to be a hard drinking brawler—his squashed nose was the proof—and that day his appearance was even more remarkable. Because his raincoat had been stolen, he wore a borrowed coat that reached down to his shoe tops.

Standing close to the rail on the deck above, squinting through the rain, he shouted about how important we were and how our wives, girlfriends and mothers were all proud of us and waiting for us to return.

"Now, you know we are in submarine-infested waters," he concluded, "and there's a good chance we will be sunk. If we are hit, I want you men to know that I will be the last one off this ship. But if we are torpedoed, be goddam sure you go over the side in a hurry!"

We appreciated this bit of humor, but it didn't lighten our mood much. No matter how many jokes were told or how much praise was handed out, we were always conscious of being in danger. When an unidentified airplane appeared on the horizon, a day before we were due to arrive in England, we were pretty apprehensive until we recognized it as a British Sunderland flying boat. Circling, it dipped its wings in friendly salute.

The last day of our voyage took us south through the Irish Sea to Liverpool. The final waterway was cluttered with sunken ships, and it seemed to us our captain was using the drowned masts and superstructures as buoys to guide us into the harbor. The amount of destruction was unbelievable. We had read and heard about the Battle of Britain, but our trek through this watery graveyard brought Britain's suffering home to us.

Apparently, the British were unprepared for our arrival. We were told to stay aboard ship for another night, so those of us who were topside went below to our sleeping quarters. Early on in the trip, four of us had opted out of the airless tomb to which we had been assigned and hung our hammocks on a steam line in a small companion way. Since we had pulled our guard duty that first night, we were not missed. Our sleeping conditions improved and so did our diet, thanks to Tommy Burns, the youngest among us, who was an experienced thief. Early on, he managed to steal a whole roasted turkey from the officers' mess. In Liverpool, he stole two boxes of apples, and we were seated on the floor munching the much-appreciated fresh fruit when the air raid sounded. Our first reaction was relief that we were in the companion way, surrounded by the steel hull, which would act as bomb shelter should the ship be hit. Relief faded to horror when the crew slammed the water-tight doors shut, sealing us off from the rest of the ship. We realized that we would die slow deaths of suffocation if our vessel joined the other sunken hulks at the bottom of the harbor. Fortunately no bombs fell nearby, and after an hour that seemed like an eternity, we heard the all-clear sound—and the following morning we marched down the gang plank to England.

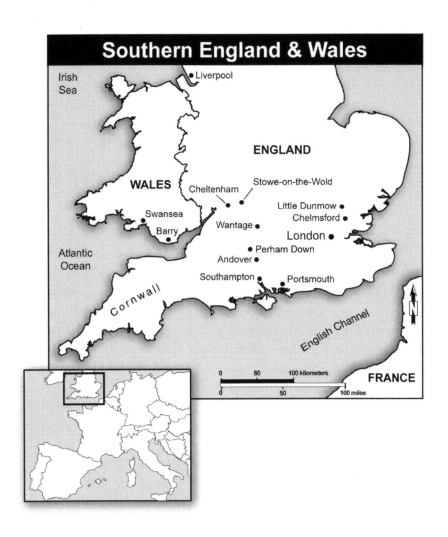

Chapter 25

WEEVIL STEW

From Liverpool, we boarded a train for Perham Down, in the south-central area of England known as Salisbury Plain. Midway on our journey, the train stopped briefly at a station where English ladies in floral dresses boarded and served us tea. No doubt about it, now; we were truly in England. These ladies obviously knew better than to ask anything about who we were or where we were going. However, another woman on the platform came up to the window and called in, "Are you Germans?"

"Hell, no!" Lou retorted, miffed. "We're Americans!"

The woman backed away, apologizing and mumbling something about helmets. Apparently our pisspot-shaped steel hats looked a little like German military head gear.

Perham Down turned out to be the home of an old Army camp that had last been used in World War I. We were met there by British officers and an army band that marched us in full gear to our billets. Marched is not quite the right word. Our step did not fit the fast British rhythm, so we shambled along at our own pace.

The second night it became obvious that the Germans knew of our arrival. The Luftwaffe pulled a low-level strafing attack, hitting the barracks next to mine. Since the air raid warning didn't sound until after the raking was all over, it was sheer luck that no one was killed. This was the first of many aerial attacks that kept us up all night. Each time the air raid sounded, the machine guns had to be carried half a mile to the top of a knoll. These were water-cooled Browning .30 caliber weapons that required four men: one to carry the gun; one to carry the tripod; one to carry two cans of water; and another to carry the ammo. By the time we got these pieces set up and ready to fire, the Germans were headed home and the all clear had sounded.

More often than not after we had returned to the barracks and climbed into our sacks, this futile routine would be repeated. After several weeks of this charade, we returned to the barracks one night to discover Bob Tie. He had not participated in his assignment, had got drunk instead, and had shit himself in his bed. Our barracks were completely blacked-out, without ventilation, and the stench was so revolting that six or eight of us dragged Bob out, mattress and all, and left him under the stars. Though we were happy to be rid of him, he had the best of the deal. He was breathing fresh air while we had to use our lungs to filter the putrid smell inside.

Our American rations had not yet arrived, so the British were charged with feeding us. Since we knew their food was rationed, we were willing to accept thin oatmeal porridge without milk or sugar and a half-slice of bread deep-fried in animal fat for breakfast. Other meals typically consisted of Brussels sprouts, small pieces of potato, and extra-large peas. Leaving the peas to grow longer in the fields increased yields but also allowed time for pea weevils to lay eggs. This resulted in a worm in every pea.

One night, when we were served a foul mutton stew with yet more overgrown peas, a food riot ensued. One of the men at our table, disgusted at the worms floating in our dinner, turned the serving pan upside down. Men at other tables followed his example. We walked out, cursing the rotten food. An hour later, our battalion was marched to a gymnasium where machine guns had been set up at every corner. The adjutant brought us to attention and the regimental commander read the riot act to us, finishing with the threat, "Yours was a mutinous act, and if you do it again, we'll use these machine guns on you. We officers eat the same food as you." Pointing to one of his lieutenants, he ordered him to tell us what they had been served for supper.

"We had mutton stew and cake for dessert."

"Cake?" we dogfaces hollered back in unison. We had never been served dessert. Embarrassed, the colonel dismissed us, and only the two leaders of the riot were given time in the brig.

After work each day, the rest of us would go and visit our two incarcerated buddies. We felt bad that they were paying the penalty for something that we had all been involved in. They didn't seem to be in any hurry to get back to the barracks, which seemed strange until they explained: they had been assigned the daily duty of cleaning the Armed Services canteen building, which might have been terrible except that three young, attractive British women worked there. The two prisoners and their guard were canoodling with these girls every morning after their work was done.

Fortunately, it was not long before food shipments began to arrive from the States, and we were able to enjoy American rations. We also were issued gas protective gear because the British felt sure that the Jerries would launch a gas attack. Construction equipment came at this time, and I was assigned to a bulldozer which had no seat. In addition to fashioning a wooden seat for the machine, I bought maintenance tools from a local ironmonger and began studying a diesel engine repair manual, so I could keep the beast running.

My first job as a bulldozer driver was to scoop out a trench for the steel columns of what would eventually be a large ordnance building. After this, we fashioned a crane by attaching a telephone pole to the dozer blade and raised the trusses in record time. Working from daylight to dark, we completed the steel work in two weeks; this was the first of many record-breaking accomplishments for our unit.

Exhausted from the hard work, only a handful of us signed up to go to a dance at the RAF base at Andover. Our officers insisted we show our appreciation to our British hosts, so about twenty-five GIs ultimately agreed to go. The officers went too, which surprised the British as their own commissioned officers and enlisted men never mixed at social functions. We Americans didn't care, and whatever our rank we soon forgot our tiredness as there were about five WAAFs to each of us. These women didn't hesitate to tell us that "Americans are fascinating." They also asked what part of the colonies we came from. My answer always was that after the Revolution there were no more "colonies," only "states". But we forgave their ignorance. These were the first of many young women who were to make us feel welcome in their country and relieve our loneliness far from home.

American women in England did their part also. The nearby village of Tidworth had been completely taken over and turned into a military cantonment. Row houses became barracks for the First Infantry Division, and the finest old home was turned into a Red Cross club. It was more than a coincidence, perhaps, that the Red Cross director turned out to be Mrs. Kermit Roosevelt.

Another famous name at Tidworth was Fred Astaire's sister, Lady Adele Cavendish, who joined Mrs. Roosevelt as a British volunteer with the Red Cross. Lady Cavendish regularly mixed with the boys, and as her part in the war effort, wrote letters home for those who were unable to do it themselves.

Chapter 25

**

From the windswept chalk downs of Salisbury Plain, we moved to a new assignment in the picturesque Cotswold Hills, in Southwestern England. Here, slow streams were green with watercress, and winding footpaths invited walking and bicycling. This was fox-hunting country, and, occasionally a huntsman in colorful habit appeared in the landscape, his well-groomed mount surrounded by a pack of hounds on their way to the hunt. The hounds clustered tightly around the horses' hooves, and all moved together as if they were one unit swooping across the countryside.

For some of us, the Cotswolds offered a different kind of recreation. In this rolling green countryside I came to appreciate the groundsheets that some British women carried rolled up behind their bicycle seats. In daylight or dark, lonely English women held trysts with equally lonely GIs—including me—on these waterproof covers under the Cotswold sky. Perhaps sex is freer during wartime because we deeply sense how tenuous life is, or perhaps it is nature urging us to replace the lives that are being lost to the madness of armed human conflict. Whatever the reason, I feel no remorse about my actions and pass no judgement on anybody else's. Our wives and girlfriends were an ocean away. We could be sent into combat at any time. We made love out of our hearts; we made love out of our desperation.

Upon our arrival in the Cotswolds, what we GIs assumed from a distance to be just another charming hill near Stowe-on-the-Wold turned out to be a masterful structure made of chicken-wire and dyed burlap. Built by the British, it was very difficult to discern from the natural topography, and concealed the Allied Forces trans-Atlantic radio transmitter and antennae. Now we Americans took it over and set about installing diesel electric generators to power it.

Those of us assigned to this secret project included civilian radio technicians from the U.S., GI military police, and a dozen engineers, of which I was one. We all worked together and could see what each group was involved in, but we were forbidden to discuss any phase of the operation. Six of us were Italian-Americans, and as we ate our lunchtime sandwiches in a communal tent we learned that others in the group, members of the Masonic Lodge, were spouting the old prejudices against us behind our backs.

One night on our way back to Cheltenham, where we were headquartered, we decided to work over one of these Masonic cadre-men. We beat him up pretty badly with no repercussions to ourselves. Subsequently, our company commander transferred all of the cadre-men except the first sergeant out of our unit, and we never saw them again.

Besides the prejudice, other reminders of my Italian-American upbringing had followed me to England. Al Lianza was sitting on the cot next to mine reading his mail, when he exclaimed, "Holy Christ! Father Appo died."

"Did you say Father Appo? The priest?" I wondered if I had heard right. I explained to Al that had known Father Appo when I was a kid in Brooklyn. Our Italian heritage had brought Al and me together; now our shared sadness at the old priest's death deepened our friendship.

Al and I both remembered Father Appo as an outstanding man— tall, handsome and dark-skinned. We assumed he was of American Indian parentage, but whatever his background, we agreed that he stood head and shoulders above other priests, not only in physical height, but in refinement. His lavish lifestyle contrasted sharply with his humility and his loyalty to the church, but like most of his parishioners, we admired him greatly.

Years later, when I was doing some research for this book, a Catholic archivist described Father Locksley Appo to me as "famous, notorious, and unique." I discovered he had been educated in Rome— which explained his flawless Italian—and he was not of Native American heritage but Haitian. He may have been the first black priest in the Catholic Church. But whatever mysteries were associated with him, Al and I had no doubts about his refinement and goodness.

By now it was December, 1942—our first Christmas away from home. Instead of Christmas cards, many of the men were beginning to get "Dear John" letters. These were always discussed after supper in the barracks, and I was mighty glad not to be the recipient of one myself. I thought of Doris all the time—more so when at a public dance at the Cheltenham opera house I met another Doris. She was married to Eric, an English sailor, and as a couple they invited me to their home for dinner. Eric and I attended a rugby match beforehand—my first and last experience of the game. It looked to me as if somebody blew a whistle and the players all rushed at one another and ended up in a big heap. It seemed like a good metaphor for the war.

Two days after Christmas we were ordered back from Stowe-on-the-Wold to Perham Down. We knew from both the stockpile of arms and ammunition and the continuing influx of Americans that the invasion of the European continent was inevitable—and that we were going to be part of it. The night before departing Stowe we sat around, depressed, discussing what we were going to do if we ever made it back home.

"What will you do, Al?" I said, expecting him he to say he was going to consummate his marriage. At Fort Dix, he had snuck away for the nuptials but had then returned immediately without spending any time alone with his new wife.

"I'm going to go into the electrical contracting business," he said.

"Well, aren't you gonna go to bed with your wife before you do that?" I was trying to help us forget our predicament.

"There'll be plenty of time for that, Big Nose," he said, grabbing the end of my nose and twisting it between his thumb and index finger.

"Hey, Clyde," I called across to an Okie buddy, "what about your wife? How come you got drafted when you have a nine-year-old daughter?"

"We're divorced," he said.

"Why'd you get divorced?"

"She had the claps."

"Did she get 'em from you?"

Clyde shook his head sadly. "I've always had trouble with women. Even here in pubs, when I go to piss after a couple of beers, the woman I've been with is gone. I can't figure out what's wrong with me."

Well, we all knew what the problem was. Clyde was a little pinched-faced fellow, five-foot-five, illiterate—anything but a ladies' man.

I figured it was time to change the subject. "What did you do for a living back in Oklahoma, Clyde?"

"I was a dishwasher in our little diner, but when I get back from the war I want to be a dishwasher in a big hotel in Tulsa," he said. The rest of us laughed at this, but Clyde was serious.

Al asked me if I was planning to go back to the Northwest or bring Doris to Brooklyn. I assured him I was going back to Anacortes to finish the house the war interrupted and settle down.

"But I don't intend to die falling off a log boom," I said. "I'm going to find another kind of work that has more of a future." Thinking of my childhood, I added. "I want to help people if I can. There'll be a way."

154

Passman was looking at his watch. "Put the lights out," he hollered to DeForest, who was nearest to the light switch.

"Shoot the goddam things out," DeForest shouted back, too lazy to get out of his bunk.

At this suggestion Billy Fender, an ex-professional boxer who had taken too many blows to the head, loaded his M-1 and fired a couple of rounds through the roof. Fearing that Billy might shoot one of us next, I went over and calmed him, taking away his rifle.

Perhaps it was due to the chaos of leaving the next morning that Billy was never reprimanded.

Back in Perham Down, Lou, Al and I were granted a day pass and decided to visit Southampton to see the devastation the Luftwaffe had wreaked upon the largest seaport in Britain. We wandered through the most heavily damaged residential area. Nothing remained except a church and a bank. An English block warden described to us what had happened when a parabomb, or blockbuster, made a direct hit on a local air raid shelter.

"The shelter was filled with about five hundred people—mostly women and children who were trapped in the rubble," he said. "We tried to dig them out, but the rescue crews were overwhelmed."

"What happened?" we asked. "How did you get them out?"

"We couldn't get them out. There was no way we could get to them. The cries and moans of the injured and dying were so terrible and hopeless that we pumped ether into the rubble to relieve their suffering."

This was our first experience of war as a killer of innocent women and children, and it made us feel glad, not for the first time, to be engineers rather than combat soldiers.

At Perham Down we were re-assigned to construction work. Another engineering unit had been relieved of duty because the steel structure they were erecting went out of plumb. Ten men from our unit were chosen to repair the listing frame. Lieutenant Stone, the officer to whom we were assigned, was a twenty-one-year-old shoe salesman recently arrived from Florida.

"These men are experienced and know what they are doing," our company commander told the young lieutenant. "Just give them their heads."

Arriving at the site, Tony Caliendo, Walt Cramoga, and I surveyed the job and debated how to go about straightening three hundred feet of roof trusses that were four feet out of plumb. We settled on a plan, and before climbing up into the structure I cautioned Lieutenant Stone and the rest of the unit not to do anything while the three of us were working above.

We straightened one truss, secured it, and moved on to the next before we noticed our new lieutenant was not following our orders. Going with some men to the far end, he cut one truss loose causing all of the trusses to collapse in a domino effect toward us.

As the other men hollered at us, we realized our predicament. Rather than dropping thirty-five feet to the ground, we decided to ride the twisting steel to the concrete below. None of us were injured, fortunately, because the steel came to a rest about ten feet above the ground. Dropping quickly down, I started for Lieutenant Stone with Walt and Tony close behind me.

"You dumb son-of-a-bitch! I told you not to do anything! I'm gonna knock your goddam head off," I lunged toward Stone, my Brooklyn street-fighting instincts coming to the fore.

Tony grabbed me. "You'll go to jail if you hit him, Johnny."

"I don't give a shit if I do," I ranted. The lieutenant had put our lives in jeopardy. I felt frustrated, too, that we had failed at our job because of him.

But I calmed down without landing a blow and we returned to the company headquarters to face the music. Surprisingly, we were not reprimanded, but we were not sent back to the job either. Soon after this, Lieutenant Stone was reassigned to another unit, while I was given a secret assignment with Browning, a truck and tractor driver.

Told nothing more than to pack all of our gear, load the bulldozer, and be ready to leave at five o'clock next morning, Browning and I suspected something big was in the wind. We knew that a beachhead had been established at Casablanca, so we thought we might be going to North Africa. The question was why we were the only two men from Company B of the 342nd engineering regiment singled out to go.

British MPs on motorcycles led us from our barracks to a main highway and a waiting convoy of six Diamond-T trucks towing lowboys loaded with bulldozers. Meandering slowly through sleepy villages,

Browning and I discussed whether or not we were leaving England, and if we would ever rejoin our parent unit.

I became increasingly demoralized with every mile. "We're obviously going into a combat zone, and our chances of making it home are getting more remote every day."

"I wonder if our wives will be waiting for us if the war continues," Browning said, making me feel even worse. "This thing could go on for years at the rate it is going now."

Every six or seven miles our MP escort was replaced by another rider. At first, we didn't understand what was happening. Finally, we realized that none of the MPs knew the ultimate destination of our convoy. They were merely responsible for escorting us for small segments of the trip.

As dusk fell we were shunted into a muddy lane under trees that would camouflage us for the night, then we were isolated behind barbed wire from anyone who might talk to us. Our travels the next day were a repeat of the day before with complete secrecy, not only about where we were going but about where we were. All English road signs had been removed for the duration of the war, so we did not know until we arrived on a dock early in the afternoon that we were in Barry, South Wales.

Again we were confined to an enclosure, this time beside an ancient tramp steamer tied to the dock. We assumed we would be going for a boat ride. The next day we helped load our equipment aboard, feeling we would be fortunate if the ship floated long enough to make its destination.

Waiting for orders to board, we witnessed the taunting of a Welsh soldier by half a dozen English Tommies.

"You're never going to be anything but a bloody coal digger," the English mocked.

"Leave me alone," the Welshman begged. Tears streamed down his face. He was small and obviously not bright enough to know how to defend himself verbally.

"Why don't you lay off him?" we shouted out from our barbed wire enclosure.

Of course, the English paid no attention to us, and this incident was not the first time I'd seen weak people tormented in the military. In our own company, our frail, effeminate bugler was razzed so badly that he lost his mind and was given a Section 8 discharge. The tense situation with the

Welshman came to a sudden end when Lieutenant Dixon gave the surprising order that we were to board a train and return to our unit.

"What about our gear?" we complained.

"A black engineering unit is taking it over. We can't go aboard and get anything off. You will be issued new gear when you get back."

A couple of months later, we heard that the ship went into Oran, North Africa. There the Germans blew it out of the water, and many of the engineers aboard lost their lives.

Chapter 26

CRABS AND FISH LADDERS

Our next assignment was at Chelmsford, in Essex, 35 miles northeast of London, where we were to build an aerodrome for the 8th Air Force bombers. The flat surrounding pastureland was punctuated with ancient chestnut and beech trees, natural umbrellas for cows and sheep. These great trees also lined the meandering country roads, entwining their limbs overhead and creating long green tunnels. The farmers' fields were defined by hedgerows and board fences, many of them with steep wooden stiles for walkers who wished to take a shortcut.

We engineers were billeted at the Warwick Estate, ten miles outside Chelmsford. The main house was taken over by the Air Force brass, obliging the resident owner of the estate, Lady Diane Warwick, to move into the servants' quarters. Lady Diane was a beautiful blonde woman in her late twenties who took the conversion of her estate into a military camp in good stride. Her husband, the Earl of Warwick, was serving in the Middle East.

I would often see Lady Diane from my bulldozer as she bicycled frequently into nearby Little Dunmow. This was a typical East-Anglian farm village with a pub, post office, greengrocer's store and thatched-roofed cottages. Lady Diane would wave and buy a newspaper for me and deliver it on her return trip.

My job was to stockpile cement and aggregate to supply the battery of twelve cement mixers. Bob Tie was still goofing off, as always, and one particular morning he was sitting on his ass while everyone else was busting theirs loading the hoppers. When Lieutenant Dixon showed up and saw Bob doing nothing, he lost his cool, picked up a shovel and threw it at him.

"Goddam you, Tie! You get up on that truck and start unloading those sacks of cement. And you don't eat until you are finished."

This was a brutal assignment because English cement bags weighed one hundred twelve pounds—eighteen pounds more than American bags—and there were fifteen tons of them to unload. Nobody sympathized with

Tie, however. He was a screw-off who deserved what he got. Soon thereafter, he was given a Section 8 discharge for mental incompetence.

As compensation for the long hours of hard work, a dance was held each week in Chelmsford at the Corn Exchange, a big hall where local farmers sold grain and auctioned livestock. Chelmsford was home to a large aircraft factory and a huge Marconi wireless plant, both of which employed many women, so finding a dance partner was not difficult, and sex was pretty easy to come by as well. But this fraternization, pleasant as it was, often led to other problems.

One afternoon Oakie, Peasley, Gorky, and I were standing around our bulldozers while Bill, a grease monkey from the air force, lubricated our machines. We were shooting the breeze about the dance in town, when Oakie piped up, "You know, guys, I've got a case of the crabs."

"It's no disgrace," I said. "Everybody gets the crabs sooner or later."

Peasley chimed in with his raspy voice, "I wonder if I ain't got the crabs. I'm itchin'. Do you know what they look like?" He opened his shirt, exposing a hairy gorilla-like chest that was covered in crabs. The rest of us backed away.

"You're alive with crabs, Peasley!" I gasped. "You better get to the medics right away for some blue ointment. I doubt like hell they've got enough to cover you. You're gonna need a whole bucket of it."

I happened to know that Oakie had been screwing a girl named Joan. She was the girlfriend of Bill the grease monkey, and two-timed with Peasley when Bill was on duty.

"You don't think you gave the crabs to Joan?" I said, out of Bill's earshot.

Before Oakie could reply, Bill joined us, lighting up a cigarette.

I said to him, "We missed you at the dance yesterday. Did you see Joan on your day off?"

"Yeah," said Bill. "I spent the night with her, and I can hardly wait for the next time. The only problem is, I think I got a case of the crabs. And I don't know where the hell I got 'em."

Well, we all had crabs, but we weren't about to admit that to Bill. We didn't say anything to him, except to advise that he get some blue ointment. As for where the crabs came from, and who gave them to whom, that question remains unanswered to this day.

Part of our job in Little Dunmow was to build hangars at various airfields in the Chelmsford area. Eleven of us, including Walt, Tony and I, worked as steel erectors.

Our third hangar was constructed at an airfield near the Henry Ford Estate. Some years earlier Mr. Ford had built an enormous mansion where he had the audacity to keep a garden tractor permanently displayed in the foyer. Combining such commercialism with the gentility of the house and surroundings offended the sensibilities of his neighbors.

Isolated at the airfield, we had to make our own entertainment. On one trip to London, Tony bought a ferret and brought it back to camp so we could hunt rabbits more efficiently. At the end of my work days I had been shaking up the stump pile with the bulldozer to scare out any rabbits and run them down. The rabbits would run around the field in circles until they tired. Then they would squat down, and we could easily pick them up. Now, we just set the ferret into the rabbit burrow, and he did the work.

Our latrine was a shed, with coal scuttles fitted with wooden seats which were used for honey buckets. The two Land Army girls who emptied these every other day were possibly two of the most beautiful women in England. They drove up in their little black Austin panel truck, emptied the buckets into a tank in the back, washed the receptacles, and replaced the loose-fitting seats. One day, they didn't replace the seat properly on one of the buckets and created a hazardous situation for one unsuspecting user.

Shannon was a big man, well over two hundred pounds, who had recently married an English WAAF twenty years his junior. He was all dressed up and anxious to get going on his twenty-four hour pass to meet his bride of one week when he was caught short and had to use the honey bucket.

Quickly pulling down his pants, he failed to notice the position of the seat as he lowered himself, and his pecker fell down between the coal scuttle lip and the seat. Dropping his great weight hurriedly, he nearly severed his manhood. Poor Shannon! The accident prevented him from doing what he had intended to do in the bucket, but, worse, it also prevented him from visiting his bride that evening.

By now, we had been in England for a year and a half, with no sign of going home. We grew more depressed with every passing day, so the Friday night dance at the Corn Exchange in Chelmsford came as a welcome relief. I drove a six-by-six truck with a load of men on the recreation run to town, parking in front of the dance hall and reminding everybody that we had to be back to the camp before ten o'clock.

The orchestra was playing "The White Cliffs of Dover" as we entered the dimly lit hall. I asked an attractive girl standing by herself if she would like to dance.

"Righto! Ta!" she accepted cheerfully, extending her hand as we moved onto the floor.

"I'm Johnny," I introduced myself.

"And I'm Muriel," she said. "What part of the colonies are you from, Johnny?"

I replied with the usual spiel about "states, not colonies," and said that I was from the state of Washington. I knew that most Britishers thought of D.C. whenever Washington was mentioned, and took pains to explain that my Washington was not the capital. "It borders on British Columbia, Canada, in the Pacific Northwest. Do you know where that is?"

"I have a vague idea," Muriel said. "I studied Canada in school. It's another of our colonies, you know."

I asked her if she had been taught in school that Britain had lost the Revolutionary War and that our particular "colony" no longer belonged to Mother England.

She ignored my question, thus avoiding an international incident. "What did you do in civilian life?" she said instead.

"I worked in the timber industry."

"What is the Pacific Northwest like?"

I described it as beautiful and green, with lakes, mountains, forests and islands. I told her I lived on an island with my wife, amidst huge trees that were hundreds of years old. "They're more than thirteen feet in diameter and over two hundred feet tall," I bragged.

Watching her as she tried to picture the monster trees in her mind, I decided I would really impress her, and asked if she knew anything about salmon.

Muriel smiled, "No, I don't have the slightest idea."

"Well," I said, "They hatch in rivers and lakes, then they go to sea and stay there until they mature. This takes two to six years, according to the species. They then return to the place where they were born. They have an instinct to return, and regardless of the obstacles in the rivers, they fight their way back. In some cases, the government has built fish ladders to assist them through rapids and dams."

Muriel looked at me in disbelief. "I have heard you Yanks tell some fantastic stories," she said. "But if you expect me to believe that fish climb ladders—away with you now!"

Before I could defend my story, the whine of air raid sirens put a stop to the dance, and by the time we reached the door, bombs were exploding nearby. It was everyone for themselves. My new friend Muriel went toward the shelter. I headed for the truck. Many of the men were already in the back saying, "Let's get going," when a large bomb exploded in a block of houses about six hundred feet away.

Bricks, stone blocks and household furnishings littered the streets of Chelmsford as we drove back to camp. Fortunately our six-by-six could navigate the rubble, and I was able to make my way without lights to the comparative safety of the two-lane highway to Little Dunmow.

Approaching camp, I noticed tracer bullets piercing the roof of one of the huts and sending brief streaks of fire into the night sky.

"What's going on?" I asked our CO, Captain Clifford, as we both ran toward the hut.

"Looks like Fender has blown his cork again, and is trying to shoot one of the airplanes down by himself," the captain replied. "I'm going in after him, John."

"I'll go with you," I said. We got down on our hands and knees and crawled toward Fender as he continued firing through the roof.

"Fender," the captain called calmly, "put down your rifle."

To my surprise, Fender handed his piece to the captain and went along to the orderly room without a word. By morning he was gone—on his way home with a Section 8 discharge.

No doubt Muriel, my doubting dance partner of the previous evening, thought I deserved a Section 8, too—but in the Pacific Northwest, salmon really do climb ladders. Honest!

Chapter 27

THE GYPSY BUILDERS

After Chelmsford, our engineering regiment of about fourteen hundred men was split up and assigned to different ground and Air Force units in England, without a parent organization to fight for it. We came to think of ourselves as "the forgotten bastards." We were sent in small groups to do shitty jobs. We got the poorest rations, and as soon as we made our quarters comfortable, we were moved on. The men who followed us would enjoy the running water and heated billets while we went ahead to start all over again. Later, after we had arrived in France, an article in *Yank* magazine (19 March, 1944) dubbed our engineering unit the "Gypsy Builders," because we moved quickly from one project to another, often stealing away in the dead of night:

> When an engineer outfit moves in, it does things in a big way... and moves on. It leaves behind water towers, and warehouses and hangars, mess halls, Nissen huts, concrete walks—wiring, plumbing, piping.
>
> These engineers don't build Boulder Dams—nothing fancy, no miracles, but only the necessary homely items of construction by which an Army lives. When they are through they fold the heavy machinery and steal off—and the Army moves in the next day.

From Chelmsford we were sent to Wantage, a small village near Oxford, where we were assigned to the 9th Air Force. We paved roads and constructed a machine shop in which Mustang fighters were fitted with larger fuel tanks and air scoops to give them greater range as they escorted bombers flying into enemy territory. These Allied air raids were taking their toll on the Luftwaffe and diminished Germany's ability to bomb England.

Wantage was also home for the time-being to some of the Italian prisoners captured by the Allies in North Africa. Unlike German POWs, the Italians were not imprisoned but allowed to travel freely between their billets in the village and the farms where they worked as laborers.

Franco and Guido were two good-looking young Italians who had sought me out because I spoke their language. Every morning on their way to work, they stopped by to visit. They were disappointed to find themselves in England. They said, "We surrendered to GIs, so why weren't we sent to America?"

"I don't know," I replied, "but you guys have it made here riding around the countryside on bicycles. The war is over for you, but it hasn't really started for us. We still have to go to the Continent and win this war."

"Oh, you'll never win this war," Franco said confidently.

"Absolutely not!" Guido said. "As soon as the Allies get to the Piedmont Mountains of Northern Italy, you will lose. That will be the end for you."

Since both men were from the Piedmont area, I understood their conviction. Italy had surrendered several months earlier, but the Germans had launched a counter-offensive down the Italian peninsula and the Allies had been having a tough fight since landing at Salerno in September, 1943.

Usually, however, my conversations with Franco and Guido were not about war or politics, but women. We had all been away from home for a long time, and talk often turned to the subject of sex. Perhaps British women were less inhibited than American women or perhaps in England they were just closer to death, but, for whatever reason, they often took pity on the fighting men, and, possibly, on themselves as well. We all clung to one other in desire and desperation, in the hope that it would make the pain of war go away—at least for a few sweet moments.

Franco and Guido were not excluded from these comforts. I listened to their stories about the beautiful English Land Army Girls with pleasure, but I warned them not to get the girls in the *famigilia* way or get "burnt."

"Don't worry," Franco said proudly. "These girls always bring their own *cappotto* (condom)."

"Italian women never do such a thing," Guido went on. "And these women want it every day!"

"Mine is the most beautiful. *Bella! Bella!*" Franco boasted.

"But mine has the biggest tits." Guido had the last word, illustrating his point by bouncing his open hands up and down below his chest.

I laughed and decided there were worse ways to get through the war than being an Italian POW in England.

Chapter 27

**

December 1943, we were still at Wantage. This was our second Christmas overseas, and with the invasion of France nowhere in sight morale was at an all-time low.

In the spirit of the season, we decided to contribute enough money to send a monthly payment to a five-year-old boy whose father had been killed in a London air raid. This small exercise in holiday generosity made us feel better in one way, but it reminded us that before the goddam war was over many children would be left fatherless and many wives husbandless back in the States as well as London. Nevertheless, the boy and his widowed mother were welcome guests at our Christmas dinner and brightened our day.

"Do you think we'll be home by next Christmas, Johnny?" Captain Collier asked as we finished our coffee.

"Absolutely!" I said. "We will positively be home by next Christmas."

"I'll bet you a hundred bucks we won't," he said dejectedly.

I called his bet and we shook hands on it. I lost the bet, of course, but it was one wager I'm certain the Captain would have preferred losing himself.

We spent New Year's that year dancing at what we dubbed "the Sweat Box," a small community hall much like our farm granges back in the States. As always, the British and American national anthems were played on the phonograph before the dance records. The Lambeth Walk was very popular at the time, but that evening I was to learn a more exciting dance.

"Coming up next—the Hokey Pokey," the phonograph engineer announced across the room.

A gal grabbed my arm urging, "Come on, Yank! Let's do the Hokey Pokey!"

"But I don't know it," I protested.

"Never mind! I'll teach you," she said, rolling her eyes in a teasing way. "Just listen to the words and do as I do":

> Put your right hand in
> Put your right hand out
> Put your right hand in
> And roll it all around

You do the hokey pokey
And shake it all around
That's what it's all about.

When the words of the music got to "the back side in and the back side out and roll it all around," every GI in the hall got a dry hump. The dance was a great hit and since it was new to us, we insisted on practicing it several times more before "Auld Lang Syne" was played. In spite of the hilarity of the Hokey Pokey the stroke of midnight turned our thoughts to other New Year's Eves in other places. Kisses mingled with tears as we GIs and our English dance partners remembered lovers and spouses far away.

In early spring 1944, Bill and I were chosen to go to Swansea in South Wales to learn how to waterproof motor vehicles so they could operate under water. We were then to go back and teach the rest of our men how to do it. This meant only one thing: the invasion of the Continent was getting close, and we would be part of it.

Until then, we made the most of things. In late March, I got an overnight pass to London. The Red Cross Club in Piccadilly was a good place to eat and frequently had lobster for fifty cents. Sometimes, I ordered two meals at a time there. Just around the corner from the club was the Windmill, a theater which had good comedy skits and a nude show. English girls were not allowed to move on stage when nude; instead, they were positioned around the stage in seductive poses. With long, slow droppings of their eyelids, they would signal the audience to survey the rest of their anatomy. Otherwise, each gorgeous woman remained absolutely still as a vocalist sang a popular wartime song, such as "Sentimental Journey" or "The White Cliffs of Dover."

Back at the Red Cross Club, I was enjoying biscuits and coffee when I ran into Walt Cramoga. We discovered we each had a bunk at the same row house near Hyde Park. About nine o'clock—curfew hour—we were signing in at our sleeping quarters when the air raid sirens went off.

I said, "Let's go and watch the action." Standing in the middle of the street, we saw the searchlight beams swinging back and forth across the sky as the concussion of exploding bombs got stronger and stronger. Then the damnedest noise we had ever heard roared out of Hyde Park over our heads. It was a few seconds before we realized that the British had fired all their rocket propelled anti-aircraft batteries at once, forming a square-mile pattern of flack in the hope of bringing down the enemy bombers.

Luckily, the horrendous sound frightened us into the shelter of a doorway. Debris from the exploding rockets fell into the street, and one of the three-foot rocket casings landed exactly where we had been standing. In the morning we read in the paper that at least seventy-eight (and ultimately one hundred and seventy-three) people had been trampled to death attempting to get down into the Bethnal Green tube station for shelter. This was the last major Luftwaffe air raid on London. From then on the Germans sent over buzz bombs and V-2 rockets instead.

Shortly after this, our whole unit was sent to Porthcawl, Wales, to train in the construction of Bailey Bridge and V-trestles, used in dock building. These were grueling exercises, carried out at night in complete darkness. No smoking, no talking, no unnecessary noise at all; we even used rubber hammers. We practiced tasks repeatedly, so we would be able to assemble these structures automatically under the worst conditions.

I designed a collapsible boom for my bulldozer, so that the blade could also be used as a crane. To build it, I had to steal material from the British Army. The material in their V-trestle was just the ticket. Realizing that most sentries, British and American, didn't know what they were looking at when an identification card was shown to them, I decided to write a trip ticket and pass it off as a legitimate reason for picking up the material.

"Hi mate," I greeted the English guard who stopped Browning and me. "We came to pick up some V-trestle pieces to use in training." He scanned the bogus identification paper, then motioned us into the sealed-off storage area. We loaded enough material for a couple of crane booms. As we passed the guard on our way out, we stopped and thanked him.

"Cheerio, mate!" he called back pleasantly.

"Righto, ta," I said.

Next day, we were building the boom when Colonel Clifford came by. He said, "John, isn't that V-trestle steel?"

There was no denying that it was, so I owned up and said, "Yup, it sure is."

"Where'd you get it?"

"We just went up to the storage site and took it. The guard didn't object at all," I said. "Do you want me to return it?"

"It's all cut up," he said. "You can't return it."

"We're almost finished with it now," I said.

"Go on and complete it, but, John, if you keep on this way you'll have us all court martialed."

He left shaking his head.

Toward the end of May we began a combat course to prepare for the coming invasion. One morning after breakfast we started out on a twenty-mile hike, reaching the bivouac area late in the day. It was in a beautiful, quiet Welsh forest, and after supper we laid out our blankets in anticipation of a good night's rest. Then we heard music coming toward us through the trees. To our extreme annoyance, our unit chaplain and his assistant, fresh as two daisies, had arrived in a truck with a portable organ.

"Come on, men, we're gonna have a prayer meeting." The chaplain, a southern Baptist, was intent on rousing us as his assistant played softly in the background.

"Ah, blow it!" Exhausted from our long hike, we weren't about to get up and listen to a holy roller.

"Ah want to impress on you all that you shouldn't be tempted by the ladies of the night," he said in his Alabama drawl. "Too many of you cannot resist the temptation, and you all have families at home to think about. Now, ah want you-all to know that my peckah gets just as hard as yours, and I resist temptation at all times."

Moans of disbelief issued from his congregation. Walt, lying next to me, said, "Listen to that bullshit. That hypocrite usually has a woman on his arm before the convoy stops."

Failing to get any attention, the pair picked up their organ and headed to the truck for their easy ride back. We rolled over in our blankets and tried once again to go to sleep, but before our tired backs could get used to the hard ground, the bugler blew reveille and the sergeants came along and told us to assemble in formation on the road in twenty minutes.

There was a lot of grumbling, but being good soldiers we did as we were ordered. Marching through the night, with short rests for piss call and smokes, we arrived back at camp by mid-morning. I had developed a varicose vein during the forced march, and the calf of my leg felt as if a hot poker was being driven in to it. We all wanted to break ranks and rest, but Lieutenant Mitchell had other ideas.

"Men, check your bazooka batteries. This is the real thing," he said.

We looked at each other and started laughing. We couldn't possibly check our bazooka batteries without firing a round that could kill somebody. The laughter embarrassed the lieutenant and we worried that he was rattled before he even got into battle.

Again, we were ordered to move out. Just a few hours after our forty-mile hike, exhausted and anxious about what was in store, we loaded our GI issue into trucks. We had orders not to take anything but official equipment with us, so we gave away our bicycles and whatever else we had acquired during our two years in Britain to the Porthcawl kids and their families. When night came, we drove away.

Browning and I spelled each other driving our truck, and the next day we were back at Wantage speculating just how close D-Day was. That night, C-47s pulled gliders overhead. Would our orders come in the morning? But the next day everything was as usual.

It was my day off, and I stopped by the Air Force repair shop to visit a buddy, Art, who said, "I hear through the grapevine that your outfit is hot." He meant that we were about to be deployed.

"Yeah, I'm sure we're close," I said. "This is June, and it would be a good month to go."

"Do you have a sleeping bag?"

"No, they haven't been issued to us yet. Our infantry packs are cumbersome as hell just as they are."

"I can get a guy to sew a mummy sack for you out of airplane fabric," Art said. "At least it will keep your blankets off the ground."

The night of June fifth, the gliders were up again, and by ten a.m. next morning the secret was out: our troops had landed in France. We were to follow two days later. Waterproofing our vehicles in case of a wet landing, we were again ordered to get rid of any excess baggage.

After supper, the officers brought a keg of beer into our hut. I was asked to dispense it and make sure no one got bent out of shape. This order was quite unnecessary because we were all feeling too solemn to drink much.

I was fairly sure I would never see Doris again because of reports that casualties from the landings were high. But though I longed to go back home to my wife and a normal life, I also wanted to participate in the upcoming beach party. I was still young and adventurous, and I had acquired many engineering skills that could be of invaluable help as our armies moved toward Berlin.

At twenty-one hundred hours the orderly came in and said our leaving time had been changed from four hundred hours to twenty-three hundred hours—within two hours—so we had to forget about sleep.

Browning and I spelled each other driving the Diamond T through the night to Portsmouth. Between the hot fumes from the newly waterproofed engine and the acrid smell of our long johns and O.D.s, which had been chemically treated to protect us from anticipated gas attacks, we were both sick by the time we arrived at our marshaling area. Half-poisoned with chemicals and exhausted from lack of sleep, we were about to fight a war!

England, 1942

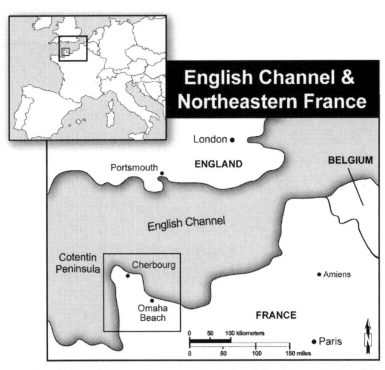

English Channel & Northeastern France

London •

ENGLAND

Portsmouth •

BELGIUM

English Channel

Cotentin Peninsula

Cherbourg •

• Amiens

Omaha Beach

FRANCE

| 0 | 50 | 100 kilometers |
| 0 | 50 | 100 | 150 miles |

• Paris

N

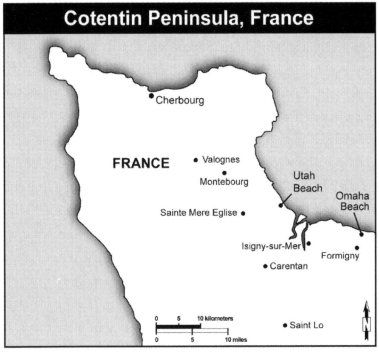

Cotentin Peninsula, France

Cherbourg •

FRANCE

• Valognes

• Montebourg

Utah Beach

Omaha Beach

Sainte Mere Eglise •

Isigny-sur-Mer •

• Formigny

• Carentan

| 0 | 5 | 10 kilometers |
| 0 | 5 | 10 miles |

• Saint Lo

N

172

Chapter 28

BEHIND ENEMY LINES

In Portsmouth, a little fresh air revived us, and by supper time we were getting hungry. The men who fed us were non-combatant Puerto Rican volunteers who did nothing else but bake and cook for transient troops. Browning and I were parked apart from the others on the side of a black-topped road when a couple of the volunteers arrived in a weapons carrier. They had large kettles of cooked food and huge loaves of white bread, jam and real butter. We asked if we could just have the bread, butter and jam— items we had not seen for the past two years. They were glad to give us anything we wanted, and handed us a large white loaf and the trimmings. Browning, a vegetarian, was even happier with our supper than I was.

After dinner, Browning made himself as comfortable as possible in the seat of the open cab, while I settled down on the canvas between two bows of the truck roof. My mind drifted between thoughts of home and whether or not we would make it on the Continent. Suddenly, the skies opened up and drenched us—so we suffered a third sleepless night.

The next afternoon we removed the fan belts from my bulldozer and Browning's Diamond T, so they could operate underwater if necessary. Now part of the 1st Army, we boarded LST 1087 at Portsmouth. The Navy fed us our "last supper" of creamed chicken and asparagus, something we had not seen since leaving the States "Here, get in line ahead of me," I said to a young sailor who was standing nearby. "I have all night to wait, so I'm in no hurry."

"We don't eat that shit," he responded with disdain. "After we dump you guys off on the beach, we'll eat steaks."

I was envious: steaks, white bread, and a bunk with sheets. If it wasn't for my chronic motion sickness, I'd have preferred the Navy. After supper, we were lying on the deck, talking quietly or thinking about what was ahead for us, when the young company clerk came by with a shoe-box full of condoms.

"Okay, you guys, take some," he said, embarrassed.

Al, who apparently wasn't interested in women other than his wife, said, "You've gotta be kidding!"

"Captain's orders," replied the clerk.

"What the hell do we need these for?" Steve asked.

"You can pull one over your head and look like a dressed-up hard-on," Al quipped.

"Only a prick like you would recognize one." Steve was not in the mood for jokes.

"Blow it out your ass," Al hollered back.

"Look guys, we're all uptight. Let's knock it off," Lou, the platoon sergeant ordered.

"Ah'll take some," Scotty said in his slow Mississippi drawl. "Maybe there'll be one of them thar French *madmazoos* on the beach, and I'll get me a piece of French ass."

"This ain't gonna be that kind of a beach party," I said, dampening Scotty's hopes. "Listen, guys, while I was at waterproofing school, I discovered a great use for rubbers. You can pull one over the end of your rifle barrel to keep it dry. You don't have to worry about taking it off because you can shoot right through it; it won't affect your aim."

I reached into the box for a whole handful of rubbers because I could imagine many uses for them in the field. Taking my watch off I dropped it into a condom, knotted it, and dropped it into my breast pocket with the end sticking out. I kept the watch that way for the next three months, reading the time through the sheer latex.

Shortly after dark, we cast off in total blackout. The deck became colder and wetter as the night dew settled down upon us. Everything was silent except for the rumble of the slow-turning diesel engine. Everyone was doubtless thinking of the possibility of getting killed in the next few days, me included.

To break the somber quiet Ed said, "Well, I can just see my wife going down the street with a ten-thousand-dollar insurance check in one hand and a new man on the other." The old joke did not seem very funny that night.

At daybreak our landing craft was in the lead, with another LST about five hundred feet directly behind us. Mid-morning the quiet of anticipation was broken by a heavy explosion muffled by water. The LST off our stern had been struck amidships by a mine. Listing in the wake from our boat, she rolled onto her starboard side.

"Do you have any casualties?" our captain hollered through a megaphone.

"Some," the other commander called back, "but we can handle it. We're taking on water, but I believe we can stay afloat."

"The tide will be right to unload in about three hours," our skipper shouted. "Come alongside us and we'll beach our boats together."

The French coast loomed into view and the moment we had anticipated and dreaded for two years was here at last. But, if anything, it was an anticlimax. The heavens did not open to reveal the face of God. The skies were not raining fire on us, and neither were the Germans. Instead, the day seemed like any other. The sun was shining, the water was calm, and all ashore was quiet.

As our LST nosed gently onto Omaha Beach, the Allied code name for this part of the Normandy coast, I thought, "Is this what we've been getting ready for?" Off to either side of us were giant steel tripods placed by the Germans to make invasion difficult, but straight ahead our beached bow opened freely to friendly white sand. Eager to be the first one ashore even though it was not a particularly valorous act under the circumstances, I ran down the ramp before anyone else, guiding Browning and his truck, my bulldozer in tow.

As it turned out, the waterproofing of our vehicles had been completely unnecessary, and we now moved on to a work area to de-waterproof them, ready for land travel. Working quickly through the day, we drank Nescafé with cold water but did not feel like eating our K rations. Evening found us exhausted, but yet another sleepless night was to come.

Immediately after dark, the Luftwaffe came over and all hell broke loose. A battery of 90-mm anti-aircraft guns off to the side of us started firing, the blast lifting us right off the ground. Flak began falling like rain around us, and a GI who had been bent over the engine on his truck hollered, "I've been hit." Fortunately, he was not wounded badly, having taken a piece of falling flak in the cheek of his ass. We led him over to a medic's tent across the hedgerow, where he was treated and—lucky guy—scheduled for evacuation.

Browning and I caught up with the rest of our unit outside of Isigny, about ten miles southwest of Omaha Beach. As we passed through the village, people waved to us. Most seemed pretty friendly, although we still had to be on our guard as we were subjected to occasional sniper fire. Obviously a few Nazi collaborators still remained on the loose.

Making camp outside of town, we set up our 20-mm cannon in the middle of a small farmyard. We were spreading the camouflage net over it when an ME 109 swooped down. Our response made the Three Stooges look like amateurs. Trying to man the gun in a hurry, our guys became tangled up in the net and fell over one another. Fortunately, one of our Thunderbolts was right on the Jerry's tail and drove the German plane straight into the ground. The gunners never did get their little cannon to fire, which was probably just as well because they might have hit the Thunderbolt.

For the most part, our foxholes were already dug for us, thanks to the centuries-old drainage ditches on the perimeter of each field. The most we had to do was a little deepening or widening in order to make a space for sleeping. On one side of each ditch, hedgerows of hazelnut, willow and other wild brush grew out of rocks from the fields that had been stacked into walls about three feet high. These walls afforded us protection against enemy fire, but they could be breached with a steady stream of machine gun fire when the infantry needed to get through during an attack.

Sleep was impossible after the air attack. We were too revved up to relax, and when our commander ordered the bugler to sound reveille at daybreak, he played to a wide-awake audience.

General Hodges suddenly appeared from across the lane and chewed out our company commander.

"What in the hell do you think you're doing?! Don't you know the German line is just fifteen hundred feet up ahead. If you're gonna win this war with a goddam bugle, I'll pull my division out, and you can take over!"
I didn't hear another bugle for the next sixteen months.

Later that same morning Browning, Cramoga and I were sent back to Omaha Beach to clear away the remaining steel tripods and mines. We had barely started when Captain Dixon came and told us to go to Carentan, ten miles away, and fill bomb craters so the tanks could get through.

I was dubious. "Captain," I said, "we heard that Carentan was lost again during the night."

"Well, I don't know anything about that," he said. "I just know what our time schedule says, and that means you go to Carentan and fill craters. I'll catch up with you guys later this afternoon."

Carentan was a vital point for both sides as it provided the only road connection between the Omaha and Utah beach-heads. These were otherwise separated by a river estuary, so whoever controlled the road controlled the strategic Cotentin Peninsula of Normandy.

Browning, Cramoga and I drove off, map in hand, trailing the dozer behind the truck. About five miles down the road we arrived in a place called Formigny and were baffled as to which of the several roads radiating from the town square led to Carentan. There were no signs, but in the very center of the square stood a large wooden cross draped with both German and American communications wires. I stood before it, feeling stunned. Somehow, somewhere I had seen this place and this cross before. Perhaps the stress of actually being in the war had thrown me into an altered state of consciousness, or perhaps I had had a precognitive dream, but whatever the reason for the déjà vu, I knew this place—and I knew beyond any doubt which road led to our destination.

The Germans had blown up the Carentan bridge, but US army engineers had replaced it with two temporary structures: a pontoon bridge and a Bailey bridge. As we approached an MP waved us to a stop, then immediately took shelter next to a high stone wall. Uncannily, within seconds an 88 shell exploded just ahead of us, hitting the pontoon bridge and sinking it, leaving the single-track Bailey bridge for access between the two beach-heads.

"How in the hell did you know that was coming?" I said.

"Just stand here quietly," he said, "and you'll see."

A few minutes later we felt the earth shaking, and the MP said, "Get behind the wall—we've got seven or eight seconds!"

It turned out that the guy either heard or felt the concussion when the Germans fired one of their many 88s at the bridge, and he knew how long it took the shell to arrive. In between times he directed traffic across the bridge. From his example, I gained a lot of respect for combat MPs. Theirs had to be one of the most nerve-wracking jobs in the army.

Between shells, we crossed over into Carentan and got our first view of death and destruction up close. A couple of Frenchmen were throwing dirt on the bodies of two dead American paratroopers. Nearby, the dead GIs' rifles had been stuck into the ground and their helmets placed on top. As we stared at the scene, the Frenchmen acknowledged four dead comrades, and then casually asked us for cigarettes. They each took two, lighting up one and saving the other behind an ear for later.

177

A couple of blocks further on, we saw some airborne guys in a skirmish line. Their medics had armed themselves in retaliation for the Germans firing at men with medic armbands. The GIs spread out to let us through, and a short distance after that we found ourselves in the middle of enemy fire. We jumped out of the truck into a hole near the church, and I worked my way back on foot to the paratroopers.

"What's going on here?" I said, more than a little pissed off.

"The Germans are all over the place! That's what's going on up here," one GI said.

"We were told that you guys had taken Carentan."

"That was yesterday. We lost it again during the night."

"What in the hell did you let us go through for?"

"We thought you were going to win the war all by yourself," a wise ass responded.

There was nothing for me to do but return to Browning and Cramoga, and figure a way to get our equipment out from behind enemy lines. Unable to turn around in the narrow old streets, we decided to continue on through the town. A Frenchman pushing a cartload of dead civilians got in the way. In desperation we hollered at him, motioning him off the street. Continuing on, we bore left as we worked our way back to our line. Cramoga and I fired steadily from the cab as Browning drove us down what seemed to be an unending half-mile of French street. Miraculously, we got ourselves and our equipment safely back over the bridge, where we awaited the arrival of Captain Dixon.

I blew my stack when he showed up. "We were behind enemy lines!"

He said, without expression, "Sorry, I had bad information."

The airborne GIs re-took Carentan, after which Browning, Cramoga and I crossed the bridge into the town once again, this time accompanied by the captain and his driver. I set to work filling the bomb craters with my dozer as Cramoga covered me against incoming enemy fire. It was unnerving as hell to see a building less than a hundred feet away get hit by an 88 and come crumbling down.

After spending the night back in our foxholes at Isigny, we returned to Carentan the next day to fill shell craters by the railroad station. I had barely got started when the Germans zeroed in on us again, and an 88 exploded on the bank above showering us with dirt.

After this an ME 109 came down the track strafing us, and we dove into a bomb crater near some airborne guys who had dug in. When things calmed down, a couple of the paratroopers came over and shared a bottle of Calvados with us.

This was France, after all, so there was plenty of liquor available. As it turned out, our lieutenant dealt with the pressures of command and the constant shelling by escaping into the bottle. Constantly drunk, he left us to deal with each situation as best we could. Still a small unit with no parent outfit, we felt more than ever like "the forgotten bastards."

Since our prime objective was to open the roads and repair the railroad to Cherbourg, on the northwestern coast of the Cotentin Peninsula, Lou, Al and I were asked next to see what could be done to repair a blown-up railroad bridge. As soon as we got there, Germans opened fire from some houses behind us. With no cover nearby, we flattened out on the ground. Slugs hit the dirt three feet from my face, but got no closer. We figured the Jerries were too nervous to take good aim, because when we decided to run a couple of hundred feet for cover they failed to hit us. A few minutes later a squad of newly arrived infantry swept in and cleaned the Germans out of the houses, where they had been holed up in the company of French collaborators.

As the battle for control of Carentan continued to rage, a terrible storm blew up in the Channel, making it impossible for the Allies to land supplies or armor. When we asked why more Allied shots were not being fired at the Jerries, we were told the Airborne was almost out of ammunition. They were limited to one 75 mm Howitzer round a day. "One shot a day! How can we win a war this way?" we despaired. If the Germans had counter-attacked at this point, they surely could have pushed us back into the water.

Grim as the situation was, it was not without its humor. Or perhaps it would be more accurate to say that under great stress we found that laughter was the only way to deal with situations that would have been repulsive in ordinary circumstances. We had just arrived at the work site when a Messerschmit 109 flew low overhead, strafing us. Everyone but a guy named Stookey took cover behind a stone wall. Stookey flattened out in the garden which, unknown to him, the Jerries had used for a toilet. Hagen, who was with us behind the wall, started shooting at the ME 109 and as the spent cartridges flew out of his M-1, they hit Stookey in the back. Stookey was sure he was being hit by slugs and buried his face deeper and deeper into the crap. When it was over, he stood up dripping with shit, and the rest of us laughed until we cried.

Everyone had one extra set of clothes, and since Stookey had no alternative but to change his, the rest of us decided to follow suit. Our chemically treated underwear had smelled more sickening with every passing day. As we peeled it off, we just hoped the Germans wouldn't use gas—and if they did, we would put our old duds back on, charge back across enemy lines, and overwhelm them with the fumes.

Normandy, July 1944

Chapter 29

DAGO JOHN, R.I.P.

As the battle for the Cotentin Peninsula continued, two platoons of our company were ordered to move on to the port of Cherbourg at the head of the peninsula. Signs of battle were everywhere as we wound our way through the devastated countryside. St. Mère Eglise was shattered and crumbled; Montebourg was burning on both sides of the road.

We stopped at Valognes where we were to secure the railroad station before continuing to Cherbourg. The infantry was already dug in when we arrived, so all we had to do was take up our positions. Scotty, the Mississippi Don Juan, had yet to find his "*madmazoo*," but he discovered a basement under a café near the station that was full of assorted wines and liquors—and he shared his prizes generously. By the time the shelling started, Torgerson was passed out under the stairway, so drunk that when plaster fell on him, he didn't rouse. About that time a battalion of tanks came by to support the advancing infantry, and as they passed us, we handed each tanker five or six bottles of spoils to buoy up their spirits.

A short while later, Al, Lou, and I got into the railroad office and found a safe full of paper money. The decision was made that I would take all of it, and we would divide it later. Throwing my gas mask away, I filled the empty case with bills and put the rest of them in my raincoat pockets.

That afternoon a Frenchman came up to me with his daughter. As an Italian-speaker I was able to understand some French also, and I had no trouble comprehending as the man told me that two GIs had held him at gunpoint while they took turns raping his fifteen-year-old daughter. He wanted me to find the men, but the best I could do was tell Lieutenant Mitchell, who simply shrugged his shoulders. Such things happen in wartime, and there was nothing he could do in this case as he had no information to go on.

The Army considered rape a serious crime, nevertheless, and some of the 142 U.S. military executions carried out in Europe during the war were for rape. These aren't much spoken about even today, but when we got to Cherbourg we received a communique that read, "Hangman wanted.

181

Tech-sergeant rating. Preferably experienced." It was signed by General Eisenhower and I understood the meaning more fully the day we moved into the Cherbourg navy yard to raise a scuttled German battle ship. On the dock was a structure that looked like a hangman's scaffold. A day later, another scaffold was erected.

"Do you want to watch the hangings on Saturday?" Walt asked.

"No thanks," I said. "I've seen enough dying."

These incidents were offset by occasional moments of spiritual redemption. In Cherbourg, we bivouacked with the infantry on Tourlaville Hill overlooking the harbor. Thousands of Germans who had surrendered in Normandy were kept next to us behind a huge and hastily-built barbed wire enclosure. Among them were about five thousand Russians from the Georgian area, whom the Germans had captured and brought to the coast to build Hitler's Atlantic defenses. At night these men sang in a great unaccompanied chorus, filling the evening air with what we could only imagine were sad love songs and melancholy longings for home. The sonorous beauty of their voices raised us temporarily above and beyond the ugliness of war.

The Germans had completely demolished the port of Cherbourg, blowing up all possible moorings in the inner harbor, as well as loading small boats with concrete and sinking them in the locks to render them useless. The town was also darkened with what we had come to call "the war cloud." For days we had noticed that wherever a bitter battle had taken place, a heavy gray cloud would linger directly above the scene. Maybe there was a scientific explanation for it, to do with the chemicals of heavy bombardment.

One morning Walt and I decided to take a look in one of the huge pillboxes above the harbor. As we entered, we could still feel the heat from the flame throwers, and a mess remained inside. Suddenly, the war cloud overhead opened and poured down a deluge of rain. The pillbox turret took a direct hit! Walt was ahead of me as we started up the stairs, which were flowing by now with a mixture of rainwater and blood. Reaching the landing, where the machine guns rested mute in their slits, Walt called back to me, "Do you want a souvenir, Johnny?'"

Before I could respond, he handed me a glove with a severed hand in it. "Walt, you bastard," I muttered, dropping the thing in disgust. "Those guys are all dead and I feel sick." I barely made it outside to fresh air.

I was assigned in Cherbourg to help Navy experts uncover large sea mines that hadn't exploded when the Germans demolished the town's main dock. This had been a steel and masonry structure with a beautiful copper roof. I was told the work involved "very little danger"—though as I was dragging the first mine out of the rubble as gently as possible with my bulldozer, I suddenly realized that the rest of the demolition team and the photographers had retreated to a safe distance.

I worked all day dragging mines out of the rubble, and at the end of it I was the only guy who didn't get a medal for doing a job under hazardous conditions. Our lieutenant, who would have been the one to recommend me for the commendation, was off looking for alcohol.

After an evening meal of K-rations, Walt and I felt like a beer ourselves, and decided to walk down the tree-lined road from our camp to a small café. We carried our rifles slung over our shoulders because there were still a few snipers around. The café was a small room, part of the proprietor's home, and just large enough for two tables with chairs and a shelf that served as bar. One of our men, Gromaski, had got there ahead of us and was drunk. Leaning against the bar, he grabbed at the pre-teen daughter of the owner as she passed to take the orders of four GIs—two paratroopers and two infantry men—sitting at one of the tables.

Walt and I ordered a glass of wine each, and watched the girl as she went back to the bar. The drunk Gromaski grabbed at her again and tried to kiss her. Walt and I felt disgusted and ashamed, but the girl's parents didn't seem to object to the guy's advances. The little waitress brought us our wine, which we paid for with our invasion money—the first chance we'd had to spend any of it.

At the other table the paratroopers and the infantry men were getting louder and louder in their argument over who had contributed more to the success of the campaign, the airborne or the infantry. All four were pretty well oiled and they grew increasingly abusive toward one another as the argument heated up. Walt and I figured seven armed GIs in a room not more than twelve feet square was at least two too many, and it was time for us to get out. Quickly downing our wine, we left the arguers with Gromaski and the French family.

We had gone about three hundred feet up the road when we heard a shot from the café and knew the best thing we could do was get back to camp. An hour or so later, our battalion adjutant led a staggering Gromaski to his fox hole, admonishing him not to leave the area for any reason.

Two days later, Walt, Gromaski and I were called, one at a time, as witnesses before a court martial board, from whom we learned that one of the paratroopers had shot and killed one of the infantrymen—as if the Germans weren't enough of an enemy.

Lou, Al and I had not gotten together since we found the money back at Valognes, but we managed to do so in Cherbourg. I was tired of carrying the money around, so we went down into one of the big pillboxes to divide our spoils. Just outside the entrance, a jeep passed us with a half dozen dead GIs piled on the back, arms and legs hanging askew. Once inside, we sat down on the steps, and peering down into the darkness, we could barely make out two Germans lying face down in a few inches of water. Not even this grisly sight deterred us from our self-serving assignment.

Because we had so much money, we decided to throw all the two-franc notes (worth about five cents), down the stairs, where they floated around among the dead enemy. We had almost finished dividing up the remainder when a couple of quartermaster GIs looked in and asked if there were any dead men in the pillbox.

"At least two," Al said.

When the GIs spotted the money, they forgot all about the corpses in their watery grave and began splashing around gathering up bills and shouting with glee. War had hardened us all.

Lou, Al and I ended up with more than two hundred dollars apiece. We were unable to send money home, but we could buy money orders made out to ourselves. I saved one hundred dollars in case I lost my bet to Collier that we would be home by next Christmas. At this point, it looked as though he was going to win.

Soon after we advanced into Cherbourg, the general commanding the Corps of Engineers came to inspect his troops, and there was a ceremony on the back of a truck bed. We were called together to see him receive a medal for being exposed to the enemy above and beyond the call of duty.

Most of us had gotten to Cherbourg three days ahead of him, but no commendations came our way.

Jack Doyle got something—though not a medal. Jack, Walt and I were sent to a beautiful estate owned by a French general near the town of Barfleur, on the northeast point of the peninsula. The estate was set deep in the woods at the end of a winding lane. We were to cut trees to be used for dock piling.

One afternoon, Jack came to Walt and me after taking a piss. He looked painfully worried.

"Hey guys, I got something wrong with my pecker, and I don't know what the hell it is," he said.

"The hell you have!" Perhaps he had contracted some horrible disease. "Let's have a look."

Embedded on the end of his circumcised peter was the biggest, fattest wood tick I had ever seen. How it could have burrowed in so deep without Jack's knowledge, I never understood until years later when I learned that ticks inject an anesthetic as they dig in. The scene seemed hilariously funny, as it occurred to me that anybody seeing Walt and me inspecting Jack's pecker would wonder what in the hell was going on.

"Better not try to pull him out," I advised. "He's dug in deep."

By then, Walt and I were laughing ourselves sick. Poor old Jack couldn't see the humor in the situation, but it was his body part that was afflicted.

"What am I going to do," he asked pathetically.

"Why don't you shake it a couple of times?" I suggested. "Or maybe you can shoot the little bastard off."

In the end we took Jack to Air Force headquarters, where a medic took a look at him. Walt and I gave the medic all the advice we could, including suggestions of amputation. When the medic left—presumably to get surgical instruments—poor Jack was in anguish. When the medic returned with a pair of tweezers, Walt and I decided we should knock off the teasing because Jack had gone through enough. We watched relatively sober-faced as the medic lit a cigarette and put the hot end to the blood-engorged body of the tick. The creature relaxed his grip at once, and the medic deftly pulled him out with the tweezers. Jack—and his penis—had survived and we thought afterwards that he should have gotten a medal for bravery above and beyond the call of duty.

Chapter 29

**

We returned to wood-gathering, loaded a trailer with logs, and were waiting for Browning to return with the truck when we decided to explore the general's chateau. It had been used by the upper echelon Wehrmacht, so we knew we had better be careful as the Germans always left thousands of anti-personnel bombs scattered in their wake. These were small devices that looked much like cans of Carter's Liver Pills, and, sure enough, there were hundreds of them lying around all over the grounds and among anything that we might want as a souvenir.

Fortunately, we had learned a few tips from one of best the guys in our unit, Sergeant George Brown. He had done a stint in the Army in peacetime and had volunteered for this war. He was single, loved soldiering, and was especially good at deactivating mines and booby traps. The Germans had taken a lot of pains to booby-trap a fine old house at a strategic point on the English Channel near Cherbourg. They had buried Teller mines in the concrete driveway, covering them with a thin layer of cement so they would not be detected.

We had discovered this maze of booby trips with our mine detectors, and Dogface Brown, as we had affectionately nicknamed George, volunteered to disarm them. This extremely hazardous task accomplished, he went on into the house where even the wooden stair treads had to be deactivated. In all, he removed one hundred thirty-eight traps.

Walt, Jack and I did not bother disarming the Liver Pill mines in this new chateau, but at least we knew what to look for and, we hoped, how to avoid getting blown up. The house was filled with treasures that included the largest and most ornate grand piano I have ever seen. In the basement we found many large chests filled with sterling silver flatware. Regretfully, we realized we probably could not get it home. When Walt reached into one of the chests, he came up with two gold medallions, each at least a quarter of an inch thick by three inches in diameter. My French was pretty good by that time, and the inscriptions on them indicated the medals had been awarded in the 1800s to a baroness for her support of the aristocracy during one of the French revolutions. In any case, they were prizes that Walt could easily carry on his person—and he figured they were the closest thing to a medal he was ever going to get.

**

Back in Cherbourg, our unit was assembling a row of stiff legs (a type of derrick) on a long concrete dock, so barges of materials could be tied up and unloaded. One day when I did not have to work, I decided simply to wander about the town to look at the damage. Finding a small café serving food, I accepted an invitation to sit with two airborne lieutenants, because there were no other tables available. A few minutes later another guy from our unit, Stevens, came in. He was drunk as hell and took the only chair he could find—the one remaining at our table.

"How the hell are all you Dagos making it?" he asked, looking at me and slurring his words as he spoke.

"Just fine," I said, not wanting to make a scene.

The two airborne officers saw that I was both angry and embarrassed by this uninvited drunk who was ruining dinner for all of us. Without finishing our eggs and fried potatoes, the three of us left. My parting words to Stevens were, "I'll see you in camp."

The more I thought about Stevens, the madder I got, but I wanted to be sure he was sober when I talked to him. The following morning I picked up my M-1, and confronted him as he sat on the edge of his foxhole. "Steve, if you ever mention one more word about Dagos, I'll blow your fucking head off," I said, holding the barrel of my rifle to his head. "You're sober now, and I just want to be sure you understand what I'm saying."

"I didn't mean you," he whimpered. "I meant all of the others."

"Well, I mean it for all of us."

Stevens never mentioned Dagos again—at least, not in front of me. That may also have been the last time I reacted so angrily to negative comments about my Italian heritage.

One morning I slipped out of my foxhole bedroll to find a makeshift cross with a dog-tag and a sign announcing "Dago John R.I.P." For the first time, I was able to laugh at a taunt about my background. Later, when a shipping crate became my apartment, I welcomed the sign "Dago John's Place" put up by some of the guys.

As the war dragged on, I grew more confident of my abilities and less sensitive to what others thought of me. In the tangle of death and violence, I was growing as a human being—and to be called "Dago John," was no longer a slur but a sign of camaraderie.

**

As the Allies cut across the Cotentin Peninsula, it was strategically important for them to take St. Lo before fanning out to secure the Breton peninsula. St. Lo was about twenty miles from Cherbourg, and at five o'clock one morning in late July we could feel the ground rumble as heavy bombers circled overhead, waiting their turn to drop their deadly cargo on the German-held French village. That day twenty-four hundred sorties were flown, with some planes returning to England for a second load. Every available artillery piece fired until dark, and the famous St. Lo breakthrough was successful. The price was high, however. Smoke markers were dropped in the wrong places, and some of our own men were killed by mistake.

Afterwards, the battleship *Texas* was brought into Cherbourg to be used as a power generator and tie into the land grid, while we engineers were assigned to rebuild the power transmission line to St. Lo. The line ran directly through an area where many of the unfortunate GIs had died, and Bourkman, one of our unit, spent his off-duty hours drying American banknotes on strings in our bivouac area at Pont Hebert. When questioned about where the money had come from, Bourkman admitted to a ghoulish routine: whenever he came upon dead soldiers, he went through their pockets.

Stringing a cable across a valley, we discovered many German bodies in a small stream that was the source of our drinking water. Fortunately, we had a water purification unit that treated all drinking and cooking water. It was easier to remove the dead than to find a new source of water.

Replacement of the towers was well underway. Ed had been a steeplejack back in the States and felt right at home in a bosun's chair. Tony was good at steel work, and Walt was just plain versatile. We decided among ourselves what each would do and then did it.

One day we were pulling the slack out of the war-weary cable when it broke. I was sighting the sag in the line from inside one of the steel towers as three adjacent towers folded like dominoes toward me. The tower I was in folded about ten feet above my head, and I climbed down unhurt, but more hesitant than ever about steel work.

The power line was eventually completed, and then we were allowed to rest for a few days, until a field evacuation hospital fresh from the States moved into the outskirts of Isigny. Now, we began working around the clock to build a surgical hut. The building progressed nicely, but winter was coming on and the nurses' tents were all but adrift in mud. We helped out by recycling their wooden packing crates, using them for sidewalks, floors and side walls. The nurses were not allowed to socialize with GIs, but they showed their appreciation by giving us their liquor rations.

I worked night shifts on the surgical hut, which allowed me to practice my French with local people during the day. Young children, like my new friends Maxim and Leona, were most helpful because their vocabulary was simple, and they were patient. I didn't realize they were hungry, however, until I saw them pick food out of our garbage cans. Then I talked to Captain Dixon about giving them our untouched leftovers, for which they and their families were very grateful. Remembering my own hunger when I was a kid in Brooklyn, I was glad to be able to help them.

I was also coming to recognize the common humanity of people, beyond nameless faces and the anonymity of uniforms. When a convoy of badly wounded prisoners was brought in and laid in rows on the floor of a receiving tent, many of them begged us for cigarettes. We were forbidden to associate in any way with these men, but knowing that they were suffering terrible pain and would probably die, we decided to ignore the rules. In our growing compassion, we would light cigarettes and drop them on the floor near their litters so they could pick them up. I liked to think they would have done the same for us had the situation been reversed.

After much bloody fighting, Paris was finally liberated on August 25, 1944. It was De Gaulle's day, and GIs were not permitted to enter the city until the Free French Forces had led the way. We were angry because we wanted to join in the celebrations in the fabled City of Light that we had helped to liberate.

I was called into the orderly tent at this time, and Captain Dixon asked if I knew where Walt was.

He said, "He's been missing since yesterday."

"Maybe he's been blown up by a mine." Walt was an avid trophy scavenger. "Or maybe he bummed a ride to Paris."

"Do you think he'd go when he knows it's off limits?"

"I sure as hell do. We're this close and we can't go. I wouldn't blame him if he did. I know he's not interested in women, but he wants to see the sights."

"That's all, John," the captain said. "I just hope he isn't dead."

Walt showed up about 3 o'clock that afternoon. He never revealed where he had been, and no disciplinary action was taken against him. I think Walt simply did what the rest of us wanted to do, and Captain Dixon forgave the transgression because Walt was otherwise a very good and dedicated soldier.

Chapter 30

A CHRISTMAS PRAYER

From Cherbourg-St. Lo, we were sent on to Valenciennes, near the Belgian border, to clear mines at a Luftwaffe airfield. This was a nerve-wracking detail, made worse by the fact that winter was upon us. Every day I could see my hundred-buck bet that we would be home by Christmas slipping away to Captain Collier.

Then the Germans launched a surprise offensive campaign in the nearby Ardennes forest. Now known as the Battle of the Bulge, this was a last-ditch attempt to salvage their war effort, and it ultimately cost them huge numbers of men, tanks and aircraft which they were no longer able to replace. But it was costly for the Allies too, and those of us who were able-bodied were reassigned to help in the fight. Disabled and older men were left behind to guard our equipment.

A quartermaster outfit picked us up from Valenciennes, and we rode all day and night huddled together for warmth in the open vehicles. At daybreak when we stopped to refuel the trucks and eat our cold K-rations, we saw a greeting between a Frenchman and a Frenchwoman that sent us into gales of laughter. Parked in front of two farms separated by a barbed wire fence, we watched as the gentleman farmer and his neighbor walked toward us through their respective fields. Apparently they were going to see what was going on with our parked trucks, but, first, they would greet each other.

The man got to the fence first, and as he waited for the woman, he unbuttoned his pants and began to piss. She continued to approach cheerfully, offering her hand to him across the fence when she arrived. He reached out with his left hand since his right hand was busy, never once slowing down the stream of pee that hit the ground near their feet. They shook hands heartily, obviously very glad to see each other.

"*Bonjour, Madame, Bonjour, Monsieur,*" I called out to them.

"*Bonjour, Bonjour,*" they both replied, smiling back at us.

We were more than smiling; we were hysterical.

"Help him out, Madame," Ed hollered brashly in English.

I'm sure they did not understand what he said, but they laughed along with us.

This small interlude helped us through the rest of the day. By dark we had arrived at the Meuse River, and were split up into two groups. I was sent to a large room in a two-story building with about fifty others. As we stretched out on the floor to sleep, families of refugees traipsed around us into adjoining rooms.

Before morning we learned that the Germans had broken through our lines, and we were to take up defensive positions on the other side of the Meuse River west of Bastogne. We were now infantrymen!

Two hundred Free French guerillas came up to reinforce us. Dressed in all sorts of ragtag clothing, the only items they had in common were berets and automatic weapons.

As we patrolled in the bitter cold, our C-rations and the water in our canteens froze, even though we carried them close to our bodies. We froze as well—in fear—as we crossed the Meuse River into no-man's land, tracer bullets streaking the sky overhead in both directions. Our concern was not only the Germans but also the trigger-happy guerillas who were liable to pop out from behind a tree or rock and shoot us in error. The Luftwaffe knew where we were, and every night in the light of the moon a German pilot flying a Junker 88 would swoop down and strafe us. We dubbed him "Bed Check Charlie," and when the moon darkened, he no longer came. Some weeks later, when Browning returned to our unit after being hospitalized, he reported that "Bed Check Charlie" had been shot down and was a patient in the bed next to him.

Before we knew it, Christmas had come again, and I had lost my hundred-dollar bet to Captain Collier. But I felt a little better when General Eisenhower announced that every GI in the European theater would have a turkey dinner. However, to the dismay of our cooks, the four birds that arrived had been chewed by rats. The chefs trimmed the ragged edges and made arrangements with the local baker to roast them in exchange for some GI rations.

As our Christmas dinner was roasting, two Belgian nuns appeared at our living quarters and invited us to a special service to be held by the village priest.

"I'm not going," I said. Months of living in foxholes had failed to cure me of atheism. "I'm not religious. I'd feel like a hypocrite."

Al said this didn't matter. "Come on, John. If the priest is going to the trouble of a special service for us, we should go."

"It won't hurt you, John. Just come along," Lou said.

I gave in and followed them to the church on the stipulation that we would all pray only one prayer—that our planes would come through and stop the Germans.

As we crossed the street under low gray skies, the town crier rang his bell to announce the special Christmas service. But the only people who entered the small stone church were we four GIs and three nuns in white-winged hats. The church was dark except for the dim light coming from the recessed windows and a few flickering candles. Kneeling down, we prayed for the planes to get through—at least I did, and I hoped the others were keeping their promise.

Ten minutes into the service, we heard the drone of bombers in the distance. My heart flickered like the candles at the altar, and I tilted my head and listened. For a moment I was in harmony with something mysterious in the universe, and I knew then that I would get through the war alive, just as the planes would get through. The experience was like that at Formigny, when I knew with inexplicable certainty which road to take.

Hours later, we learned that our planes had been able to drop their bombs on the enemy through an opening in the clouds that presented itself at the very time we were praying. By then the wonder of the feeling of oneness with the universe had passed, and I was back to analyzing the situation with my twentieth-century mind. It had to be coincidence that the clouds opened at that precise time on that particular Christmas Day. Clouds don't respond to prayer, and it wasn't enough to restore me to "Katholicism." Nevertheless, it was an experience I have never forgotten.

As the winter wore on, the cold became even more brutal, and so did our feelings toward anyone who shirked their duty. A soldier who failed to show up to relieve his man at the forward observation post wasn't just AWOL, he was considered a deserter. Captain Dixon wanted to execute on the spot a twenty year-old who failed to show up on time, but other officers intervened at his court martial hearing, and he was given a five-year sentence—a high price to pay for a night in bed with a local mademoiselle.

The Germans were dropping paratroopers behind our lines. After patrolling all night we would have barely laid down to rest before we were sent out again to hunt the enemy. Frightened, exhausted and suspicious, I almost shot two of our own men who approached on a motorcycle and did not heed my warning to halt. The driver was a Canadian paratrooper whose headgear looked much like a German helmet; his passenger was a friend of mine, although I did not immediately recognize him in the dark. They did not stop until I aimed my gun at them, and they realized I meant business. The Canadians were laying mines in the area, and the guy driving the bike was coming to borrow an air compressor from us to drill the frozen ground.

Perpetually cold and fatigued, we were beginning to fall ill, but the situation was desperate. The order came out that no soldier could report for sick call if he was ambulatory. That same morning I found Lou lying bundled up in blankets on the floor of his quarters.

"The Captain says you are to take a detail across the river," I said, kneeling down beside him.

"I'm sick, Johnny. I'm too sick to go," Lou said, shivering noticeably beneath his covers.

When I reported back to Captain Dixon he retorted, "What the hell's the difference if he dies here or on the other side of the river?"

Perhaps it was rage at the heartless response, but Lou found the wherewithal to pick himself up from the floor and do as he was ordered. But he vowed to kill the captain. "If that son-of-a-bitch comes across the river, I guarantee he won't come back alive."

A few days later we were reinforced by the 17th Airborne Division, which had been training in England for the Rhine River crossing. The German breakthrough in the Ardennes changed their plans and gave them a taste of battle sooner than expected. On occasion we would encounter some of these troops, who were also on patrol. One night I spotted a man in the darkness, and not knowing if he was a GI or not, I stuck my rifle barrel in his stomach and gave the password for the day. At the same time he stuck an automatic weapon in my belly.

"Clara," I spit out at him.

"Bow," he answered instantly, as happy as I was that we had not shot each other.

We were now in Belgium. I had been ill for two days, but managed to keep going. On our way to Antwerp in the northeast, I asked the driver to stop in La Louvière where the medical corps had set up a hospital in the university.

"You are a sick man," a medic said, shaking his head at my temperature of 105 degrees. "We'll get you into bed right away."

I not only had pneumonia, but a strep throat as well. Fortunately, penicillin and sulfur drugs were available and I began to feel better after a week or so. I learned then that I had been close to death.

"Hi, soldier!" a young nurse said one evening. "Your doctors thought they were going to lose you." She felt my forehead. "But you're gonna make it now for sure."

I noticed she was wearing a purple heart. She told me it had been awarded for her work at the Anzio Beachhead.

"We were under constant fire there," she said. "Just about everyone in our hospital unit was wounded at one time or another."

It occurred to me then that she was very attractive—another sign that I was getting better.

I said, "You are a living image of Joan Crawford."

She smiled, "I've been told that before."

From that time on, I addressed her as "Joan," never mind that she was a lieutenant and could have pulled rank on me. She was certainly more impressive than another lieutenant who was admitted as a patient with little more than a cold. Given a bed at the end of my row, he immediately began complaining about his lack of privacy.

He continued his hell-raising until the nurses hung blankets from the ceiling to partition him off.

"I guess he doesn't think he should be in a ward with us dogfaces," I said.

"We treat everyone the same," my nurse said. "Rank doesn't get special privilege here."

A couple of weeks later, I was astonished to see Captain Dixon standing beside my bed.

"Are you sick, too?" I queried, unable to believe that he would take the trouble to visit me.

"No, I'm not sick. This is the first chance I've had to catch up with you. I just wanted to know how you are doing," he replied. He handed me some mail and a carton of cigarettes, and I felt glad, after all, that Lou hadn't carried through with his threat to shoot the guy.

**

After five weeks of bed rest, I joined my unit in Antwerp. I was a little weak but happy to join up with the old gang. A couple of the guys were gone, having cracked up with the strain of working under constant shellfire, strafing and bombing. Those stresses, coming after we had been overseas for nearly two and a half years, were beginning to take their toll.

Antwerp was known as buzz bomb alley, as you could see and hear the V-1 bombs coming for a couple of miles. They looked like small fighter planes, hurtling toward us six or seven hundred feet above the ground. Since they were set to explode on impact, we had to sweat them out until they had passed overhead. Adding to our anxieties, the German radio propaganda artist Axis Sally interspersed her American music broadcasts with uncannily accurate predictions of each buzz bomb attack. Just as demoralizing, she knew our unit number and location.

One of our biggest jobs in Antwerp was to clean up the debris of a movie theater that had taken a direct hit from a buzz bomb. Hundreds of people were killed or injured, more than half of them Allied soldiers and other military personnel. We were among two hundred rescuers who labored for a week with bulldozers and other construction equipment, digging through the wreckage looking for bodies.

After this gruesome detail, we were sent from Antwerp to Herstal, on the outskirts of Liège on the Belgian-German border. There we were bivouacked in a comfortable brick schoolhouse. At nearby Neuville we were to complete a chapel at an American cemetery that took the overflow from Henri Chapel near the German border. The Neuville cemetery was situated on an old estate with tall poplar trees lining the narrow dirt lane that led to the graves. Here, Christian and Jewish GIs were laid to rest side by side. We had all fought for the same cause, and the graves gave me the feeling that part of me would be staying in Belgium also.

When the chapel was complete, a Christian cross was placed on the steeple. We thought we were finished, but a couple of days later we were ordered to remove the cross and replace it with the Star of David. That symbol was subsequently ordered removed, also. This switcheroo process continued for a couple of weeks, with every possible combination of symbols being tried. When the job finally came to an end, the steeple was bare, which made it non-denominational.

At this time I was given orders to move on—alone! No other member of my unit was to go with me.

Captain Dixon explained: "Base section headquarters needs someone who speaks French and drives a truck. You fill the bill, so you are to report to Lieutenant-Colonel Bianco in the morning."

I sensed that some intrigue was involved, as well as a change of pace. To whom would I be speaking French? Where and why would I be driving a truck? I could hardly wait for the next day to find out.

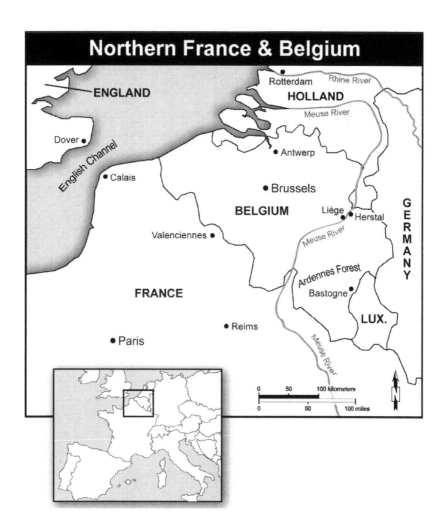

Chapter 31

THE HIGH LIFE

Reporting to Colonel Bianco, I found myself in a luxurious manor house that had been commandeered for American officers. When I arrived, I was shown to the basement, now a kitchen and dining room for the unit officers assigned there. Attractive Belgian women were serving breakfast, and as they poured coffee, they gave a peck on the cheek to each man. A few of the officers—obvious favorites—received even warmer kisses. I was surprised and envious that the officers lived in such luxury, and in the company of such charming women who were apparently eager to cater to their every need. The thought ran through my mind that a lot of the officers would not have enjoyed that sort of high living back in the States.

After breakfast Colonel Bianco took me to his office and gave me orders to report to the Givet Furniture Factory for any duties that were required. The factory had been damaged by a buzz-bomb attack; I was to help get it back into production, under the direction of the factory owners, the Savoie family.

Monsieur Savoie was nattily dressed in a dark business suit and homburg hat. His factory was large, so he was undoubtedly wealthy, and his speech and manners indicated that he was well-bred. He did not speak English, however, so I was introduced to his multi-lingual son, Marcel, who would be my civilian liaison. Like his father, Marcel was dressed in a smart suit, and he, too, appeared to be well-educated and upper class.

The first day Marcel and I drove to pick up a load of cement at a little village outside Liège. At noon, we stopped at a roadside café that Marcel obviously knew well. The proprietress greeted us warmly and a young woman in a petite white apron served us a lunch of black market eggs, fried potatoes, a Belgian endive salad, and two bottles of wine.

After this excellent meal, as we sat enjoying the last of the wine, Marcel asked pleasantly in his Belgian-French accent, "Would you like the waitress? I'm paying."

At first I thought he must be offering to order something more from the menu. But in Marcel's dark eyes I saw a twinkle.

198

He said, "These girls are very nice, and it is safe."

When had we first entered the café, I had seen Marcel exchange charged looks with the proprietress. Now it was clear to me. Marcel wanted to lay her and he was suggesting that I might like to do the same with the pretty little waitress who had served us.

"No, thanks," I said, attempting to give the impression that a quick roll in the hay with a strange girl after lunch was as commonplace to me as it evidently was to Marcel Savoie. "I gotta get on and pick up the cement or I'll be late getting back to camp. Besides, I'm afraid of getting a dose of *chaude pisse.*"

The waitress gave me a dirty look. Marcel did not look pleased either, but he did not argue with me. I mused as we drove on that I just learned an entirely new meaning for the term "sack lunch."

The next morning, Marcel insisted that I accompany him home to have a drink with his mother. I looked at him carefully but could not figure out his intention. "Why in hell does he want me to meet his mother?" I wondered. I was no one special, just Dago John—Johnny Bananas!—from Brooklyn and Anacortes, an ordinary GI who had survived three years of war in Europe. I was not the sort of guy who met upper-class women for tea at nine in the morning.

"Thanks, Marcel," I said, "but I'd better not. I was sent here to get this furniture factory on line, and there's a lot to be done."

Marcel was not to be put off.

"I have told my mother about you," he said. "She wants very much to meet you."

For me, the war had been a series of adventures. This latest assignment was shaping up to be yet another—so why not go with Marcel and see what developed?

Marcel directed me to park the army truck in front of a great house that overlooked the city. From there he led me into the garage that housed his father's French car, a vehicle that had been kept in immaculate order and was apparently still running in spite of the wartime gasoline rationing. The garage was grander than most people's homes, with white tile wainscoting and gilt-framed old paintings on the walls.

Marcel led me into the dining room, where his mother and father were having their after-breakfast coffee at a table that was large enough to seat thirty people. The furniture around them was intricately carved and the walls were adorned with yet more paintings.

I shook hands with Monsieur Savoie, and he introduced me to his wife. Wearing a long satin dressing gown, she was the most astonishingly beautiful woman I had ever seen. Tall with reddish-blond hair and blue eyes, she was quite unlike Marcel, who was short with curly black hair. Perhaps she was his step-mother, as she was at least thirty years younger than her husband, although Marcel did not look much like his father, either.

Mystified as to why I was there, I followed Marcel obediently into an adjoining room. It, too, was sumptuous, with tall cabinets of carved wood that held hundreds of bottles of liquor behind doors paned with beveled glass. Marcel poured me a large snifter of Pernod with a cognac chaser and seated me so that I faced his mother through the archway; his father's back was toward me. Disconcertingly, Madame kept smiling at me over her husband's shoulder. I sipped slowly at my drink and thought, "What is this assignment? Why am I here? The furniture factory doesn't seem to have anything to do with the Army. My sitting here early in the morning downing alcohol doesn't seem to have anything to do with the Army either. And what's with Madame Savoie—is she giving me the eye?"

Marcel disappeared several times without explanation, leaving me alone. Madame and Monsieur were talking in low voices in the other room, and I got the definite feeling that they were discussing me. "What in hell is going on?" I asked myself for the hundredth time.

Marcel reappeared and asked if I wanted another drink.

"No, thanks," I replied. "That's all I can handle. I've got to drive, you know."

The elder Savoies stood up to bid me goodbye. I shook Monsieur Savoie's hand formally, but when I stepped forward to do the same with Madame, she grasped my outstretched hand with both of hers and gave it a meaningful squeeze.

Marcel and I then drove to Holland to pick up building materials.

Next morning, when I appeared at the factory, Marcel greeted me by saying, "Let's go."

"Sure. What are we doing today?"

"We have to go to my house again."

"Do you have to pick something up there?" I said. "Did you forget something?"

We were in the truck by now, and we drove for a couple of blocks before he answered, "*Voulez-vous* fuck *ma mère?*"

I was so surprised that I couldn't speak for twenty or thirty seconds. Finally I found my voice. "Marcel, do you know what you're saying? Do you know what 'fuck' means?"

"*Oui, Jean,*" he replied in French. "My mother wants you to go to bed with her."

In France I had seen little boys and girls pimping for their sisters and mothers, but I just couldn't fathom this aristocratic young man offering me his mother.

"What about your father, Marcel?" I said. "And I've got a wife back home. One of these days I'm gonna go back to her."

"Don't worry about my father. It's okay. No problem," he said emphatically, easing my apprehension at even thinking about screwing his mother. "My mother wants you," he repeated.

The temptation was too great. I had been away for three years, and Madame Savoie was very, *very* attractive. "Shit," I thought to myself, "She won't be the first woman I've slept with since I've been over here. I'll probably be sent on to fight the Japs after this. I don't know if I'm ever gonna make it home. And, craziest of all, I have the blessing of her husband and son!"

"What are you gonna do, Marcel?" I asked, still a little disbelieving and wondering what the hell was really going on. Would he be wandering around the house while I was in bed with his mother?

"Oh, *Jean*, I will be downstairs in bed with the maid," he assured me. "Don't worry. No problem."

The situation seemed surreal to me. I had grown up in Brooklyn with nothing. Now I was being wined and dined in Europe and offered the sexual favors of a beautiful upper-class woman.

Two blocks from the family chateau, I made up my mind to go to bed with Madame Savoie.

She greeted me in the salon and poured me another snifter of Pernod. I learned later that this stuff contains absinthe, a high-proof alcohol made from wormwood and herbs. It has mind-altering properties, which caused it to be outlawed in the States, and I had already figured out that it messes with other parts of you too. To corrupt an old saying, "absinthe makes the heart grow fonder."

"Marcel tells me you are married," Madame Savoie said conversationally as we sipped at our drinks.

"Yes," I admitted.

"How long has it been since you saw your wife?"

"Almost three years," I said. "My wife has never seen me in a soldier's uniform."

"Haven't you been home on leave?"

"The American Army doesn't allow its soldiers to return home during wartime. Not unless they get shot up. And when this part of the war is over, I'll be going to Japan," I said, feeling a little sorry for myself.

"It doesn't seem right," she said, obviously feeling sorry for me, too. "Husbands and wives should not be separated for that long. And do you have children?"

"No, no children, Madame. And you?" I asked. "Do you have any children besides Marcel?"

"We have a daughter who attends a boarding school in Antwerp," she answered.

I thought of the bodies in the rubble of the cinema. Many of them had been young women. The Savoie's daughter could easily have been one of them.

I could feel the alcohol beginning to take hold, but before I could grow morose, Madame Savoie set down her drink, held out her hand, and led me up a grand curving staircase to her bedroom. This was the most magnificent room I had seen yet. It was grander than anything I had ever seen at the movies, even, and I couldn't help thinking that I had taken a step up from my army life. The huge bed with down comforters was certainly an improvement over a GI cot, let alone my foxhole in Cherbourg, and the great square bathtub encased in marble in the next room was a far cry from the makeshift GI showers—more so as Madame Savoie had thoughtfully taken it upon herself to fill the tub before my arrival.

"What would your wife think if she knew this?" Madame asked, sitting on the edge of the bath as I sank down into the luxury of hot water with bubbles.

"She's not gonna find out," I replied.

"*C'est la guerre*," she said letting her gown slip from her shoulders.

This was too much for me. "And what about your husband?" I asked, climbing out of the bath and reaching for a towel.

"He is an old man, *Jean*, and he does not care," she assured me.

"You are a beautiful woman, Madame," I whispered, drawing her toward me.

"I am not 'Madame,' *Jean*. My name is Claudette."

After that, all thoughts of spouses and war faded away, and there were only two people who existed in the world: Claudette and me.

Time had no place in that Belgian boudoir, and it was early afternoon before we rose from the bed.

"Do you want to see me again?" Claudette asked, giving me a last embrace before I descended the stairs.

Of course, I wanted to see her again. "*Oui, oui*," I said breathlessly. "When?"

"Tomorrow?"

"That's for you to say, not me. I have been assigned to work for you. I am at your disposal."

"I want to see you again, *mon cheri*, and soon. Work is not important and we had a wonderful time today," she whispered.

My head was still swimming when I returned to my unit that evening, and it wasn't just from all the absinthe.

"How's the new job going?" Jerry asked.

"Great," I said.

"Just what do you do?"

"Oh, I drive a 6 X 6 and haul material for a furniture company. And I translate and do a few other things."

There was no way I was going to tell Jerry or anyone else about Claudette. Even if I felt like boasting about her, that would only spoil things for me.

The next morning at the factory, after greeting Marcel, I turned sheepishly to Monsieur Savoie. He smiled and shook my hand warmly, and I felt reassured that he wasn't about to shoot me.

"Your family is Italian," he said in French. "Are you a Chicago gangster?"

"No," I replied.

"Then you must be a cowboy. The cinemas always portray Americans as one or the other."

"I was a cowboy for a couple of months," I said, thinking of Coney Island, "but now I work in the forest industry. It's hard work. A man must be very strong."

"Have you met any Belgian women beside Claudette? They are known for their beauty and their passion, you know."

Clearly he knew all about my liaison with his wife. Where was this leading? I still had no idea.

Monsieur waved us off cheerily as we left the factory for my day's assignment. I didn't mention my impending date with Claudette to Marcel. I wanted to see if she had actually meant what she said.

"Where to today, Marcel?" I asked him brightly.

He looked askance at me and said, "To our house, of course. Don't you remember?"

"Yes, I remember. I just wanted to make sure I wasn't dreaming."

"My mother likes you," Marcel assured me.

This was the second day of what was to become a daily dalliance. Claudette and I began each morning with a snifter of Pernod, which I drank sparingly, not wanting to be oblivious to the delights of the boudoir. Claudette was starved for intimacy and responded with enthusiasm to my advances, but our encounters were strictly sexual. It was not a love affair, and there was never any expectation that we would see one another socially. Claudette spent her afternoons and evenings with other people.

The war and my illness had made me thin and serious-looking, but I was strong, clean-shaven and neat, and though still young at twenty-seven, I was more mature than many of my fellow GIs.

"Why have you chosen me?" I asked Claudette the second day.

"Because, *mon cheri*, you will go back to America and not tell anyone there, and since you do not socialize here, you will not tell anyone here."

After making love, we would go downstairs, where Marcel served us magnificent lunches of Belgian endive salad, steak or eggs, *pomme frites*, or crêpes. I knew the steak and eggs were only available on the black market and atrociously expensive, and I just couldn't believe that I was living so well.

Each afternoon Marcel and I would drive somewhere to pick up material for the factory. I soon realized I was useful to the Savoies in other ways. On my second or third day Marcel announced that his father needed gasoline for his car and asked me to get some. In fact, the car would need gasoline every day. Each morning I arrived with eight full jerry cans on the running board of my truck, and Marcel would help himself to the contents of six of them. My reasoning, which was ridiculous, was that I was absolved from stealing since I did not literally give the gasoline to Marcel, but allowed him to take it while my attentions were engaged elsewhere.

When Marcel offered to lend me a thousand francs and assured me I needn't worry about paying it back, I realized I was involved in a black market gasoline operation. I took the money, but with considerable misgivings. Then Marcel began giving me bottles of liquor. I could accept this more readily than the cash, and shared it with my buddies. However, as time went on, I began to feel that there was something subversive in what I was doing. I was being showered with sex, money and liquor to keep supplying the Savoies with gas—and to keep quiet about it.

It occurred to me that I had been sent to the job by my company commander, and if I offered him some of the booze I would incriminate him also, which either would give me some protection or we would both go down together. But the CC accepted it willingly, even agreeing to store some in his foot locker for me. I felt relieved to know that that I was not alone in the intrigue—more so when I noticed a German burp gun in his footlocker. We GIs had been required to surrender ours, but the CC had kept his illegal booty.

My detail with the Savoies lasted for a couple of months. Then the war with Germany came to an end. On V-E night the streets of Herstal and Liège were alive with people who cheered any passing GIs as "liberators!" The cafés were crowded, and the Belgians were dressed in their finest clothes, though we learned later that their celebrations had been more restrained than those that took place in the States. The Germans had been driven from their country some months earlier, and the Belgians had already started on the long road toward recovery. The final surrender of the enemy was merely the icing on the cake.

The next morning we were told there would be no work detail that day. Instead, we would all attend the movie "Two Down and One to Go." Italy and Germany had been vanquished, but Japan, as I had feared, was still very much in the fight.

"Come on," I said to Turk Thompson, "I can't phone the people I've been working for, so I have to drive over and tell them I won't be available today."

Turk's eyes widened when we arrived at the chateau. "You've been working here?"

"Not exactly. I'll tell you later," I said.

"You are early, *Jean*," Marcel said when he answered the door. He invited us both in for a drink.

"Yes, well, I can't work today because we all have to see a movie."

Claudette floated down the stairs in an elegant pink sleeping ensemble. Turk gasped, and I knew he must be thinking, "What the hell is this?"

"What is it, *Jean*?" she asked, obviously distressed. "Are you going back home?"

"No, Madame." I addressed her formally so Turk wouldn't get any more suspicious than he already was. "It's just that I can't work today. And I surely will not be going back home. We still have the war with Japan to win."

Marcel poured us each a generous Pernod and cognac chaser in the salon. Claudette came and stood behind my chair, placing her hands affectionately on my shoulders. Turk looked slyly up at me from his snifter as if to say, "Why, you son-of-a-bitch!"

Marcel poured drink after drink. By the time we left, Turk and I were pretty well bombed.

"I'll see you in the morning," I promised, as we all shook hands in the foyer.

Back in the truck, Turk could hardly wait to begin the interrogation. "You bastard! You're screwing her, aren't you?"

"No," I lied.

"Well, I think you are. It looks to me like you're more than just friends."

I continued to deny everything all the way back to camp, but Turk remained unconvinced.

Chapter 32

EIGHTEEN CARLOADS OF SILVER

Though the war with Germany was over, my work detail with the Savoies continued and I resumed my daily routine at the chateau and the factory. I had the feeling that I was involved in something more than the gasoline racket, but I couldn't figure out what it might be.

When I arrived at the factory one morning in early June, Marcel greeted me with the news that we had to go to the railroad yard right away. "We have a big job to do," he said.

"What is it?" I asked.

"You'll see," he replied cheerfully. "You'll see."

Well, I saw all right. At the station were eighteen rickety box cars guarded by GI sentries. These old wagons were of a type known as "forty-and-eight," as they had been designed to carry either forty troops or eight horses to the front during World War I. When Marcel opened the door to one of them, my eyes all but popped out of my head. Shining dimly in the darkness of the car were hundreds of silver ingots, an incredible treasure, the likes of which I had never expected to see in my life. I recalled seeing pictures of such ingots stacked on Philadelphia or New York docks when nations made their payments to each other—but to be in the physical presence of that sort of wealth was overwhelming.

I stared incredulously at Marcel as he explained, "There is this much silver in all eighteen of the cars. We have to move it to the warehouse at the furniture factory."

Still somewhat stunned, I tried to pick up a bar but could only lift one end.

"Who's gonna move this stuff?" I gasped, realizing it represented a huge operation.

"You are going to move it, *Jean*, and you can have as much of it as you want."

My head was swimming. There had to be big people, important people, involved in this operation I was sure—maybe even generals. "Shit,"

I blurted out, "I can hardly lift these goddam things, let alone move them to the warehouse. I'll talk to the colonel and see if I can get help."

Back at base section headquarters, I told the colonel about the silver. "There's something funny going on with it," I said, not dreaming that he might be involved.

He looked at me as if he had never seen me before. "And who are you?"

This guy knew perfectly well who I was, and it took a couple of minutes for me to realize what was going on. He had assumed I would go along with the heist, and now that I was questioning it, he pretended not to know me. Without either of us saying anything more, I turned around and left. I then reported to Captain Dixon and explained that there was an illegal operation underway. The next morning he came with to see for himself.

At the factory we found about twenty Italian prisoners, guarded by American sentries, neatly stacking the silver bars in the warehouse. Looking closely at the ingots, we discovered bronze plaques indicating that the treasure had come from French Indochina and had been consigned to Deutsch Bank in Hanover. It would have required high-ranking Army officials to arrange for its shipment by rail to the furniture factory in Herstal.

Marcel was nowhere to be seen, and the sentries did not challenge Captain Dixon and me. I figured we could have ordered the Italian prisoners to load our command car with silver and no one would have stopped us. Instead, I spoke with a couple of the prisoners in Italian. "You're working very hard. The silver is heavy."

"We've been working all night," they said. "We're tired but we're almost finished now. Are you Italian?"

"My family came from Italy, but I'm an American," I answered. Turning to Captain Dixon I said, "Well, what do you think of this operation?"

"Christ!" he exclaimed, "This is a king's ransom! Let's get out of here, and I'll talk with Colonel Clifford."

Colonel Clifford was our commanding officer. He went to inspect the silver operation at the warehouse and decided, like us, that there was definitely something crooked going on. When he went to base section to clarify the matter, he was told to "back off and forget the whole thing." We assumed the big wheels running the enterprise were probably generals at either end.

Unfortunately, that incident brought to an end the best tour of duty I had in the Army. No more crêpes; no more Pernod; no more boudoir sessions with the beautiful Claudette; and no silver ingots for me either. All I could take with me were fond memories of a dreamlike interlude at the end of the war.

It was the Fourth of July when I reported to the 1143rd Engineer Combat Group at Laon, about fifteen miles from Reims. I was angry and depressed that I had been chosen from among thousands of other GIs to remain in Europe to prepare for ending the war in Japan.

Many of my friends had already headed back to the States. I thought of them as Major Ross outlined my duties. I was to run a saw-mill to cut lumber for crating machinery headed for Japan. "You'll have fifty German prisoners working for you," he said, "and they will be guarded by liberated Poles. The Germans used them as forced labor to build the West Wall. They'll have German rifles to give the prisoners a taste of their own medicine, if necessary. By the way," he continued "there are some people here who know you."

"Who," I asked eagerly thinking it might be Walt or some of the other fellows I had been separated from.

"Captain Collier and Colonel Clifford," he reported smartly. "You do know them, don't you?"

"I sure as hell do!" I was convinced those two bastards were responsible for my being chosen to stay on Europe. They both knew me and my work.

That night I ran into Collier. He greeted me with, "Hi, Johnny! How are you?"

"I'm pissed off! That's how I am. I think you're responsible for this assignment. The rest of them are going home, and I'm still sitting here, headed for Japan."

The captain said nothing. He just turned and walked away.

There was nothing I could do, of course, but get on with the work. I found myself supervising a crew of German POWs at a portable sawmill that had been manufactured in Corinth, Mississippi. Two of the older prisoners ran a mobile machine shop, and since there wasn't a lot of repair work to be done they passed the time making souvenirs out of a German airplane propeller. Paul was busy making me a ring when a commotion with a lot of hollering began. Hearing a shot, I ran out of the shop and saw a German prisoner lying dead on the ground.

The only legitimate reason a Pole could have for shooting a prisoner was if that prisoner was trying to escape. The dead German had allegedly been running toward the woods and did not heed the guard's warning to stop. The translator told me the man had been headed for the latrine when he was shot, but that seemed doubtful since he was more than a hundred feet beyond the slit trench.

I shook my head in disbelief that any of the Germans would try to escape. The machinery for their repatriation was already in motion, and if the dead guy had only waited, he would have made it safely home.

The war was over for the Germans, but it wasn't over for me until the atomic bombs were dropped on Japan. But even after that happened I still wasn't issued orders to go home. I had been overseas for three-and-a-half years, and I had come to the end of my rope. I meant to return to Doris and the Pacific Northwest, regardless of the consequences.

I was hitchhiking to Reims when Colonel Clifford came along in his command car.

"Where are you going, John?" he said, gesturing that I should get into the vehicle.

"I'm headed into base section headquarters to find out why I haven't received orders to go back to the States," I said. "I feel I've done my share in this thing. You can put me in jail, or whatever you want to do with me, but I'm not going to do Army work anymore." I felt the same determination I had felt when I told the policeman Marvin Beebe in Anacortes to put me in jail if he had to, but I would not stop cutting wood.

Colonel Clifford took me to his office and called in Major Ross. He asked the major to take me to Reims and make sure that my name was on the next set of orders to go home. As it happened, their intervention was not necessary. My name was on the orders that had been cut that morning. I was on my way home!

Two German prisoners had been assigned to me as orderlies. Back in my room, I told them I was going back to the States. One of the men pointed to a map on the wall and asked where I lived. I showed him, and he said "California?" Apparently it was the only state he had heard of.

"Not California," I said, emptying my barracks bag as I spoke. "Washington State." I gave the men some candy bars, and perhaps it was this gesture, or perhaps it was just that I was going home and they were not, that caused one of the men to cry.

My heart went out to them. I assured them in my broken German that they, too, would be going home soon, and hoped for their sake it was true.

On the train to Marseilles, we were pensive. What would we find when we got home? Would it all be the same or would things have changed? We had been away so long and seen so much tragedy, not to mention stupid accidents, that even now we remained apprehensive as to whether we would make it home or not. As it happened, two men were killed on that very train trip. One was hanging out too far from the train step and hit the side of a tunnel. The other stepped in front of a "galloping goose" that sped past us while we were stopped. Nor would danger end in Marseilles. Assuming we made it aboard our homeward ship, there was still the possibility of being sunk by drifting mines.

Our ship was not yet in port, and we did not know when it would arrive, so the situation was one of "wait and hope." Miraculously, my old buddy Walt Cramoga happened to be assigned to a tent next to mine, so we waited and hoped together over beer at a local café.

Then, finally, the day we had been dreaming of for nearly four years arrived. We climbed with our gear into a truck and headed for the dock, still fearing that something would keep us from our appointment with our ship. My intuition proved correct. Winding down one of the narrow streets, we had to slow almost to a stop behind forty or fifty people plodding along behind a horse-drawn hearse. The cart was so rickety it seemed unlikely to hold together long enough to get the corpse to the cemetery.

"You know, that's a bad omen," I said to the guy next to me, and sure as hell, when we arrived at the harbor, there was no ship.

But the next day, a proud Victory ship named the *Marine Raven* was tied up at the Marseilles dock—and I was on my way home.

PART IV

ANACORTES

1945-2016

Chapter 33

HOME AT LAST

The last leg of my journey home from Europe was both the shortest and longest of the entire trip. After getting off the train in Mount Vernon, Washington, I set out to hitchhike the last twenty miles to Anacortes. Mr. and Mrs. Kack, who knew Doris and her family, stopped to pick me up and offered to take me right to my door.

The Skagit Flats were a blur to me as we drove along—not because of our speed, but because of the turbulence in my head and my heart. I was overwhelmingly grateful to be alive, and my head spun at the thought of seeing Doris.

We crossed the Swinomish Slough bridge to Fidalgo Island. As my anticipation increased, the car speed decreased—or so it seemed to me. The road through Summit Park was only two miles long but felt like it was ten times that. Eventually we arrived at Deans' Corner, with its small service station and grocery store just as I remembered them. Four miles to go, but they, too, seemed to have stretched. "How could the road have lengthened like this?" I agonized, as we wound interminably along the shoreline of Fidalgo Bay, past the railroad trestle and Weaverling Spit, and crept slowly up the hill at the south end of town.

At the crest of the rise, Anacortes spread out before us. The stores, the mills, the houses—and one of those houses was mine!

A few more blocks down Commercial Avenue, up twenty-second street, right on N Avenue, and I was home!

I fear I did not say "Goodbye" or "Thank you" to the Kacks as I tumbled out of the car, because Doris had flung open the door and was waiting for me on the porch. She was more beautiful than I remembered—her face sweeter, more mature. All of the suffering and loneliness of the past four years seemed to evaporate as we fell into each other's arms.

That night I lay awake long after Doris had fallen asleep. Our new house was still unfinished and the old one to which I had now returned was in no better shape than when I had left four years earlier. I could still see the stars through the holes in the roof, just as I had done when we first bought the place. Back then I had felt like I was in heaven. I felt the same again now.

The next morning I walked down to the police station, where the cop on duty was none other than Marvin Beebe, the guy who had confiscated my rifles the day after Pearl Harbor. Like most cops, he hadn't been drafted into military service but had stayed behind to keep the peace at home. His back was toward me as I entered the office, and when he turned around, his face blanched.

"I've come for my rifles and ammunition," I said in my most contemptuous voice.

"What? Now?"

I was sure Beebe had heard me, but clearly he was shocked and stalling for time.

"I want my guns and shells back," I said.

"You've been gone a while."

"I want my rifles and ammunition," I repeated, in no mood to make small talk.

Beebe produced the rifles, and as he handed them to me he admitted that much of the ammunition was missing because several local men who had not gone to war had used my guns and shells to hunt deer in my absence.

I was still angry at having been thought a danger to my country when I had been more willing than my detractors to fight for it, and I could have made a scene with Beebe. But the missing ammo seemed a small thing to argue about, and I let the matter go. I knew the war had made me stronger. I had learned many engineering skills, I had come to appreciate home and family more than ever, and I knew what was, and wasn't, worth fighting over.

I had also come to terms with my Italian heritage. On my way home that day, rifles in hand, I remembered the morning I had awakened in my fox hole in Cherbourg to find a cross hung with a set of dog tags and the sign "Dago John RIP." I smiled to myself, recalling the good-natured sniggering of my buddies who had pulled the joke. But they had been right, too. From that moment on, I had known that Dago John would truly "Rest in Peace."

**

Johnny Bananas (not to mention GI *Jean*!) had long since been dispatched to the same place as Dago John. In their place, John Tursi, now honorably discharged as a Tech Sergeant from the U.S. Army, had to set about making a living. The GI Bill was one possibility, but with only an eighth grade education I figured it would take me too long to earn a degree, and I could learn just as much simply by reading and doing. After moving around so much, and dreaming of home for so long, I was also determined to stay in Anacortes.

Going back to being a log boom man wasn't an option, because my feet had been frostbitten in the Battle of the Bulge and I wasn't as agile as I had been. (My dancing days were over, too, unfortunately, though I soon found a new role as square dance caller. This boosted my social confidence, and helped lay to rest the very last of my anxieties about being an Italian-American in Anacortes.)

I applied to the fire department, but quit after a single day; polishing the fire truck while waiting for action was not the life for me. I did ordinary laboring work, spading gardens and other odd jobs, and I briefly worked in a hardware store. Eventually I got a job in one of the salmon canneries, and though these were going the way of the mills— forced into mergers or shutting down completely—I made myself useful in the machine shop. As I had done with my bulldozer in the war, I got to know the machines I was working with. Eventually I was hired by the cannery in a permanent capacity, first as foreman and later as head machinist.

I stayed with the cannery for almost nine years, though I was tempted early on by an offer from my former company commander in the 342nd engineers to go back over to Europe to help provide technical assistance under the Marshall Plan. The colonel knew me as a hard and resourceful worker with a range of construction skills; I could also speak several European languages. But I turned the job down. I had done enough traveling for a while, I had a decent job at the cannery, and I had finally finished building our new house—which had enabled Doris to cut her business overheads by selling the Kulshan Beauty Shop and work out of home.

Then, in 1955, the Shell Oil Company announced that they would be building a refinery on March Point—the small pastoral peninsula I had contemplated from the railway trestle in my crab poaching days. The oil would be shipped from Alaska, and the refined products shipped onwards

217

from Anacortes by sea or rail. This would provide a great economic boost for the town, which was past its peak as a fishing and mill town and was losing people by the month. Many of us saw the refinery as an opportunity for well-paid, long-term employment. Shell was hiring construction workers, and they offered better benefits than the cannery, so I decided to try my luck with them. I was hired as a construction inspector and started work as a Shell employee on July 5, 1955.

As the refinery took shape, I was responsible for the alignment of pumps, engines and other machinery attached to piping. As I had done at the cannery, I also worked in the machine shop, eventually becoming supervisor of mechanical equipment. I was interested in, and studied, pumps, turbines and so forth, and was able to repair most mechanical problems without having to call in technicians and engineers from the companies that had supplied the machines. My immediate bosses came to see me as "valuable," and so did the higher ups. I began to be sent to different places around the country where new refineries and chemical plants were being built. Although I lacked formal training as a mechanical engineer, I was given that job title, along with the responsibility for getting new refinery units up and running.

I was also called to troubleshoot ongoing problems in older refineries. In one instance I redesigned the faulty valves of a certain type of gas compressor so that these machines would run for months, instead of days, without a breakage. Another time, I designed a seal to stop toxic gas leaks in places where men were working. This was a chronic problem in refineries all over the country, and a common (and understandable!) cause of work stoppages. Shell's regular engineers didn't know what to do about it, but I had an idea, built the parts in my machine shop in Anacortes, and they worked fine. I addressed some other issues in the process, and was loaned out by Shell as a consultant to other refinery companies experiencing the same problems.

I was very well paid for this work, and ultimately remained with Shell for twenty-three years, until my retirement in 1977. Meanwhile, Doris and I had sold our house in town and built a new one in 18 acres of woods near Sharpe's Corner.

As my salary increased, I became interested in investing. When I started with Shell, the company paid ten percent of our salary into its provident fund—a safe but low-return pension scheme. When the economy picked up during the Kennedy Administration, I drew out some of this money and invested it in higher-return CDs with Washington Federal bank. I also started watching the stock market and began to invest in it, too. I was pretty successful at this, and plenty of people asked me over the years about my "strategy." In truth, I never had one; there was never any "science" to what I did. I didn't bother with formal advice from stockbrokers; I read the newspapers, watched TV and relied mostly on intuition. Sometimes I bought low-priced stocks with funny-sounding names ("Apple"!). I also did well following tips from Warren Buffet, including his advice to invest in foreign capital and businesses. I bought stocks in a Canadian oil company that was drilling in Tashkent, and in Chinese oil. In my entire investing career I only ever took one major beating, and that was from Martha Stewart.

Doris was never interested in the stock market. Her only concern was that we could pay our bills. Perhaps it was our Depression-era upbringing, but we both remained pretty frugal even when we no longer needed to be. Our houses were nice, but Doris never asked for flashy jewelry or other material things, and I had to talk her into buying a fur coat. A friend asked why I didn't buy a Mercedes. "Can't afford it," I told him, though I was lying. I probably could have bought three, but that just wasn't our style. Doris and I would joke about putting turkeys on other people's Thanksgiving tables while we sat down to oxtail soup.

One thing we did spend money on was traveling and seeing the world. We made our first trip in 1968 and over the next three decades we visited sixty-five countries in Europe, Asia and Africa. We had many exciting adventures, which we shared with local schools, senior centers and community clubs through slide shows and lectures. I was especially drawn to places that were "off the map": if I saw a tour to some place away from the usual tourist routes, I'd make arrangements for us to go. In 1978, we were among the first Americans to tour China, as part of a group that traveled to that country from Yugoslavia. We found Chinese history and culture fascinating and returned to China twice more. We also visited Russia before the fall of the Berlin Wall—again, we "snuck in" with another foreign tour group—and we went to Tibet before it became fashionable. That was probably our worst trip. There was little to see, the people were dirty and seemed to have nothing to live for. It was obvious to me that the Chinese would move in sooner or later to develop it and extract its mineral resources.

We visited plenty of civilized places too, including France, although the one place I could never bring myself to revisit was Omaha Beach. Too many disturbing memories, I guess.

After Doris died, in 2005, I lost interest in further investing and decided to cash in my portfolio—including a pile of Warren Buffet's Berkshire-Hathaway stocks. I figured I'd made enough money and I couldn't see any sense in making more. As it happened, I got out of the market the day before Buffet announced he was selling his own stocks in Berkshire-Hathaway. I had no idea he was going to do this, but my intuition remained my best friend as an investor right to the end.

Chapter 34

LONG JOURNEY TO THE ROSE GARDEN

Doris and I never had children. For the first fifteen years of our marriage, my work situation was so tenuous that I did not want to bring children into the world if we couldn't raise them properly. The memories of my hungry Brooklyn childhood stayed with me, and Doris's upbringing hadn't been much rosier. We adopted a number of dogs over the years, however, and became faithful supporters of local Humane Society. Doris, in particular, loved animals and made overtures to all the wild creatures that inhabited our wooded acreage at Sharpe's Corner. One of my favorite memories is of the two of us walking up a trail near our house. I had got a little ways ahead, and when I turned around to check on Doris, I saw not only her but our two pet nanny goats, our dog, our cat, and a mama raccoon with three babies, all following along in a line.

As our circumstances improved, we began helping people in the Anacortes community who needed a boost. In this, I was fulfilling the idea I had formulated during the war, when we knew the invasion of Europe was imminent and Al, Clyde and I, among others, had discussed what we would do with our lives if we ever made it home again. I would have gratefully accepted some practical kindness from time to time when I was a starving kid—and now, in midlife, I was in a position to offer it to others. As my investments began to pay dividends, I reinvested some but also allocated a portion of the profits to an assortment of philanthropic causes. Doris shared my view on this, and we began by paying grocery or milk bills for families that could not pay for these things themselves. Some of these were households headed by single moms who could not afford to have their kids join the Boy Scouts. I recalled being excluded from the Scouts in Suffern because I was too poor—so I started up a troop in Anacortes, financing it myself so the kids could get out into the woods and have plenty to eat on campfire nights. Doris and I eventually sponsored four troops of Scouts, and now I see kids who are the grandchildren of our original members.

Chapter 34

I joined the Anacortes chapter of the Veterans of Foreign Wars, at the coaxing of a neighbor who was a World War I vet. I found the meetings slow—the members were mostly old men not interested in doing much but squabbling and trying to get more benefits for themselves. Eventually we bought an old church and remodeled it as a place to hold our meetings. That gave us a new focus—and it was this group that worked to secure the disability pension for my Italian-American compatriot Tony Campano.

Doris joined the Soroptomists, and with two other women they started up a little thrift shop on 32nd Street. I helped them raise additional funds over the years by running salmon barbecues and the like. At one of these dinners someone mentioned that the former Salvation Army building in town was for sale. It needed work, but I decided to buy it, after which I patched it up and handed it over to the Soroptomists for their new thrift shop. Doris continued to work there as a volunteer into her eighties, even after she became legally blind. She also served as president of the Anacortes Soroptomists for some years, and as president of the VFW Womens' Auxiliary, the Eagles Auxiliary, the Anacortes Museum, and the Skagit County Historical Society.

I became interested in local history also—perhaps because in my CCC years I had been a part of it! It seems a long time ago now, but the structures we built at Deception Pass State Park—buildings, picnic shelters, guardrails—endure to this day, as does the bridge, which carries some 32,000 vehicles daily. At a ceremony in 2010 commemorating the seventy-fifth anniversary of the opening of the Deception Pass bridge, I was the only CCCer of my unit still alive (or in good enough physical shape) to attend it.

I did a lot of much-needed carpentry work on the Anacortes Museum building, but fell out with the museum director so Doris and I transferred our allegiance to the Skagit County Historical Museum in La Conner, which was undergoing an expansion. I designed and built many of the new exhibits, and salvaged lumber from old barns to build a replica of both a barn and a blacksmith's shop. Doris and I served as docents at this museum for about a dozen years.

My retirement years became even busier as I became a volunteer driver for the Department of Social and Health Services and began taking people to Seattle hospitals for medical treatment. I did this for twelve years, after starting out as a pall bearer at funerals for dead veterans who didn't have enough buddies left to carry their coffins. As a DSHS driver, I had to be vetted by the local police, the State Patrol, the FBI, and every other police outfit in Washington State. This brought back a few memories of Marvin Beebe and the war years. American society has matured, however, and my Italian-American heritage was of interest only because I could speak languages other than English, which made me useful as a translator. I covered an area from Bellingham to Tacoma, driving people to cancer treatments and so forth. Some of my passengers were prisoners and sex offenders; some were destitute; most simply didn't have a car of their own, or the means to get where they needed to go. I drove one cancer patient to Sedro-Woolley for at least thirty chemo treatments. By this stage of my life I had multiple claims on my time, but sick people always had priority—and it was a revelation to me how many organizations needed people to drive other people around for them.

I guess someone was keeping track of my activities, because one morning in 1985 a letter arrived in the mail from the White House. I thought it was just another piece of junk mail and put it aside to be thrown in the trash. Something special about the letter must have caught my eye, however, and made me open it:

The White House
Washington, D.C.
April 12, 1985

Dear Mr. Tursi:

As you may know, April 22nd-28th has been declared national volunteer week. During this week the President will be participating in a number of activities honoring outstanding volunteers and voluntary organizations.

On behalf of President Reagan, I would like to invite you to join him for a Rose Garden ceremony honoring outstanding senior volunteers from the Retired Senior Volunteer Program on Friday April 26, 1985.

You should plan to arrive no later than 10:15 am at the east visitors' entrance on east Executive Avenue with photo identification. Please RSVP to the office of Private Sector Initiatives by April 18th with your date of birth and social security number if you plan to attend.

We look forward to seeing you on the 26th.

Sincerely,

Frederick J. Ryan
Director, Private Sector Initiative

So it was that with a great deal of gratitude and humility Doris and I entered the Rose Garden that cloudless spring morning. My life which had begun in poverty on the edges of crime, moved to the forests and waters of the Pacific Northwest, taken me to Europe in World War II and back home, now culminated in this honor. As President Reagan spoke to us from the steps of the White House, my thoughts drifted back to my family beginnings in Italy. I imagined Papa as he must have sat in his cave-dwelling at Genzano, pondering his emigration to America. Never in his wildest dreams could he have thought that any son of his would be honored at the White House by the President of the United States.

When the first edition of this book (then titled *Long Journey to the Rose Garden*) went to press in 1989, that morning in the Rose Garden seemed like the pinnacle of everything I had worked for. I was proud of what Doris and I had achieved together, and grateful, too, for the acknowledgement. But life went on, and in the years that followed, even as we continued our volunteer work and wrote checks to worthy causes, we found a new cause for our philanthropy: the Anacortes Community Forest Lands.

Anacortes occupies only the northern portion of Fidalgo Island. The rest comprises rural subdivisions, lakes, rocks, and several thousand acres of beautiful Douglass fir, cedar and hemlock forests. I had cut down my share of trees as a young man before the war, in order to make ends meet, but when I heard in the early 1990s that 400 acres of forest land near Heart Lake, at the base of Mt Erie, had been earmarked for selective logging, I decided then and there that I would try and preserve them. I went to City Hall and said I would write a check for $100,000 there and then to save Mt Erie. The city officials I spoke to just about fell off their chairs.

I gave more money in the years that followed, and many other people in Anacortes have contributed too, and now the city has over 2800 acres of community forest lands preserved into perpetuity. This includes a number of pocket parks (including the John and Doris Tursi Park, dedicated in 2009), and some areas stewarded by the Skagit Land Trust, including most of the 18 wooded acres that Doris and I owned at Sharpe's Corner. After Doris died and I moved into a senior living center in town, I made sure that as much of our property as possible was protected by a conservation easement.

I believe the Anacortes Forest Lands are one of the city's greatest natural assets: Anacortes has more property protected under conservation easements than just about any other place I know of. It gives me great satisfaction every time I go past the 400-acre tract by Heart Lake to think that I helped to preserve it for walkers, bikers, and the wildlife that lives within it. These days, houses can be built just about anywhere, but this is a pristine place—and there simply aren't many of those left. It does my heart good to know they always will be there, even when I'm long gone.

Doris died on March 6, 2005, at the age of 89. As the newly revised edition of this book goes to press, I'm still going at 98.

I consider my life to have been an honest one. Had the CCCs not given me a way out of Brooklyn, it might not have been—I would almost surely have gone the way of my brothers, and resorted to crime as the only way to make a living. I told a few lies, mostly to the priest in Suffern who seemed to expect them from me. I broke a few of my marriage vows to Doris during the war years, but I presume she forgave me. Indeed, when Thelma Palmer and I talked about writing this book after the Rose Garden visit—what to include, what to leave out—Doris's response was, "Oh John, just go ahead and write it as it was. After all, it's been fifty years."

I consider myself extremely fortunate—to have escaped Brooklyn; to have been sent by the CCCs to Anacortes; to have met and married Doris; to have survived the War; to have found good work and financial prosperity in later life; to have been able to give something back to the community that has been my home for the past eighty years. But I believe a person can make their own luck, too. I was successful because I was always willing to work at any job that was asked of me, and I worked hard without complaining. In return, I was given positions of trust—beginning with my assignment as a "powder monkey" in the CCCs—that gave me confidence in myself and my abilities. These things feed on one another, and if I have any concluding advice to offer, it's this: if you have a good attitude—to work and to life—someone will notice you.

Made in the USA
San Bernardino, CA
16 April 2016